Religious Reform in the Late Ottoman Empire

Religious Reform in the Late Ottoman Empire

Institutional Change and the Professionalization of the Ulema

Erhan Bektaş

I.B.TAURIS
LONDON • NEW YORK • OXFORD • NEW DELHI • SYDNEY

I.B. TAURIS

Bloomsbury Publishing Plc
50 Bedford Square, London, WC1B 3DP, UK
1385 Broadway, New York, NY 10018, USA
29 Earlsfort Terrace, Dublin 2, Ireland

BLOOMSBURY, I.B. TAURIS and the I.B. Tauris logo are trademarks of Bloomsbury Publishing Plc

First published in Great Britain 2023
This paperback edition published 2024

Series design by Adriana Brioso
Cover image: Constantinople, Ottoman Empire, ca. 1895.
(© Granger Historical Picture Archive/Alamy Stock Photo)

A catalogue record for this book is available from the British Library.

A catalog record for this book is available from the Library of Congress.

ISBN: HB: 978-0-7556-4547-3
PB: 978-0-7556-4551-0
ePDF: 978-0-7556-4548-0
eBook: 978-0-7556-4549-7

Typeset by RefineCatch Limited, Bungay, Suffolk

To find out more about our authors and books visit www.bloomsbury.com and sign up for our newsletters.

To my family

Contents

Figures

Tables

Preface

This book is a portrayal of the formation of professional ulema identity in the late nineteenth century with a specific focus on the educational and professional experiences of the Ilmiye members. It argues that the career paths of ulema in educational and professional life experienced a major transformation after the reestablishment of the Şeyhülislam (chief of the ulema) office at the beginning of the Tanzimat. A number of regulations that allowed for more intervention in the procedures with respect to how members of the Ilmiye were educated, appointed, and promoted were designed by the central authorities to re-identify both their educational and professional practices. From this period forward, the ulema in the nineteenth century was affected because of various dynamics stemming from the transformation; consequently, a professional ulema identity became more apparent. The important steps that constitute the professional ulema identity, the reorganization of the Şeyhülislam Office, and the transformations experienced in the educational and professional life of the ulema are within the scope of this study.

This book also aims to explore the social origins, careers, social and political networks, and relations among Anatolian ulema who were officially assigned to the Ilmiye between 1880 and 1920 with reference to the archival documents using a prosopographical method. It also responds to a narrative that is far from comprehensively explaining the actual place of the ulema. It thus illuminates the social and professional history of the late Ottoman ulema by bringing their main experiences into focus.

This book is organized into five main chapters and a conclusion. In the first chapter, the historical framework of the institutionalization of the Şeyhülislam Office and religious affairs through a political process as well as the practices of centralized state control over the authority of the Şeyhülislam in the nineteenth century will be outlined. This chapter draws attention to the transformation of the Ilmiye class into professional officials of the state while showing the reorganization of the office of Şeyhülislam over time. After the Tanzimat, the state's new approach towards religion and the positioning of the ulema in the newly centralized state show that the Ilmiye members transformed into state officials who served the imperial center's goal of institutionalizing the office of

Şeyhülislam and helped to create a proper state religion in the second half of the nineteenth century.

The second chapter aims to explore the educational background of the provincial ulema to explain the general rules of becoming an *alim (scholar)* and evaluate the educational quality of the provincial ulema. The ulema's educational path helps to explain the story behind the entrance of the Ilmiye organization with a clear picture of the madrasa *(Islamic college)* education of an *alim*, the curriculum of the madrasas, and the examination system for both graduation and appointment to the Ilmiye posts. In parallel with the expansion of institutionalized and professionalized demands by the state, the ulema's professional training in the madrasas was a priority for being appointed to a vacant Ilmiye position in the nineteenth-century Ottoman Empire. In this sense, unlike traditional state structure, the privileges of aristocratic ulema families, their personnel influence over the state system, and patronage were not common in appointments to the Ilmiye positions. There was a definite procedure and criteria to hold the Ilmiye posts in the Şeyhülislam Office that included the madrasa education of ulema candidates.

The third chapter emphasizes the formal stages of the career paths of the Ilmiye members, such as *müderris (*scholar in a madrasa*)*, kadı (judge), naib (the deputy of judge), and mufti (jurisconsult). The professional background of the ulema is one of the main factors that formed the Ilmiye institution, and studying their professional lives allows the exploration of the professional transformation of the Şeyhülislam Office in the nineteenth-century Ottoman Empire. In this regard, the greatest opportunity in the study of the Ilmiye class and their social, educational, and professional backgrounds is the examination of the personnel records of the ulema in the Meşihat Archive of the Istanbul Mufti's Office. Looking at the personnel registry files of the ulema has guided me to answer the questions about how the Ilmiye members professionalized under the Şeyhülislam authority and how laws and decisions about the Ilmiye members and the Şeyhülislam Office were implemented in practice. Moreover, questions like how ulema actually obtained positions and won promotions in the Ilmiye hierarchy will be explored while studying different professional groups within the Ilmiye system. This study emphasizes the ulema as a group instead of focusing on specific muftis or scholars *(müderris)* in order to reveal the main orientations of the Ilmiye organization as a whole.

In parallel with the importance of ulema biographies, the career paths of ulema will be examined as a prosopographical study in the fifth chapter. The method of this section is twofold. The first is to present profiles of particular provincial ulema in the late nineteenth century on the basis of their personnel records. The second is to clarify the appointment mechanism of the ulema to the Ilmiye posts. This chapter will deal with biographies of some by considering the social, political, and intellectual conditions of the period. It analyzes the career paths of the ulema and their network of relations in comparison with other members of the state bureaucracy. This part also focuses on the early childhood as well as educational and professional careers of the Ilmiye members working at the Şeyhülislam Office between the years 1880 and 1920. The sample biographies show that the late Ottoman Ilmiye system was much different to how it is normally depicted. The curricula vitae of sample ulema highlight the need to reconsider basic prejudices about the career lives of the ulema in this period.

Chapter 5 deepens the discussion of the mediatory role of the ulema representing an influential group in provincial areas. This shows how the ulema were perceived both by the government and provincial community by looking at them as mediators, as well as examining the ulema's effect on decision-making processes and their occasional partnership with provincial powers. This part will explain the survival of ulema as both state agents and religious leaders in contrast to the narration of ulema that has largely been on the basis of a decline paradigm. From this point, this section aims to eliminate the state's approach toward religion and the position of the ulema in the newly centralized state. Certain decreases and increases in the educational and professional role of the ulema will be traced by reformulating the ways of thinking about the function of the Ottoman ulema and scrutinizing the centralization of religious affairs.

Acknowledgments

This book emerged from my dissertation, which was completed at Boğaziçi University in 2019. Many people contributed to the writing of this book. First of all, I would like to express here, my thanks to those whose contributions have been invaluable throughout this dissertation process. I cannot imagine how it would have been accomplished without the various contributions of my Ph.D. supervisor Nadir Özbek of Boğaziçi University. Throughout my graduate study, he has been a source of scholarly inspiration and he has been a model teacher for me. He enriched my historical thinking enormously by reading and discussing my chapters with me.

I thank Cengiz Kırlı, Bilgin Aydın, Abdurrahman Atçıl and Umut Türem for their careful readings of the drafts and their constructive criticism. I am wholeheartedly grateful to them for their essential conceptual, theoretical, and historical contributions as well as unconditional help. Their guidance and feedback at different stages renewed my belief in this study. I also have to thank Jonathan Phillips who carefully and patiently copyedited the book.

A number of scholars shaped my thinking and have had an impact on my academic orientation. I am indebted to Zafer Toprak, Şevket Pamuk, Edhem Eldem, Çağlar Keyder, Asım Karaömerlioğlu, Aydın Babuna, and Seda Altuğ for creating an academic environment in their classes.

It has been an honor and privilege for me to have such a distinguished academic circle and colleagues from Üsküdar University, Nevzat Tarhan, Mehmet Zelka, Niyazi Beki, Ümit Taş, Uygar Aydemir, Mert Akcanbaş, Yusuf Teke, Selçuk Duman, Sabri Kazanlı, Hüsna Yıldırım, Eda Yetimoğlu, all contributed to my intellectual growth through their vast knowledge and their valuable contributions.

I cannot express my thanks to my all friends who generously shared with me their intellectual wisdom; I benefited from the sound advice of Ekin Mahmuzlu, Alp Kadıoğlu, Faruk Yalçın, Turan Keskin, Yener Koç, Gülseren Koç, Sema Yaşar, Gizem Cimşit. Derya Dali, Naz Baydar and Burhan Duymuş.

There are no appropriate words to express my gratitude to Ayda, who provided a loving atmosphere for me with her patience and unforgettable memories. She put in as much effort as I did, spending long hours re-reading the drafts, correcting mistakes, and editing the whole text. She was always ready to help me. I would not have been able to write and finish this book on time without her endless support and assistance.

Abbreviations and Acronyms

A.}MKT.MVL.	Sadaret Mektubi Kalemi Meclis-i Vala Evrakı
A.}MKT.NZD.	Sadaret Mektubi Kalemi, Nezaret ve Devair
A.}MKT.MHM.	Sadaret Mühimme Kalemi Evrakı
A.} AMD.	Sadaret Amedi Kalemi
A.} DVN.	Sadaret Divan Kalemi
BEO.	Bab-ı Ali Evrak Odası
BOA.	Başbakanlık Osmanlı Arşivi (Prime Ministry Ottoman Archives)
C. ADL.	Cevdet Adliye
C. MF.	Cevdet Maarif
DH. MKT.	Dahiliye Nezareti Mektubi Kalemi
DH. MUİ.	Dahiliye Nezareti Muhaberat-ı Umumiye İdaresi Evrakı
DH. SYS.	Dahiliye Siyasi Kısım
DH. EUM. AYŞ.	Dahiliye Asayiş Kalemi
DH. TMIK. M.	Dahiliye Muamelat
EV.d.	Evkaf Defterleri
EV. BRT.	Evkaf Berat
FTG.f.	Fotoğraflar
HR. TO.	Hariciye Nezareti Tercüme Odası
HR. SFR.4.	Hariciye Nezareti Paris Sefareti
HSDTFR1.	Satın Alınan Evrak Rumeli Müfettişliği
IRCICA.	İslam Tarih, Sanat ve Kültür Araştırma Merkezi
ISAM.	İslam Araştırmaları Merkezi
İ. DH.	İrade Dahiliye
İ. DUİT.	İrade Dosya Usulü
İ. MMS.	Meclis-i Mahsus İradeleri
İ. MVL.	İrade Meclis-i Vala
İ. TAL.	İrade Taltifat
MA.	Meşihat Archive
MV.	Meclis-i Vükela Mazbataları
MF. MKT.	Maarif Nezareti Mektubi Kalemi
ŞD.	Şura-yı Devlet

TDV.	Türkiye Diyanet Vakfı
TS. MA.e.	Topkapı Sarayı Müzesi Arşivi
USAD.	Ulema Sicill-i Ahval Dosyası (Personnel Records of the Ulema)
Y. PRK. UM.	Yıldız Perakende Evrakı Umumi
Y. PRK. DH.	Yıldız Perakende Evrakı Dahiliye
Y. EE.	Yıldız Esas Evrakı
Y. MTV.	Yıldız Mütenevvi Maruzat
Y. PRK. BŞK.	Yıldız Başkitabet Dairesi Maruz
Y. PRK. ASK.	Yıldız Askeri Maruzat
Y. PRK. AZJ.	Yıldız Arzuhal Jurnal
ZB.	Zabtiye Nezareti Evrak

1

Introduction: The Decline Paradigm of the Ulema Reconsidered

The ulema[1] have not attracted much attention by Western or Turkish scholars in spite of their socio-economic, cultural, military, political, and educational effects on society in the nineteenth century. The reason for the lack of interest in the function of the ulema and *the Ilmiye* (learned class) in the official version of Turkish historiography may be the identification of the ulema with backwardness, conservatism, and obscurantism from the Tanzimat Edict (Imperial Edict of Reorganisation) to the mid-twentieth century.[2] However, today's historians are examining the influence that the ulema had on nineteenth-century reforms in order to bring to light such issues as hand secularism, the place of the Directorate of Religious Affairs, and religious education in public schools, which are still unresolved in today's world and are rooted in nineteenth-century reform movements. In the limited current literature, the ulema is generally studied in only one respect: their attitudes against the Ottoman reforms. Nevertheless, the reaction of the ulema towards modernizing reforms has been controversial since it began to be studied by historians.[3] Most studies about the ulema describe it as a reactionary, hardline conservative group standing in opposition to efforts to modernize.[4]

Some historians generally analyze the decline of the influence of religious affairs and the Ottoman ulema in public life as a requirement of modernization and centralization in the nineteenth century.[5] Most authors who study the Ottoman ulema attribute their loss of importance to their anti-modernization attitudes. Those authors are generally encouraged by the idea that the Ottoman government was in decline in the nineteenth century. Advocates of this argument say that the first three centuries of the empire were its expansion years and that the Ottomans experienced their golden age after these first three centuries. When the empire neared its end, stagnation was inevitable, and this regressive period in the empire's history developed into regional contraction and political corruption. Conventional historians describe the nineteenth century as a period of crises, weakness, and decline that lasted until the empire collapsed in 1922. Aside from this paradigm of decline, some historians interpret the nineteenth century as a period of the formation of a modern state that developed out of new institutionalization efforts. However, approaches that only identify the nineteenth century either as a period of modernization or as a period of weakness, crises, and decline are Eurocentric, Western viewpoints. Particularly "Turkish nationalist" historians who want to draw a line between the Ottoman State and the republican era define the empire in later periods as a state in which officials were unsuccessful at modernizing society. Meanwhile, society was tied to traditions and could not shake the past. This was a different kind of decline paradigm of the empire. But a key fact that doesn't fit this decline paradigm is that the institutionalization efforts of the nineteenth century, which started in 1789 with the enthronement of the reformist Sultan Selim III, represented a long, multifaceted period. The institutionalization efforts were undertaken to save the empire from European encroachment, not from decline and backwardness.[6] Although the nineteenth century is called "the longest century of the empire,"[7] this longevity or these long attempts at the resistance that resulted from efforts to ensure the empire's survival by implementing the reforms did not save it from collapse.

Older literature on the Ottoman ulema predominantly offers a picture of decreasing power and effect of the ulema in society, especially through the analysis of the reformist policy of the empire. This literature also generally emphasizes the ulema's attitudes against reform movements and their weakening power. Most of this literature describing the ulema and religious institutions is about how the power of the ulema decreased during the nineteenth century. This is another important problem in the Ilmiye literature, apart from the lack of studies on the social history of Ottoman ulema. Although this book is an examination of the Ottoman ulema's role in the nineteenth century, it differs significantly from earlier studies on the Ottoman ulema's power with respect to its unconventional approach to the questions and different answers and standpoints vis-à-vis the same questions. Also, previous mainstream studies with a few exceptions generally do not provide data in terms of the social origins, profiles, and functions of the ulema during the reformist era. The narrative shared by these studies is bereft of any analysis of archival documents. The ulema are described as composed of insignificant political actors who disobeyed the reforms. These studies do not appreciate the support of the ulema for reform and their place within the new government bureaucracy.[8] They ignored the ulema's adaptation to social, political, educational, and professional life in the nineteenth century. In contrast to the one-sidedness of previous studies, this book aims to depict the roles of the ulema in formal and social life to generate a complex picture of the Ilmiye members.

This book evaluates the prevalent tendency in the current historiography towards the belief in a decline paradigm with respect to the ulema in the nineteenth century. It argues how the ulema adapted to the new situation and requirements by criticizing the paradigm of the decline of ulema institutions in light of first-hand documents. It also offers a different interpretation of claims regarding the decline of the Ottoman ulema's power through an analysis of the educational and professional life of the ulema in various regions during the late nineteenth century. In this regard, the present study diverges from conventional Ottoman historiography in at least two respects. First, it identifies the impact of a new form of government policy on the professionalization[9] of the Ilmiye members and the capacities and activities of the ulema in the Ilmiye office through a study of who the ulema were. Second, it sheds light on the exact processes of their educational, professional, and social missions in detail.

One primary focus of this book is the ways in which the ulema maintained their position in the eyes of the people, especially in the peripheral regions. The functionality of the ulema to the government in developing its infrastructural capacity at the periphery of the empire constitutes the scope of this study. It will also be evaluated how the Ottoman ulema interacted with and influenced the decision-making processes of the empire. This book offers a different perspective on literature that advocates the decreasing role of the ulema in the nineteenth century. In spite of the existence of deficiencies within the Ilmiye institutions, the powerful networks of these institutions and the quality of education and professional experiences of official ulema will be focused on as central and real agents of the administrative structure.

Major Themes in Studies on the Decline of the Ottoman Ulema

The core of the Tanzimat reforms was actualized in two parts—the first composed of taxation and provincial administration reforms and the second educational and judicial ones. Reforms in education and justice are given as the reason for the declining role of the ulema. The weakening of the ulema's position is considered to be the reason the Ottoman ulema lost their political significance as legal and educational civil servants with the centralization and bureaucratization that resulted from reform movements. This belief is accepted as fact in conventional historiography.

In this regard, some authors querying the ulema's power in the nineteenth century examine the ulema's attitude towards reforms mainly according to their socio-economic structure. They also observe that the ulema were not a monolithic class and therefore the relationships among different groups of ulema were characterized as an imbalance. They generally divide the ulema's attitudes towards reforms into three. The first group of ulema was the high-ranking ulema and they supported reforms to a full extent because they continued to receive new posts and status in the new system. This group is smaller than the other groups. The second group of ulema was the low-ranking level ulema and they opposed reforms since they were uncomfortable and against the government's political, traditional, and religious reforms. The main concern of this group was to maintain its autonomous position in the public arena. They carried on the values and concerns of traditional religion. By contrast, the third group of ulema constituted the vast majority who did not have a clear opinion about the reforms. They neither supported nor reacted to the reforms.

Uriel Heyd's approach to the ulema from a class perspective is one of the most important representatives of the socio-economic approach. According to Heyd, while high-ranking ulema supported modernization, low-ranking ulema were strongly against the reforms. Uriel Heyd says that high-ranking ulema supported the reforms because of the decreasing power of the empire and raison d'Etat, the government's hostility to Janissaries, and Bektashis who were important supporters of the ulema.[10] Therefore, high-ranking members of the ulema did not constitute a social body standing against the government's reformist politics, but "many ulema in the lower ranks remained extremely hostile to European innovations."[11] The ongoing struggle between higher and lower class ulema reflected their place in social and political life. He argued that low-ranking ulema had to withdraw from the political scene because of their resistance to the reforms, in contrast to high-ranking ulema supportive of the reforms who preserved their place and importance on the political stage.[12]

Also, Arnold H. Green analyzes the frustration of the lower-ranking ulema with the authorities because of rules and regulations that prevented their advancement in the new government system during the Tanzimat. As a result, they mainly took a stand with reactionaries like the Janissary corps, the Bektashi lodges, and some other popular revolts against the sultan. On the other hand, the higher ulema supported the sultans to protect the continuity of the regime.

Because the high-ranking ulema were part of the ruling bureaucracy, they wanted to protect their position in the system. So they cooperated with the Sultans' reformist policies.[13] In other words, high-ranking ulema were keen on maintaining the stability of the state.[14] Similarly, Avigdor Levy says that low-ranking ulema showed hostility towards Westernization reforms and began to lose power in the nineteenth century.[15] Levy also notes that Sultan Mahmud's appointment of low-ranking ulema as *imams* in the newly established army was an exception. Even though low-ranking ulema opposed the reforms, they supported the sultan against the Janissaries having been recruited into the new military system.[16]

Some other studies, however, tend to treat the decline of the ulema only as an indicator of secularism and modernization, like the establishment of modern education and secular courts, rather than as an institutional transformation that requires an explanation in its own right. These scholars argue that all ulema's power began to decrease in the nineteenth century, regardless of their socio-economic positions. Bernard Lewis was one author who said that the Ilmiye class started to lose importance at the beginning of the nineteenth century. Lewis argues that in the new government structure of Sultan Mahmud II, the Sublime Porte and the palace expanded their influence to a great extent. The administration of the new bureaucratic structure was left to bureaucrats who were educated in Western values and trained in the Translation Bureau. This group lived isolated from the rest of society. As a result of the modernization reforms during this period, the Ilmiye class started to lose power and the ulema turned into a pseudo-ulema. Lewis contends that during the Tanzimat period, the Islamic character of the government was damaged. Secularism gradually expanded to government offices and legislation. Secular laws adopted from the West were applied in many areas, and secular education became popular. This modernization movement affected the relationship between the state and religion. The religious character and Islamic appearance of the state structure started to change progressively. Also, Lewis says of the government's authority over other semi-autonomous institutions within the centralization movement: namely, Janissaries, provincial notables *(ayan)*, and ulema affected the distribution of political power by the government. The abolition of the Janissaries, the reduction in the influence of the *ayans*, and the gradually decreasing role of the ulema in politics caused the government to adopt an authoritarian structure.[17]

Similarly, Niyazi Berkes argued that the power of the ulema decreased with modernization and the transformation of the bureaucracy. He first states that the şeyhülislam, who was the person leading the Ilmiye class, was excluded from the government administration by Sultan Mahmud II, who made him an ordinary religious official.[18] In this period, Sharia law's conservative power in government affairs began to evaporate. That *Divan-ı Ahkam-ı Adliye* established the secular justice system in 1868, became another step in the reduction of the power of the ulema.[19] Moreover, Berkes argued that during the first constitutional period, the ulema started to be one of the main opposition groups that used pamphlets, meetings, and agitation among madrasa students.[20] For Berkes, all these developments were indicators that the government had begun to lose its theocratic structure and that the scope of the ulema class diminished in the nineteenth century. Berkes also stated that the Tanzimat Edict of 1839 was a significant break with the past in terms of the centralization, rationalization, and bureaucratization reforms of the Tanzimat state. Berkes explains the conventional point of view that the ulema declined as the state introduced centralization and bureaucratization programs in the Tanzimat era that were not supported by the ulema. In the end, the ulema became powerless and lost their sovereignty in most cases. The ulema's supreme aim was the preservation of the traditional order, not change or reform.[21] Also, Berkes said that in the same period, important individuals belonging to the Ilmiye class, such as Cevdet Pasha, began to work in bureaucratic positions. İlmiye members expected their position in the government to increase again with these kinds of posts, but these expectations were not met by the government, and the Ilmiye members continued their decline, he says.

In describing the main features of the ulema, Richard Chambers indicates that the position of the ulema was relatively stable until the Tanzimat period. At the onset of modernization, when the empire experienced bureaucratization and centralization, both the importance and influence of the office of the Şeyhülislam in particular and the Ilmiye group in general steadily declined. Chambers explains the reasons for this decline as mainly their inability to compete with a rising civilian bureaucracy and newly opened educational centers, their lack of military support after the elimination of the Janissaries, and the destruction of their financial resources. Also, he asserts that the influence of the şeyhülislam on government affairs started to decrease with the Tanzimat Edict of 1839 and the Islahat Edict of 1856 by transferring some duties of the şeyhülislam to newly established councils, such as the Supreme Council for Judicial Regulations *(Meclis-i Vala-ı Ahkam-ı Adliye)* and the Supreme Council of the Reforms *(Meclis-i Ali-i Tanzimat)*.[22] In the end, Chambers says, the reasons for this decline were increasing secularism, the loss of financial autonomy, the cutting of waqf income for the ulema, and the rise of modern schools as alternatives to traditional madrasa education.[23]

Another author who argues that the power of the ulema decreased in the nineteenth century is Nikki Keddie. For her, given the continued growth of government power as well as the expansion of the army, bureaucracy, and secular education, even in villages, the political power of the ulema probably continued to decline in the nineteenth century as it had in the last half of the eighteenth century. Also, the founding of Western-style schools and the disintegration of traditional madrasa institutions led to the loss of the ulema's position and influence.[24]

Stanford and Ezel Kural Shaw discuss the bureaucratic position of three groups in the Ottoman Empire in the nineteenth century. These groups were the *Mabeyn-i Hümayun*, formed by the sultans and some attendants; the *Bab-ı Seraskeri*, representing the military class; and the *Bab-ı Meşihat*, made up of the ulema. The authors say that the weakest in political terms in the nineteenth century was the Meşihat. They began to lose the support of both the government and society with the reform movement. At first the ulema reacted defensively toward reforms. They worried that their privileges would be harmed by the reforms, and they were therefore cautious about the movement. They were worried that they could be abolished or that their influence could be decreased since there was a possibility that centralization would isolate them from the educational and judicial arenas. They were perceived only as religious leaders in the nineteenth century. They lost their influence in jurisprudence and education as a result of the reform movements. The ulema were never as strong as when they had the support of the Janissaries.[25]

According to Carter Findley, the reasons for the decline of the Ilmiye class were both the bureaucratization and abolition of the traditional religious education system due to its failure to solve the problems faced by the government.[26] The replacement of religious educational institutions with modern educational institutions changed the education system that was established between the Treaty of Küçük Kaynarca (1774) and the Russian invasion of Crimea (1783). Findley says that in the nineteenth century, the ulema's educational concerns were limited to religious matters in contrast with earlier periods when the ulema were trained in a wide range of subject areas—from astronomy to mathematics.[27] As a result, the Ottoman ulema began to be excluded from important decisions made in government institutions starting at the beginning of the nineteenth century, especially regarding reforms in the field of education. Also, Findley argues that much of the money once allocated to religious foundations began to remain in the government treasury in the nineteenth century, especially after the removal of Janissaries (Auspicious Incident, called Vaka-yı Hayriye, the Beneficent Event, in Ottoman historiography) in 1826. The ulema, who had support from the Janissaries, were alone as a movement against the administration following the removal of the Janissaries.[28] Findley says that mosques and religious foundations in many parts of the empire did not have adequate funding, not even to cover minor repairs, during the modernization period, and eventually, the ulema lost their importance in politics, jurisprudence, and education.

Another author well known for his works on the Ilmiye and ulema is Mehmet İpşirli. According to İpşirli, the establishment of the Ministry of Pious Foundations (*Evkaf-ı Hümayun Nezareti*) was an important reason for the declining role of the Ottoman ulema because the incomes and administration of religious institutions and endowments were diverted from the ulema to central authorities and the treasury by this ministry.[29]

Ahmet Cihan divided the Ottoman ulema's relationship with rulers into three periods: the first was the formation and development phase from 1300 to 1600. The second period of stagnation from 1600 to 1770 was followed by the third phase of reformation from 1770 to 1876. Also, he divided the third phase into two. Between the years 1770 and 1830, the first period the ulema pioneered reforms. In a second phase of rerouting between the years of 1830 and 1876, the ulema were gradually excluded from Ottoman political life despite their active participation in the reforms.[30] Although Ahmet Cihan says the ulema were strong at the beginning of the reform years, their power decreased thereafter. Cihan says that the ulema were used as a decision-making mechanism in government during the reform years, especially from the 1770s to the 1830s. In that initial period of the reformist era, the ulema and the Ilmiye were pioneering reforms and sharing the risks and official responsibilities for the reforms and their power increased.[31] However, like most of the literature on the ulema's power during the nineteenth century, Cihan argues that the ulema began to be gradually excluded from political life starting in the 1830s because they had to share governmental positions, especially in the educational and judicial fields, with Western institutions as a result of the reforms from 1830 to 1876.[32] Although Cihan said that the ulema withdrew from Ottoman political life by abandoning the educational and judiciary areas to the emerging Western institutions and persons that came with the Tanzimat reforms, this transformation in the reform period can be interpreted differently. Likewise, the ulema continued to be involved in education and the administration of law by incorporating themselves into the newly established European institutions.

Amit Bein also published a comprehensive book that covered a wide range of topics related to the ulema of the late Ottoman period and early Republican era.

In contrast with earlier narratives about the negative branding of the ulema, he argues that the ulema's most esteemed members supported the reform movements and that madrasas trained brilliant and talented religious scholars. However, an identity crisis ensued with the new republican regime. They were caught between their roles of the "agents of change and the guardians of faith". Amit Bein argues that this secular regime transformed the ulema into a pragmatic group, and the ulema began to engage with the new political scene in the early republican period. Also, Bein explains that the effects of the reforms in the context of centralization and bureaucratization were more apparent in the institution of Religious Affairs (Diyanet). The new republican government made Diyanet responsible for all religious affairs. Most functions of the Şeyhülislam were taken over by newly established government institutions during this time. The ulema's authority was limited, and they were transformed into an institution that controlled only the Diyanet. The Diyanet, as a continuation of the Şeyhülislam office, lost its old popularity but it was still a source of legitimacy for the new republican regime. However, the ulema came to a grim end, withdrawing from the political scene as a result of the modern education system.[33]

The book by Susan Gunasti, *The Qur'an between the Ottoman Empire and the Turkish Republic*, is the product of a comprehensive study examining the social, professional, and, intellectual side of a leading religious scholar, Elmalılı. Rather than presenting the decline of ulema narratives, this book emphasizes the powerful place of an eminent late Ottoman scholar and his Qur'an commentary.[34]

Yalçınkaya's book comprehensively evaluates the changing and expanding Ottoman views and debates on science and values in the nineteenth century. It emphasizes how the ulema adapted to the new discourses on science and how the ulema became the representatives of new discourses on knowledge and science by using the Islamic and traditional concepts. It also offers a different interpretation of Ottoman ulema regarding science through the contextual analysis of the discourses on scientific knowledge formed by the new elite. According to Yalçınkaya, the ulema succeeded in forming alliances with the new Ottoman elite although the financial and administrative autonomy of the ulema was restricted.[35]

Rethinking the Decline of the Ottoman Ulema

It has been frequently argued that the paradigm of the decline of the Ottoman ulema has been overturned for several decades. The common view in the ulema and the Ilmiye literature is that the secularist, modernist, Westernization reform programs starting with the Tanzimat Edict resulted in a decrease in the ulema's political and social power as important members of this class. In the analyses of the scholars who argue that the power of the ulema declined in the nineteenth century, the secular, modernist politics of the government were represented in opposition to the ulema and religion.

Most historians in their studies about the ulema and their attitudes during the nineteenth century failed to take into account the individual perspectives of members of the Ilmiye. Their approaches towards the loss of the ulema's power were compared to the decline of the clergy's power in contemporaneous Europe. They draw the conclusion that modernization led to a similar result for the Ottoman ulema as for the European clergy. This situation reflects the paradigm of endless crisis between modernity and tradition. However, this approach overlooks the historical role of the ulema in Ottoman society because it perceives them as standard-bearers of traditional culture.[36] Also, this paradigm of the declining power of the ulema conceals the major role of the ulema in the transformation of the Ottoman state from an empire to a nation-state. These studies show that the modernist bias is inadequate for analyzing the decline of the Ottoman ulema in the nineteenth century and proving this claim. As an alternative, this book argues that ulema-state relations continued to be a major source of concern for Ottoman ruling elites even in the post-Tanzimat era, contrary to what is generally portrayed. There was a mutually supportive relationship between the ulema and the government, molded to suit the political authority's needs. Because the religious structure was dependent on the favors and support of the ruling elite,[37] the ulema developed an intense relationship with the government. The ulema facilitated the shaping of this relationship by providing legality to the rule of the sovereign under the light of Islamic rules. They were committed to the defense of the empire, and their first target was to protect the raison d'Etat rather than enforce their power or serve their interests.[38]

The Ottoman ulema were aware of the political problems faced during the Tanzimat period, such as territorial disintegration and the growing penetration of European powers into the empire. The conditions the empire experienced in the nineteenth century damaged the existence and stability of the government. This book shows that in such circumstances, the Ottoman ulema's approach to reorganization under the Tanzimat reforms was above all to protect the government's existence and stability. The dominant opinion of the ulema towards the reformation was that "we are all in the same boat."[39] The ulema advocated for the importance of obedience to the sultan while the sultan was making his reforms, and they supported the military reforms of the Tanzimat period on the grounds that jihad was a sacred task vis-à-vis European threats. The basic argument was that all Muslims were required to obey the orders of the sultan so long as his actions did not contradict Sharia. They also believed that support for the sultan and the existence and stability of the empire would determine the fate of Islam. Hence, the Ottoman ulema supported the sultan and his reforms for the sake of religion and the state. In contrast to arguments about the ulema's degeneration, both the high- and low-ranking ulema were generally complacent and sometimes supportive with respect to the reforms. For instance, İlber Ortaylı evaluated the attitude of the ulema toward modernization more positively and with a level-headed approach.[40] He argued that the Ottoman ulema did not support modernization unconditionally, but supported the Westernization efforts of the central government.[41]

David Kushner also provides invaluable data and emphasizes the job opportunities in new government departments alongside traditional ones for the ulema during the nineteenth century. He perceives that the Tanzimat "opened new avenues to those who sought their careers as ulema."[42] Therefore, the ulema, excepting neither high nor low-ranking *alim*, were still powerful on the political scene in the nineteenth century.[43] The ulema could challenge the reforms and continue to hold powerful, prestigious places in society, but the government required the ulema's support and religious legitimization to implement its reforms. In this regard, the ulema became indispensable allies of the government as a channel of political communication.

According to the proponents of the declining power of the ulema, the impact of the long nineteenth century on the decline of the ulema was manifest in the modernization and secularization of the government, such as the opening of new, modern schools and secular courts. Because a new elite group educated in secular government schools of the Tanzimat took the place of the ulema, the latter was no longer the only group representing Islam. Therefore, the proponents of the paradigm of the declining power of the ulema say that traditional madrasa education lost popularity and that the ulema started to assume a few bureaucratic positions in government offices when this new system of education began. After these developments, the role of the ulema—both as individuals and as an institution—was thought to have deteriorated. The opening of new schools could be seen as a radical break upsetting the traditional position and status of the ulema in the nineteenth century. However, the ulema's encounter with new secular schools did not result in a decline of their power. The ulema maintained their standing by securing seats in new institutions as officials.

Another focus of proponents of the declining power of the ulema is the increasingly centralized system of modern government. Although changes took place in the political authority of the Ottoman Empire, the content of the religious centralization program of the government did not change over time. Therefore, the proponents of the decreasing power of the ulema say that the Tanzimat state, which was determined to develop new strategies to provide religious centralization in both central cities and provincial areas, attempted to minimize the ulema's autonomy and maintain control in order to centralize its power. The Ottoman government gradually became more concerned with the ulema and the contents of their sermons in the mosques. Indeed, the government's attempt to check the movements of the ulema was a development to which the Ilmiye class was not accustomed. Therefore, the ulema's response to the challenges of modernization was first tied to their desire for self-preservation. Even if the Tanzimat brought about more government intervention for the ulema, this was not peculiar to the Ilmiye class. This regulation and bureaucratization affected almost all government institutions. The attempt of the government to control the ulema was not intended to reduce the power of the Ilmiye class; indeed, there was no amendment to the role of the ulema. The government's attempts entailed a general bureaucratization movement and centralization policy of the government. However, this bureaucratization did not negatively affect the position of the ulema. This study reveals that the members of the Ilmiye in general and the ulema, in particular, took part as active officials in the empire's new, emergent institutions.

Furthermore, many scholars have thought of the Ottoman ulema itself as an outside bureaucratic organ in the nineteenth century. However, in contrast to the decline doctrine, the new, centralized government incorporated the ulema into government mechanisms. More recently, scholars such as Halil İbrahim Erbay[44] and Jun Akiba[45] examine the ulema in this sense. Specifically, they have shown the importance of the ulema by focusing on their educational careers and their involvement in the newly established government system. The educational and intellectual mobility of the late nineteenth century did indeed create a professionally trained and qualified ulema class in the Ottoman Empire that filled the new bureaucratic positions. In this sense, the centralized government system threatened the position of the ulema but at the same time offered them new opportunities and status. The balance of power between the central administration and the ulema developed new dimensions, through which new alliances were formed. The centralization movement of the government aimed to increase the government's capacity by redistributing new titles to the ulema.

The government wanted the ulema to provide trained personnel to fill new bureaucratic positions in the Tanzimat era. The government's concern with centralizing the civil ulema by placing them within the bureaucratic system was the result of an inclination for salaried, obedient civil servants. The Ottoman ulema were successfully integrated into the Ottoman bureaucracy as official civil servants. Many new posts were granted to the ulema in various ministries and they were appointed as the new scholars in modern schools. The new ulema bureaucrats had the necessary skills to staff such positions. Graduates of the madrasas, which were used to fill the new positions, played a crucial role in the formation of a new bureaucratic cadre in the empire. Although most madrasas lost their monopoly over education, many of the ulema maintained their access to power in the government.

Another point of criticism of the pervading view concerns the situation of the Şeyhülislam in the Tanzimat era. Even though some authors argue that the Ottoman ulema's power decreased in the nineteenth century and that the authority of the Şeyhülislam started an incremental decline, in fact, the role of the ulema and the Şeyhülislam were always important on the political stage. Even though the reformist period of Sultan Mahmud II affected the position of the office of the Şeyhülislam, these reforms did not neuter it; the sultan simply tried to bureaucratize the Ilmiye by restructuring it. Sultan Mahmud II found support from the ulema for these reforms because the sultan resolved the duality between religion and the government and did not remove religion from society. Furthermore, Sultan Mahmud II made a great effort to prevent the Ilmiye opposition to the reforms. One of his most important efforts was to create new jobs for the ulema, like high-status military positions. In addition, government officials conferred with the ulema on a regular basis, participated in Ramadan activities conducted by the ulema, and constructed or endowed mosques and religious schools. Sultan Mahmud, therefore, both facilitated reform plans and controlled the ulema through the privileges given to them.[46]

Another common argument for the breakdown of the Ottoman ulema's political authority in the nineteenth century is that they lost the respect of the populace because secularization encroached on all aspects of life. This situation made the ulema increasingly ineffective, those scholars argue. Contrary to the proponents of the decreasing power of ulema in the post-Tanzimat era, however, when the government was secularizing, there was no distinct break with religion. For instance, the inception of secular law did not entail a completely different government structure. In reality, the fundamentals of Islamic law were protected until the end of the empire; at least, Islamic law continued its ostensible existence.

In this sense, the ulema were always influential among the public through their Islamic discourse and knowledge. Therefore, the government wanted to win the ulema's support for maintaining the government's existence by granting them status, salaries, and posts in the administration. Under these conditions, the ulema usually had cause to support rulers and their centralizing policies, and in many cases, the ulema were among their chief supporters. They wholeheartedly embraced reform projects and thereby protected their independent positions in the religious and political fields. After the Tanzimat reforms, the ulema's political sphere and discourses were accordingly reformulated and gained new meaning.

Moreover, the ulema provided an influential counterattack to various streams of religious thought that began to worry the Ottoman administration in the nineteenth century. The increasing effects of Wahhabism, Shiism, and foreign missionary activities in the Ottoman realm endangered Ottoman sovereignty in this century. In response to these various religious comments, the Ottoman Empire attempted to disseminate official Islamic propaganda through the ulema. To avoid the rise of factions within Islam, the Ottoman ruling elite standardized Islamic doctrine and promoted a unified Islamic order. They did so with the help of a new printing policy for religious books, through the institutional identity of educational centers, and through attempts to centralize the Ilmiye and tariqa institutions. The ulema's attempts to preserve religious unity and harmony served as a guide for the next generation. Hence, the ulema had a significant role in the adoption of Tanzimat reforms with the purpose of ensuring the government's perpetuity in the nineteenth century.

Lastly, some of the literature argues that the great *mollas* (*molla* is a superior rank in the Ilmiye hierarchy) sought to ensure their sons' futures and regularly promoted and awarded their sons the necessary certificates to be appointed to official government posts in the nineteenth century. This resulted in many unqualified madrasa graduates holding teaching posts.[47] Although the ulema sons were in positions to protect their status thanks to their fathers' professions, the sons were not appointed to their fathers' office as long as they did not have the necessary scientific qualifications for the Ilmiye hierarchy. There were always men who followed the necessary order of advancement to take their graduation certificates *(icazet)* and earn posts in the Ilmiye hierarchy. The presence of this substantial number of qualified trained ulema contradicts the narrative of degenerated ulema and madrasa institutions.

To sum up, the relationship between the central elite and the ulema was based on mutual interest in the nineteenth century. The capacity for state control over administrative practices, the loyalty of Muslims to the state, and the maintenance of state order in provincial areas was limited owing to the lack of qualified bureaucrats, and financial resources. At this point, the government needed the ulema's support in order to rescue the empire and consolidate state power, so the state strategically incorporated the ulema into the administration and tried to regulate society with their help. One essential function of the ulema was to help the ruling class to preserve order *(nizam)* in provincial places. Similarly, the ulema needed the state's protection to preserve their privileges. Therefore, a large number of ulema aided the state's reformist policy. The ulema's prestige depended on their collaboration with the rulers. Under this partnership, the ruling elite obtained legitimacy and the ulema maintained their dignity in society so long as they supported state policies.

In contrast to the narrative of the decreasing power of the ulema within the context of the new centralized administration, the state of the ulema was not socially, economically, or intellectually weak at the dawn of the nineteenth century. Their importance continued to grow even in the Tanzimat period. The Tanzimat reforms threatened the ulema's privileges and position in the government hierarchy, but they also provided new opportunities for them to increase their wealth and vigor. Therefore, the sultans' early modernization reforms in various fields were supported and even carried out with the cooperation of many ulema. For instance, Ahmed Cevdet Pasha's support for secular education was followed by that of Arif Hikmet Bey, who was appointed as the Şeyhülislam in 1846 by Sultan Abdülmecid. The list of ulema concerned with secular education is not limited to Ahmet Cevdet and Arif Hikmet Bey. Selim Sabit Efendi and Hoca Tahsin were among other famous supporters of the Tanzimat's secularist education policies. Arif Hikmet Bey and Ahmet Cevdet were proponents of the judicial reforms of the Tanzimat, and Sahhaflar Şeyhi-zade Seyyid Mehmed Esad Efendi supported reform initiatives by Sultan Mahmud through his writings.[48]

Conclusion

Despite numerous works of mainstream historiography on the Ilmiye and ulema, the literature on the Ottoman ulema is far from comprehensive as far as the true place and function of the ulema during the nineteenth century is concerned. In the current historiography, most works focus on the paradigm of the declining power of the ulema, concentrating on increasing secularism in the empire, the ulema's loss of political autonomy, and the rise of modern, Western forms of education as alternatives to traditional madrasa education. In these studies, the ulema are represented nearly as conservative instructors of Islamic religion, and they have a deeply rooted tendency to conceptualize the ulema as a traditionalist opposition to the reform movements of the Tanzimat period. However, this perspective needs to be questioned. Through a quantitative analysis of primary sources found in the Meşihat Archive and Prime Ministry Ottoman Archive, this book argues that the Ilmiye class expanded its position and role in newly created institutions, becoming the voice of the provincial population and an effective partner of the central government in the organization of new judicial and educational systems in the nineteenth century. In contrast to the extant literature that mostly overlooks the ulema's actual role in the application of reforms and regulations during the reform period, this book contributes to filling the gap on the ulema's educational, professional, institutional, and social role in the literature.

In contrast with the basic assumptions by mainstream historiography about the total decline of the Ottoman ulema, this chapter evaluated the ulema and the Ilmiye as part of a transformative process in a changing Ottoman Empire. It focuses on the emergence of new types of social and administrative roles of the ulema who hold a variety of positions in society as active and qualified, trained officials of the central government in the late nineteenth century. From this perspective, the central government turned the ulema working under the office of Şeyhülislam into an institutionalized class and minimized the role of the ulema as power brokers, unlike their predecessors. In this regard, this study aims to contribute to the further understanding of the new identity of the ulema which became more uniform and permanent under the direct control of central authorities.

2

The Re-organization of the Şeyhülislam Office (1826–1914)

To eliminate bureaucratic weaknesses, the Ottoman Empire entered a new phase of state-building, institutionalization, and centralization—known as the Tanzimat reforms—in almost every field of state bureaucracy in the nineteenth century. The Tanzimat state aimed to end the autonomous rulers and re-establish the empire's governmental system, so the ruling elite generated a new perspective on bureaucracy, society, economy, religion, and all other forms of life. The purpose of this project was to fortify the state with absolute authority and overcome the empire's decline through the centralization of state institutions. Parallel to the restructuring process, the learned class *(the Ilmiye)*, one of three main administrative offices of the Ottoman State, the others of which were the military class *(seyfiye)* and the bureaucrats *(kalemiye)*, was most exposed to constant state intervention in the nineteenth century.[1] The effects of the restructuring and institutionalization movement on the establishment of the new office of the Şeyhülislam will be the topic of this chapter.

The main task of the Ilmiye class in general and the ulema, in particular, is to protect the faith and guide Muslims in the difficulties and challenges they face by interpreting and analyzing the sources of the religious law.[2] Since the ulema were Sharia's practitioners and almost all of the day-to-day issues of the state were determined by the Sharia, the services of the ulema were essential in the social, political, and economic arenas of the Ottoman Empire. The Ilmiye class, which had a prominent role in the resumption of the Islamic function of the state, had a special position within the centralized state structure because of the Islamic character of the Ottoman Empire. Therefore, the evolution of the Ilmiye institution, which was one area where the transformation of the Tanzimat reforms was felt, and the role of the ulema as its main instrument is an issue that needs to be addressed.

The ulema as part of the Ilmiye institution adapted to the new circumstances of nineteenth-century concepts of centralization and institutionalization and engaged as an essential part of the Ottoman state order with the new departments under the Şeyhülislam Office. In other words, Ottoman authority engaged the ulema and restructured its relationship with religious affairs through state-centered religious mechanisms in the nineteenth century. In this regard, it will be concentrated on the development of the Ilmiye authority and follow its evolution chronologically, focusing on the Şeyhülislam Office in particular. So, the consolidation of the institutionalized Ilmiye system, the desire of the government to create religious integrity, and the creation of a new centralized religious environment under the influence of the bureaucracy can be better understood.

The institutionalization of the Şeyhülislam Office had two main concerns: First, it focused on a solid control mechanism of the central state over religion, and religious authorities. Thus, semiautonomous attitudes and characteristics were prevented by the government. Second, this institutionalization process handled the creation of a new office for the Şeyhülislam and the establishment of new departments under the Şeyhülislam Office. The number of departments and personnel increased as a result of the new departments and these new personnel performed their duties in accordance with an institutionalized and professionalized bureaucracy.

Expanding Central Government Control

Systematic social control and supervision in the Ottoman Empire became a new mechanism to regulate state–society relations towards the middle of the nineteenth century.[3] The state's capacity to dominate and control religious affairs was limited at the beginning. However, the Tanzimat was a turning point in terms of the interaction between the government and religion in the empire. The government's first demand of ulema within the centralization context was to stay out of political matters that opposed the interests of the government. The Tanzimat was a period of creating a single official religion as well as an attempt at greater state intervention vis-à-vis the ulema and their activities in the Ottoman Empire.

In the nineteenth century, the oppositional movements of some Islamic groups against the state interests justified the state's involvement in religion and with religious authorities. The state needed a centralized religious administrative tool as a mechanism to supervise religious affairs, to disseminate this official state religion, and to reject alternative understandings of religion.[4] In this regard, the Tanzimat state founded the committee of the Ilmiye inspectors under the Şeyhülislam Office to supervise the activities of the entire Ilmiye class. These inspectors were in charge of control over the madrasas as well as examining the duties of all of the Ilmiye members. These inspectors checked the Ilmiye officials' professional qualifications and prepared official reports for the office of Şeyhülislam.[5] By using the Ilmiye inspectors to supervise the functionality of the professional Ilmiye organization, the government realized control over the ulema. The state thereby fulfilled its wish of controlling the ulema with the help of the Ilmiye inspectors to police the functions of the Ilmiye organization.

First, the Ilmiye institution was reconstructed to gain the favor of Muslim subjects and to suppress alternate, opposing religious interpretations. The central state aimed to replace varied interpretations of Islam with the one true Islam of the state for the sake of society's solidarity and unity. The Ilmiye hierarchy turned into a representative of "ideal", "real" Islam through their teaching design to encourage religious harmony and solidarity among the Muslim subjects in society. According to the proper Islamic definition of the state, the central state attempted to establish a single authority for the Sunni religion, and the Ilmiye class was reorganized to counterattack the increase in radical Islamic religious sects and factions. This government intervention vis-à-vis the multiplicity of religious views resulted in the monopolization of religious affairs and the diminishment of pluralist views about Islam. In other words, Sunni Islam in the Ottoman Empire was equated with the "state religion". Maintaining a traditional Sunni understanding of religion and culture was expected to produce territorial unification, a sense of solidarity, understanding within communities, and loyal subject of the state.

The Şeyhülislam was responsible for constructing a disciplined religious body to avoid the formation of alternative understandings deviating from the official Sunni Islam and to disseminate the proper, state perception of Islam. In this system, the mission of the ulema was to provide an integrated society under the root of Sunni understanding. In pursuit of this goal, firstly, the respected ulema were sent to the provinces of the Ottoman Empire for protecting this single religious understanding.[6] For example, the government appointed ulema to Syria, Iraq, and Middle Eastern provinces to spread the Sunni understanding in contrast with the increasing fragmentation of Islam.[7] Secondly, the government removed from office those ulema that were sympathetic to alternative Islamic interpretations. For instance, Abdülvahid Çelebi from among ulema members and a Mevlevi sheikh was accused of being Bektashi by the Konya governor and the mufti. According to reports sent by the provincial governor and mufti in

Konya in 1898, Abdülvahid Çelebi was an influential figure in society and was deemed a dangerous figure who was weakening the Sunni understanding.[8] Because the official Sunni religious discourse was effectively encouraged by the government and was opposed to other beliefs like Shiite and Bektashi beliefs, the state closely followed the activities of Çelebi Efendi.

Second, the government made use of the power of the ulema to supervise the state's educational capacities. The traditional madrasas were strictly checked by the Ilmiye inspectors. Madrasa students who made a number of disobedient movements such as boycotting or not participating in classes were punished with dismissal and deportation.[9] The government thought that such disturbances were organized by madrasa students who had no references when registering for the madrasa. Therefore, it was decided that unidentified persons without references would not be admitted into the madrasas starting in 1849.[10] The office of Şeyhülislam inspectors recorded all of the Istanbul madrasa students individually along with their references in a special notebook.[11] This inspection committee also prohibited students from walking around in groups of ten or fifteen people and from walking around with guns in the bazaars and city centers. Central elites thus tried to prevent separatist organizations. Also, intoxicated students were reported in confidential reports to the office of Şeyhülislam by the inspectors, and such students were punished by the office of Şeyhülislam.[12]

Apart from controlling traditional madrasas, the state also strictly supervised the newly created modern schools with the help of the ulema. For this reason, the Ilmiye class was employed to teach religion in modern schools. The religious education in these newly established schools was taught by the ulema who were state officials, and the design of the religious curriculum of modern schools promoted ideals, among official Islamic thought of students as well as loyalty to the central elite.

Third, the central government increased involvement in religious affairs to use them as state agents according to the interests of the state. The government intended to use the ulema to control society and to include all religious organizations outside of state control into the state system. Therefore, the central administration developed new control strategies within the established religious order and intervened more to mold the ulema's viewpoint in line with the current political will of the state. All the religious activities and institutions in the empire were under absolute state control. For instance, the book of the religious teacher Hacı İbrahim Efendi on the doctrines of Islam (*Kavaid'ül İslam*) was not allowed to be published due to mistakes concerning basic religious doctrine.[13] To give another example, although the leader of the Rufai tariqa, Ebü'l-Hüda held the highest Ilmiye rank as Rumelia kazasker during the reign of Sultan Abdulhamid II,[14] his book about Abdulkadir Geylani was checked, and rejected by the Şeyhülislam Office. The reason for the prohibition of the book of Ebü'l-Hüda was the depiction of Abdulkadir Geylani as a non-religious man and the fact that Sheikh Ahmad Rufai was the only tariqa leader to be praised in the book. The Şeyhülislam Office viewed this as a violation of the Sunni understanding of Islam and feared that this booklet would cause disorder among Muslims. For this reason, the Şeyhülislam Office demanded that authorities immediately confiscate any copies found and prohibit this booklet from being printed.[15]

Also, the government perceived control over the Ottoman ulema's sermons and religious works as a prerequisite for the management of religious order in social life and the establishment of a true religious understanding among the people. In this context, the central government took strict precautions to constrain and manage the ulema's interpretations of Islam in or out of mosques and madrasas. The government started to supervise the ulema's Friday sermons,[16] the prayer leaders' *(imams)* sermons, and the mufti's fatwas in ensuing years with the council of examination of written works *(Tetkik-i Müellefat Encümeni* and *Teftiş-i Mesahif-i Şerife Meclisi)*. In this sense, the Friday sermons of the *imams* were always under the control of provincial administrators and the Ilmiye inspectors. The suitability of religious sermons and speeches was determined by the verdict of the provincial governor or provincial muftis who regulated their content according to the government's requests.[17] The attendance of the whole Muslim population in the Friday sermons in the mosques was of great importance so that new messages and political discourses of the government reach the public. Therefore, the khutbas and speeches had great power to influence the masses. In the past, the contents and subjects of the sermons and khutbas were personally determined by the ulema, and preachers *(vaiz)* added their own interpretations of the doctrines of the Quran and hadiths. However, according to the regulation on the writing of sermons, it was decided that the content of sermons such as exegesis *(tefsir)*, hadith, and homily *(sermons)*[18] would be determined by the office of Şeyhülislam.[19] With this regulation, the central body organized and monitored the content and subject of the Friday sermons, khutbas, and speeches. Central elites charged provincial governors with keeping all of the ulema's actions and even the contents of their sermons on Fridays under control.[20] Through this activity, the state wanted its politics to be compatible with the contents of ulema's sermons, khutbas, and speeches as an instrument of obedience and trust in the political ruler.[21] The ulema's personal interpretations and ideological analyses that opposed the wishes of state authorities were categorically rejected and disallowed in sermons by the central elites. If the preachers did not obey the rules of the government, the ruling elite did not hesitate to act ruthlessly toward them. Therefore, non-compliant ulema faced the risks of being excluded from religious professions, deportation, imprisonment, and temporary or life-long exile according to the specificities of each crime.[22] In this respect, many ulema were dismissed from duty. One of the most common reasons for dismissing was criticism of the current political matters of government. For instance, preachers of the Hagia Sofia and Fatih Mosques, Hayri, Osman, and Tatar Hoca were punished for inappropriate sermons. They were immediately reported to the Şeyhülislam Office because of their ideas that contradicted internal and external state politics and their criticism of exiling of Sheikh Abdülaziz Çavuş by the government in 1912. Such sermons from the mosque lectern *(kürsü)* were not accepted by the government.[23]

Similarly, the government also controlled the fatwas[24] in the context of centralization and institutionalization in the late nineteenth century. The obedience to a fatwa of the ulema was a fundamental of Islam for Sunni subjects.[25] Through fatwas, the ulema strengthened the community's confidence in the central government. In this regard, fatwas were not decisions limited to one person or place. They included the public at large and were applied with the consideration of religious customs. Their influence in increasing the obedience of subjects to the government and their religious and moral power increased in the nineteenth century as a result of some social, economic, and cultural shifts. In this respect, the Şeyhülislam Office's fatwas continued to legitimize the ruler's policies in this century. Therefore, the institutionalization strategy started to be applied by the central government through the establishment of the institutional fatwa office which played a key role in Muslim subjects' world views.

At the same time, the central government started to be interested in ulema's graduation certificates and to certify their ability to preach a sermon or teach in mosques and madrasas. Each member of the Ilmiye who gave sermons in the mosques had to graduate from a madrasa or obtain a religious certificate issued by the office of Şeyhülislam. The provincial governors and muftis were charged with checking ulema's preaching certificates.[26] In this regard, the government took significant precautions to check the ulema's speeches, attitudes, and competence. For instance, except for official ulema, the wearing of the Muslim style turban *(sarık)* was banned by the government in order to prevent preaching by non-graduates and imposter ulema wearing a *sarık*.[27] The government also checked the ulema's graduation certificates, and the ulema who did not have the required documents were forbidden from giving advice.

The forbidding of ulema's sermonizing, providing reading materials and issuing fatwas without the permission of the Şeyhülislam, and checking the ulema's graduation certificates illuminate how fundamental religious knowledge and perceptions were strictly regulated and monitored by the strong intervention of the state. In the exercise of this state control mechanism, provincial administrators were valuable state agents. The central government used provincial administrators effectively to oversee the ulema's activities.[28]

A New Office in the Şeyhülislam Office: Ağa Kapısı

In the reorganization process, the Ottoman center engaged in religious affairs on a wide scale under the Şeyhülislam Office for the sake of centralizing state power, strengthening imperial unity, and making provinces more accessible to the center. In this sense, the transformation efforts significantly affected the Şeyhülislam Office, and the Şeyhülislam Office was restructured in the face of changing needs and expectations. The Şeyhülislam's authority, which is called "*Şeyhülislamlık Kapısı*," "*Bab-ı Meşihat*," "*Fetvahane*" or "*Bab-ı Vala-i Fetva*," the main target of government institutionalization and centralization. The reorganization of the Şeyhülislam Office was conducted in two ways: The first was a new office for the Şeyhülislam and the second was the establishment of new departments under the Şeyhülislam Office.

The aim of the government in the institutionalization of the Şeyhülislam Office was to create a professionalized ulema and bureaucratic authority. However, the implementation of this institutionalization was no short process. One of the major activities of central elites to institutionalize the Şeyhülislam Office was to establish a permanent place in the center to supervise religious activities. The Şeyhülislam—the home of which used as their office until the nineteenth century—obtained a separate office, which was called *Ağa Kapısı (the residence of the janissary chief)*. Before the allocation of *Ağa Kapısı* for the Şeyhülislam in 1826, Şeyhülislams used their private house as their offices. They divided their houses into two, using the *selamlık* (the public area or ceremonial suites) as their office and the *harem* as private areas where they lived with their family until 1826. Therefore, a change of Şeyhülislam meant the constant change of the location of Şeyhülislam's office in contrast with the structure of a bureaucratic state. However, with the abolishment of the Janissaries, the headquarters of the chief commander of the Janissary corps, which was called *Ağa Kapısı*, was allocated to the Şeyhülislam for his office. The conversion of the headquarters of the Janissary corps into the permanent office of Şeyhülislam was declared in the Hatt-ı Hümayun (imperial edict) by Sultan Mahmud II in 1826.[29] After this declaration, this place started to be called the *Bab-ı Meşihat*, furthering efforts to forget the name Janissaries. Thus, the Şeyhülislam who used his house as an office until 1826 gained new authority, and an important step in the institutionalization process of the office of Şeyhülislam was taken. The Şeyhülislam Office started to operate in a fixed place determined by the central government. While the Şeyhülislam and the *fetva emini*[30] and some civil servants under these two authorities served at the Şeyhülislam Office until 1826, from this date forward, the Anatolian and Rumelian kazasker (chief judge) and the kadı *(judge)* of Istanbul started to serve at the *Fetvahane*.[31] The *Fetvahane* was initially established under the Şeyhülislam Office to answer all kinds of religious questions concerning private and public law. An *alim* (scholar) who had graduated from the *Madrasat'ül Kuzat* and had the best knowledge of the Islamic jurisprudence *(fiqh)* was assigned by the Şeyhülislam as *fetva emini* to the *Fetvahane*.[32] In 1836, the Anatolian and Rumelian kazaskers were moved to an office allocated to them within the *Fetvahane*. Through this regulation, the collection of the Sharia courts was carried out in one center.

In the nineteenth century, the growing importance of Şeyhülislam was again put on the agenda, and his central government was extended as the head of all religious institutions in Ottoman territories instead of just the capital city's mufti. With the emergence of the new organization of the office of Şeyhülislam, which was the highest religious authority of the government, he became responsible for all religious, educational, and judicial affairs. The government gave direct authority to the Şeyhülislam to organize and administer Islamic affairs, so it can be said that the Şeyhülislam had both religious and political authority.

Accordingly, throughout the nineteenth century, the Şeyhülislam Office controlled religious affairs in the empire in the following two ways: First, new departments in Şeyhülislam Office were founded as an effective bureaucratic organization, and all religious offices were included in the state bureaucracy under the office of Şeyhülislam. Second, systematic, formal recruitment through centrally organized regular exams and a mechanism of surveillance was instituted. The central appointments of *müderrises* and the operation of all madrasas and Sharia courts as well as the nomination of all judges were under the supervision of the Şeyhülislam Office.[33] During the Tanzimat, such institutionalization and professionalization of the Şeyhülislam Office also helped develop bureaucratic authority and well-trained civil officials at the central and provincial levels. The government's approach towards religion and the ulema transformed them into a subservient agency that served the political interests of the state.

New Departments under the Şeyhülislam Office

The great institutional expansion in the nineteenth century included the creation of a centralized bureaucratic administration through the creation of new departments. The institutionalization of the Şeyhülislam Office continued with the establishment of new departments. The positions and authorities of the Şeyhülislam Office were reorganized and underwent structural changes with new departments and authorities in this century. The new departments established under the Şeyhülislam authority show that the central government was trying to bring a professional character to the ulema working in the Ilmiye hierarchy, apart from the growing importance of institutionalization and professionalization. Also, the Şeyhülislam was transformed into an institutional-based bureaucratic authority on account of professional specialization in the Ilmiye hierarchy.

Firstly, an important step was taken to supervise the appointment of civil servants in the Ilmiye hierarchy via the İlmiye Penal Code (*Tarik-i İlmiyeye Dair Ceza Kanunnamesi*) of 1838.[34] According to this decree, the appointments of the Ilmiye servants would be made with the recommendation of the Rumelia and Anatolian kazaskers[35] and the final approval of the Şeyhülislam and sultan. It was also decided to make new ulema assignments with exams to prove their qualifications to serve in the Ilmiye offices. All assignments, promotions, and changes of the position under the Şeyhülislam Office were made with exams. A central procedure was put into practice regarding regulations for the examination of madrasa graduates to be assigned to the Ilmiye class. The ulema also entered exams for reappointment to new jobs and promotions within their professions. Therefore, in the nineteenth century, the graduation, appointment, and promotion of the Ilmiye members were completely dependent on examinations. At the same time, this law stated that non-qualified or non-authorized ulema who did not have an *icazet* could not take positions in the Ilmiye hierarchy. An *alim* who lost his *icazet* would be subjected to an exam again and could regain his *icazet* according to this law. However, having an *icazet* was not enough to take a position within the Ilmiye system. If the ulema do not behave in accordance with the norms of the Ilmiye hierarchy, they would not be given a position irrespective of their education and *icazet*.[36] For instance, with the İlmiye Penal Code, bribery[37] and unearned income were strictly banned, and the Ilmiye

Table 2.1. New Departments under the Şeyhülislam Office

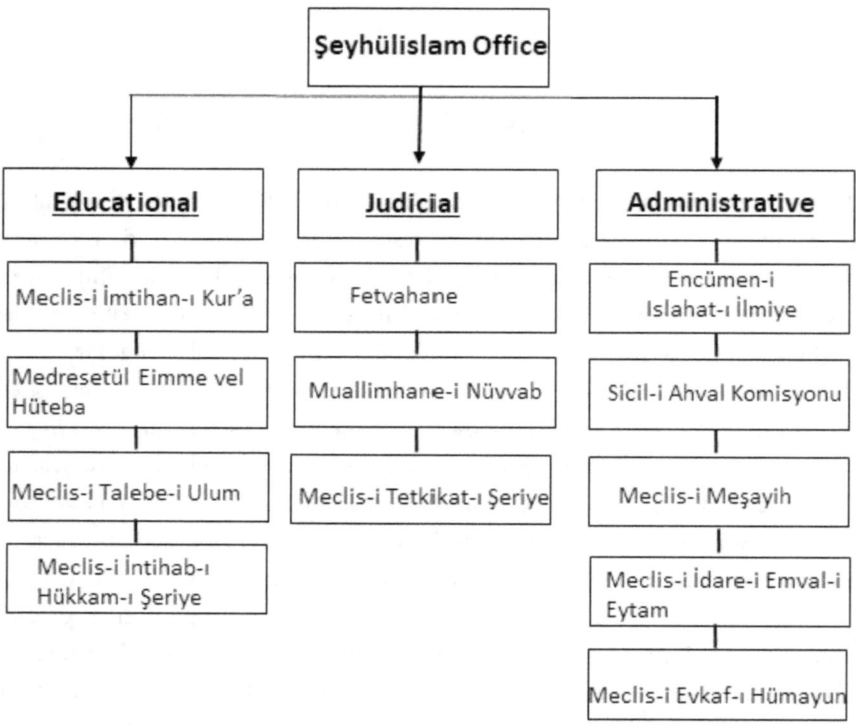

members who took bribes or had unearned incomes were penalized. In cases where the ulema were understood to have received bribes, those ulema were penalized with reprimands, warnings, revocations of their titles, imprisonment, and beatings.[38]

Another regulation made as part of the institutionalization concerned the conscription of madrasa students. In the Ottoman Empire, a conscript system with the drawing of lots was started in 1834 in order to meet the needs of soldiers of *Asakir-i Mansure-i Muhammediye*, the new army established after the removal of Janissaries in 1826. Men of the age of military service (twenty to twenty-five years old) were subjected to this lottery and those named in the lottery were conscripted.[39] However, madrasa students were exempt from military service in this period. This led to the possibility of students registering for the madrasa to avoid military service. Therefore, madrasas could become gathering points of fugitives from the military instead of the scientific center. In 1846, the central state formed a council of examination for madrasa students called the *Meclis-i İmtihan-ı Kura* within the framework of the Şeyhülislam to prevent this irregularity.[40] The government included the madrasa students aged between twenty and twenty-five years old in the lottery. Madrasa students chosen in the lottery were subjected to an exam covering the courses they studied in the madrasa by this council. Students who did not pass the exam were considered cheaters who had enrolled in the madrasas to avoid military service, and those students were conscripted.[41]

The other important step in the name of professionalization was the *Muallimhane-i Nüvvab* (Training School of Judges) established in 1855 to educate the kadıs and naibs.[42] Before the foundation of the training school of judges, naibs and kadıs were trained in Istanbul courts. During this period, Istanbul courts were the places to gain experience and places for evaluation as the internship. Those who wanted to become a member of the judiciary after their internship period were assigned to take an entrance exam for vacant positions in the Ilmiye hierarchy and were appointed as members of the Ilmiye in case they succeeded. However, in 1855, it was decided to establish a new type of school where kadıs and naibs would receive education on judging. The *Muallimhane-i Nüvvab* was founded as a result.[43] This school specialized in ulema who wanted to work in the judiciary part of the Ilmiye class and educated the judges of ecclesiastical Sharia courts. The legal curriculum in this school was based mainly on Islamic jurisprudence.[44] In this sense, this school was an important initiative because it provided special training for ulema who wanted to be in the judicial field. The scope of the education in this school was broader than classical madrasa education. Legal methodology and foreign languages like French were taught to students as well as classical legal education. The students of the *Muallimhane-i Nüvvab* took a combination of old and new methodological courses.[45] With the establishment of *Muallimhane-i Nüvvab*, the central government also aimed to control the judiciary by introducing new regulations for the education of the Ilmiye members. This school was transformed into a unit of the office of Şeyhülislam in 1878 within the scope of institutionalization. The name of this law school was changed as *Madrasatü'l-Kuzat* or *Madrasatü'l-Nüvvab* in 1885. After 1913, it started to be called *Mekteb-i Kuzat* or *Mekteb-i Kudat*.[46]

The introduction of a five-grade system in order to arrange the appointments of judicial members in 1855 was another provision in the judicial field. The kadıs, naibs, and other judicial positions were divided into five categories by the five-grade system.[47] This also entailed a categorization of regions that varied according to a district's scale and importance. In other words, after the regulation, the position of naib was divided into ranks according to importance.

The degree of a district changed according to its distance from the center. The fifth-grade regions were furthest from the center and the first-degree districts were the central areas.[48] Therefore, high-level judgeships (*mevleviyet*)[49] were appointed directly to these first-grade regions. Provincial kadıs who were down a degree from the center comprised the second class. The remaining ones were tested and categorized according to their knowledge level into the third, fourth, and fifth grades. To arrive at first-grade judiciary positions at this categorization, rank, and reputation as well as exam results were the main criteria. Judiciary members of the Ilmiye were appointed to vacant positions corresponding to their grades..

In 1855, there was also made one more important regulation to reduce the workload of the Şeyhülislam. In the nineteenth century, the kadıs and naibs, except for the Anatolian and Rumelian *mevleviyets* (one of the higher ranks in the Ottoman Ilmiye hierarchy), were appointed directly by the Şeyhülislam. In the same way, reappointment and promotions of these judicial officials were carried out by the Şeyhülislam according to determined criteria. However, in this century, there was a great demand for the Ilmiye members due to bureaucratic reform in the empire. The need for trained personnel increased as the state bureaucratized; even the *mülazemet* period was shortened and madrasa graduates were appointed without waiting.[50] On the other hand, the appointments of provincial naibs by the Şeyhülislam increased his workload enormously. It was difficult for the Şeyhülislam to determine the competence and knowledge of each of these ulema who will be appointed as kadı or naib himself. Therefore, in the nineteenth century, corruption in the appointment procedures for judiciary members due to the heavy workload of Şeyhülislam, like appointments with diplomas received with bribes, was inevitable and uncontrolled. In order to reduce the Şeyhülislam's workload and prevent irregular appointments and promotions of incompetent officials, the *Meclis-i İntihab-ı Hükkam-ı Şeriyye (Şeriye Mahkemeleri*, the Committee for the Selection of Sharia Judges*)* was founded in 1855.[51] The Şeyhülislam Office assigned the *Meclis-i İntihab-ı Hükkam-ı Şeriyye* with defining the standards and carrying out the examinations that measured the competence of Sharia judges' appointees.[52] After the establishment of the *Meclis-i İntihab-ı Hükkam-ı Şeriyye*, the Şeyhülislam Office requested documentation of the educational histories of the ulema, their madrasa graduation certificates, and their exam results from the *Meclis-i İntihab-ı Hükkam-ı Şeriyye* before they were appointed to the Ilmiye service. If a madrasa graduate was not sufficiently competent, he would not be given the Ilmiye position.

With the regulation of 1873 on the *Meclis-i İntihab-ı Hükkam-ı Şeriyye (Meclis-i İntihab-ı Hükkam-ı Şeriyye Nizamnamesi)*, the committee started to determine candidates who wanted to be appointed as *kadı* and directed them to the *Muallimhane-i Nüvvab*. Those who did not study *Şerh-i Akaid*[53] were not accepted into the *Muallimhane-i Nüvab*, and this process was supervised by the council. Only madrasa students who had studied *Şerh-i Akaid* and passed the entrance exam for the *Muallimhane-i Nüvvab* were able to register. The Şeyhülislam Office appointed those who graduated from *Muallimhane-i Nüvvab* (Training School of Judges) to judicial positions in the Ilmiye hierarchy according to their knowledge level and competence considering the decisions of this commission.[54] However, the decisions made by the council were always carried out under the control of Şeyhülislam. Also, the regulation of 1873 on the *Meclis-i İntihab-ı Hükkam-i Şer* regulated the conditions of becoming a naib. According to Article 11 of the regulation, only third-, fourth-, and fifth-grade judges were eligible to be naib and they were required to pass the exam in Istanbul. Even experienced judges were obliged to pass the exam to be certified as naib.[55]

Furthermore, in this century, as a part of a fair, equitable central state, a high-level court was needed to defend the rights of defendants unsatisfied with judiciary decisions and to resolve important cases such as the freeing of slaves. As a result of this growing need, a committee called *Meclis-i Tedkikat-ı Şeriyye* (Supreme Court) was formed in 1861. This commission undertook the role of a supreme court for the Sharia court system. The members of the council, who were the judges of Istanbul, Bursa, and Edirne *(Bilad-ı Selase)* as well as some officials of *Bab-ı Fetva*, convened under the chairmanship of the Rumelian kazasker. The cases of defendants who did not like the rulings of the kadı and cases involving matters of vital importance were decided by this council. The council, which was initially provisional and unpaid, was made permanent in 1862. The commission convened twice a week to examine the documents of complicated cases and make final decisions.

The establishment of the *Meclis-i Meşayih* (the Committee for the Administration of Sufi Orders) in 1866 was another step in the institutionalization of religion in the nineteenth century. Since the Ottoman Empire had a religious characteristic, many Ottoman bureaucrats, officials, and ordinary Ottoman citizens were members of different tariqas (religious orders). Thus, the central government wanted to supervise the tariqas and established the *Meclis-i Meşayıh* in 1866 to centralize the tariqas and regulate the relationship of autonomous religious sects with the government. This council administered all the Sufi orders in all provinces of the empire to control them.[56] It was possible to oversee all of the Islamic monasteries, *tekkes*,[57] and tariqas with the *Meclis-i Meşayih* because this institution took responsibility for the administration and inspection of all Sufi orders in Istanbul, while *Encümen-i Meşayih* carried out this task of administration in the provinces.[58] The regulation of *Meclis-i Meşayıh* prevented the establishment of *tekkes* and appointment of tariqa leaders without the approval of the government and the central authority, thus circumventing the autonomy of tariqas vis-à-vis religion in the empire. Tariqas, which had acted independently to some extent until 1866, started to be taken under the control of the state together with the *Meclis-i Meşayih*.

Another regulation was prepared in 1891 in order to tighten central administrative control over the functioning of the tariqas—namely, the *Meclis-i Meşayih Nizamnamesi*.[59] This *regulation* forbade the performance of religious rituals, ceremonies, and activities by scholars outside of government mosques. The government tried to prevent religious ceremonies from being held outside its control with this regulation.[60] Due to this regulation, the government converted all independent, private mosques into state-controlled *tekkes*. Another article of the *Meclis-i Meşayih Nizamnamesi* gave the assignment of sheikhs to the *tekkes* and tariqas to the central elites of the government.[61] This regulation was the direct outcome of the endeavor of the government to keep tariqa leaders under state control. The regulation of the *Meclis-i Meşayih* within the scope of bureaucratic centralization reforms became a turning point for the *tekkes* and tariqas, the religious activities of which were directly controlled thereafter. This was the institutionalization of the management of the tariqa within the central system. If the leaders of *tekkes* and tariqas coincided with the political interests of the central government, the state sponsored their financial needs.[62]

Furthermore, in 1874, a council to deal with orphans was established under the name *Meclis-i İdare-i Emval-i Eytam* under the chairmanship of the kazasker.[63] The decisions of this council were made with the unanimous consent or the majority of votes and the approval of the Şeyhülislam. The *Muhtacin-i Eramil* and *Eytam-ı İlmiye Sandığı* (The Charity Fund) were also created in order to pay the salaries of widows and orphans of deceased Ilmiye officials with the *Meclis-i İdare-i Emval-i Eytam* in 1874. A month's salary of the newly appointed and promoted Ilmiye officials were transferred to the fund of *Meclis-i İdare-i Emval-i Eytam*.[64]

Another important step made in the name of institutionalization after the Şeyhülislam Office was established as a self-contained authority was the promulgation of the *Fetvahane Nizamnamesi* in 1875. The *Fetvahane* was rearranged by regulation in 1875. With the regulation of *Fetvahane* dated on

19 February 1875, the number of persons serving in the *Fetvahane*, the appointment procedures, and the salaries were systemized.[65]

Central elites also took major steps in order to provide the centralized and institutionalized Şeyhülislam Office—one of the important ones of them was the establishment of the Educational Council, *Meclis-i Talebe-yi Ulum* in 1878. The central authorities aimed to take control of madrasas and madrasa students with this council. The council changed its name a year later to *Meclis-i Mesalih-i Talebe*.[66] The inclusive council checked many issues, ranging from the income of madrasa waqfs to the courses taught in the madrasas to the total training period to the livelihoods of *müderrises* and madrasa students. The central government intended to construct a centralized education system and religious materials in order to avoid the speculation of nonofficial materials and the formation of nonofficial courses in the madrasas with this council. In this sense, the Educational Council, *Meclis-i Mesalih-i Talebe* facilitated and supervised the courses taught in the madrasas and identified the characteristics of students to be admitted to the madrasas. Also, this council recorded the number of madrasas, their foundations, the number of their rooms, and the number of students who stayed in these rooms.[67]

Regarding the waqf institution, the ulema managed the incomes of waqfs of such institutions as schools, mosques, and hospitals, the funds of charitable endowments and minority groups, and other forms of urban property. However, the central state wanted to supervise the financial activities of the ulema in the context of the institutionalization and centralization of the nineteenth century.[68] Therefore, the Inspectorate of Imperial Foundations, *Evkaf-ı Hümayun Müfettişliği* was established for the purpose of supervising and protecting waqf property belonging to the Şeyhülislam Office and the Ilmiye in 1878. The name of this inspectorate was changed to Council of Inspection for Imperial Pious *(Meclis-i Teftiş-i Evkaf-ı Hümayun)* in 1895.[69] Through new regulations regarding waqf income, this council, and an inspection mechanism, the central government aimed to reduce ulema interest in waqf incomes.

The central elites also strictly controlled the religious materials of the ulema with the Council of Examination of Written Works *(Tetkik-i Müellefat Encümeni* and *Teftiş-i Mesahif-i Şerife Meclisi)* established in 1889. Control over materials was regarded by the government as a challenge to superstitious belief and as preservation of a harmonious community among subjects. In the process of controlling religious materials, the Şeyhülislam Office decided to reject or approve religious books according to their suitability for official religious doctrine. The *Tetkik-i Müellefat Encümeni* and *Teftiş-i Mesahif-i Şerife Meclisi* engaged in checking the contents of the Quran and religious books to determine whether they were suitable for publication. These commissions prohibited reading materials not approved for distribution and printing by the Şeyhülislam Office.[70]

Apart from control over the religious sermons, rituals, and books, the central state surveilled the Ilmiye members directly. The personnel registry files *(sicill-i ahval registers)*, which included personal information on and the backgrounds of ulema working in the Ilmiye hierarchy, started to be formed in 1892 as a result of this desire of the government.[71] the Ilmiye officials were individually identified as a result of the central government's registration policy to oversee every part of life. The personnel registry files were used in cases of appointments, changes of office, and promotions. The personal records of the Ilmiye officials registered by the government resulted in increased government control over the Ilmiye officials.

Furthermore, the Council of Official Islamic Academy *(Encümen-i Islahat-ı İlmiye Darülhikmetül İslamiye)* was established as a department of the office of Şeyhülislam to enlighten Ottoman subjects on religious and ethical issues and to distinguish "proper" religion from superstition.[72] The central Şeyhülislam Office planned to inform Ottoman subjects about missionary activities and non-religious thinking with this unit. This was considered of great importance in terms of the security and order of the Empire.[73]

The control mechanism over the religious institutions on the part of central elites deeply affected the position of the preacher, too. The profession of preaching a sermon was not practiced by a separate person in the provinces; preaching in these districts was among the duties of the *müderrises* and muftis of the region.[74] In the context of institutionalization, a separate group of ulema started to be assigned from the center as a preacher, called *vaizin* or *huteba*. Therefore, in Istanbul, a madrasa called the "*Madrasatü'l-Vaizin*" *(*Preachers' Madrasa*)* was established to train *vaizin* and *huteba* (preachers) to be assigned to central mosques in 1912.[75] The education at this madrasa lasted four years. The office of Şeyhülislam started to determine the basic rules for the supervision of the actions of graduating preachers from this madrasa in the public sphere, like the contents of their speeches *(vaaz)*.[76] The central government also recorded a given preacher's name, the mosque or waqf in which they could give a sermon, and their *icazet* in order to supervise all their activities.[77] Similarly, in 1913, a madrasa called "*Madrasatü'l-Eimme ve'l-Huteba*" *(*Madrasa for Prayer Leaders and *Preachers)* was established to train prayer leaders *(imams)* and prayer collars *(muezzins)*.[78] In time, these madrasas were combined under the name "*Madrasatü'l-İrşad*'. Lastly, in 1914, all the Istanbul madrasas were unified under the name of *Darü'l-Hilafeti'l-Aliyye (*Madrasa of the Abode of the Caliphate*)*.[79] The institutionalization of the Ilmiye class was completed by this last move.

Conclusion

This chapter examines the expanding bureaucratic organization of the Şeyhülislam Office during the nineteenth century. It argues that the government ensured the institutionalization of the Şeyhülislam Office by building new departments and rules into the office. However, new departments never completely negated the old ones. The government re-identified the duties of the old offices of the Şeyhülislam by creating new offices and directly, centrally organizing the permanent personnel of the office.

The newly established departments under the Şeyhülislam started to serve the central government with better coordination, high performance, and efficiency in both the center and periphery. In these new offices, the appointments of the Ilmiye members, changes to their duties, their performances, and retirement were directly made by the Şeyhülislam Office. As new departments were added, the number of staff working at the institution started to increase. In other words, all these new departments meant an increase in the number of civil servants working in the Şeyhülislam Office in the nineteenth century in accordance with its increased duties and powers. All employees of the institution were widely recognized duties and rules by instructions. Apart from the new departments and the increasing number of staff, professionalization became another important tool of institutionalization. The institutionalization process of the Şeyhülislam Office was completed with the centralized appointment of the Ilmiye to all provinces of the empire and the centralized regulation of all the Ilmiye members and institutions.

Furthermore, the central control of the Ottoman government was reestablished in the Şeyhülislam Office with newly created institutions from the beginning of the Tanzimat. The central government turned the Ilmiye members working under the office of Şeyhülislam into an institutionalized class. In this process, the government minimized the autonomous power of the Ilmiye members and maximized its effect on religious life. All religious hierarchies were attached to a well-ordered Şeyhülislam Office that was concerned with the matters of recruitment, promotion, appointment, discipline, and professional characteristics of the Ilmiye members. From this perspective, this study contributes to the further understanding of the institutional identity of the Şeyhülislam Office which became more uniform and permanent under the direct control of central authorities.

3

Ulema's Educational Career

The institutionalization project of the nineteenth century became a turning point for the education system of the Ottoman Empire. Ulema education was taken under the absolute control of the central government; the Şeyhülislam Office became responsible for closely coordinating and administering the educational structure. The most important development in the field of education in this century was the turning of traditional madrasa education into a center of more systematic, and formal education. The aim of institutionalizing madrasa education was to enhance the infrastructural capacity of education for specialization and professionalization in the Ilmiye class. It is necessary to acquire knowledge including systematic information to meet the state's requirements and gain the title of ulema in the nineteenth century. For those seeking a career in the Ilmiye hierarchy, the government set the formal requirements to receive a long, proficient training such as receiving a graduation certificate and passing central examinations. In this regard, patterns pertaining to the training of madrasa students underwent certain transformations in the nineteenth century. With the development of institutionalization, receiving a quality education in a madrasa began to play a significant role in securing work in high-ranking Ilmiye positions.

During the nineteenth century, the attempts of the government to transform education like the standardization of examinations and rearrangement of the curriculum in the madrasas and the adaptation of madrasa students to this new educational structure provided a more formal, standard education. These major transformations deeply affected the educational quality and intellectual capacity of Ottoman Ilmiye members. In this regard, this chapter will shed light on the exact stages of the educational backgrounds of Ottoman ulema from their primary education in *sibyan mektebs* to their graduation from formal madrasas to becoming a *scholar*.

Sıbyan Mektebi

Basic Ottoman education began in the *sibyan mektebs* or *mahalle mektebs* (primary schools) that can be thought of as the continuation of the earlier Islamic educational centers called *daru't-talim, daru'l-huffaz, taş mekteb*, or just *mekteb*. With a decree issued by Sultan Mahmud II in 1824, primary school education in the *sibyan mektebs* became compulsory for all children. The *sibyan mektebs* remained the first step of education during the Tanzimat period. The *sibyan* education period was set at four years by the General Education Regulation *(Maarif-i Umumiye Nizamnamesi)* in 1869.[1] Children *(talebe-i ulum)* were introduced to the *sibyan mektebs* at a young age in the Ottoman primary education system. The entrance age to *sibyan mektebs* generally varied from between six and nine.[2] Since the maximum age to begin studying in the *sibyan mektebs* was nine, it can be inferred that students of *sibyan mektebs* graduated at the latest at the age of thirteen. The ceremony marking the first day of school for a student in the Ottoman Empire was known as the Amen Parade *(Amin Alayı)*. It was also the first day of school to be an *alim* before pursuing madrasa training. Ottoman children who were at the age of six to nine could join the formal educational ceremony and attend primary school. Dozens of students, the *sibyan muallims* (teachers),[3] and several senior government officials went hymning to the houses of potential students ready for *mekteb* education.[4] Then, the parents put their children on a pony and the child was taken to the *mekteb* in fancy dress. After the child took the first *mekteb* course from his *müderris*, parents gave small gifts to the students attending the ceremony and their *müderrises*, and meals were served.

Although personnel records of the ulema show that the *sibyan mektebs* were available in almost all towns and villages around the empire, there were a few regions where there was no *mekteb*. In districts where the number of *mekteps* was insufficient or there was no school, some district madrasas provided the services of a *mekteb*.[5] In such situations, the initial education of the *talebe* was provided by the neighborhood *imam* instead of by the *sibyan muallim*.[6] There are also examples of students who studied with their fathers or other family members instead of being educated in a *sibyan mekteb*. For instance, Ahmed Hulusi Efendi of Ankara began his education with his father, Hacı Halil Efendi, receiving a primary education at home at an early age. He learned basic mathematics, reciting the Quran *(Elifba)*, the recitation rules of the Quran *(tecvid)*, a concise manual of Islamic faith, worship, and ethics *(ilmihal)*, and Arabic grammar rules *(sarf* and *nahv)* from his father instead of in a *sibyan mekteb.*[7] Similarly, Hacı Hüseyin Feyzi Efendi of Konya came from ulema families and was taught by his *alim* father, Arpacızade El-hac Feyzi Efendi, without having studied in a *sibyan mekteb.*[8]

The language of instruction in primary schools was the native language of the students. It was intended that every citizen have the ability to read and write, have some basic religious education, and be able to do simple calculations via the four-year compulsory *mekteb* education. Reciting the Qur'an, reading and writing (grammar rules), worship and ethics, the recitation rules of the Qur'an, and calligraphy *(hüsn-ü hat/ nesih* and *sülüs)* as well as Ottoman and Islamic history, geography, and basic mathematics were taught in these *sibyan mektebs.*[9] Also, some *mektebs* required memorization of the Qur'an and penmanship. Most of the hafiz have memorized the Qur'an in the *sibyan mekteps.*[10] The curriculum of the *sibyan mekteb* could be changed according to the region or the *sibyan mektebs' müderrises.* Sometimes even more advanced courses were taught in *sibyan mektebs.*[11] The training program in the *sibyan mekteps* varied according to the requests of the students *(talebe)* and the capabilities of their *müderrises (hocas)*—with the exception of basic courses that were required to be taught, such as the alphabet, basic mathematics, reciting the Quran, the recitation rules of the Quran, and a concise manual of Islamic faith, worship, and ethics. There was no regular, standard curriculum for the *sibyan mektebs.* However, the major requirements for graduation included reciting the Qur'an from beginning to end at least once, writing and reading in Turkish and Arabic, and learning to make basic mathematics. After the completion of *sibyan mektebs*, some students preferred to attend a *rüşdiye (secondary school)*[12] and others went directly to study in a madrasa, a decision which would affect their future careers.

Education in the Madrasa

The education pattern of an *alim* candidate started with the completion of one's elementary education close to home and then going to formal madrasas. Beginning a career in the Ilmiye during the nineteenth century would start with *sibyan mekteb* education and then involve entering a madrasa. Every madrasa in the Ottoman Empire was a respected place of learning. One of the primary functions of the madrasa system was to create a professional class of scholars having an important effect on all Muslim society.[13] The madrasa education allowed the ulema to maintain their prestige because madrasa-educated ulema constituted a privileged social group. Education in the madrasas was difficult and achievement in this education system was no easy process. The education of ulema finished at the end of a multidirectional and different social and educational process. Formal academic training in the Ottoman Empire was well planned and intensive. Each ulema candidate was expected to attain basic Islamic knowledge.

The madrasa education for the student was a place of specialization in religious science that involved reading the Qur'an, mastering the hadiths (reports of the traditions or sayings of the Prophet Muhammad), logic, and theology, and recording the rules and sayings laid down by the Prophet Muhammad as the guide of Islam. The transmission of knowledge by the *müderris* was key to reinforcing religious authenticity in their professional life. Although the training requirements for the madrasa changed according to time and place, the ulema's main expectation from madrasa education was to contribute to their intellectual capacity and help them enter the Ilmiye service.

Madrasas were major components of Ottoman teaching and learning as well as educational centers that Ottoman subjects had to attend to obtain the necessary qualifications to be an *alim*. The *alim* title was given at the end of long years of training in the madrasas. Ottoman madrasa students were known as "*talebe*," and the plural form of which is "*tullab*," or they were called "*müste'id*" or "*suhte (softa)*."[14] Madrasa students were called by several titles until they graduated from the madrasas and became the ulema.

Anyone who wanted to be a scholar or judge or to pursue some other profession in the Ilmiye hierarchy needed to complete a long, difficult education process. The education of the ulema and the production of knowledge was a result of madrasa learning which formed the basis of the Ottoman higher education system. As the most influential authority in the educational framework, the whole education system in the madrasa was carried out by ulema of different ranks and categories, ranging from pre-madrasa teachers to fully fledged professors *(müderris)*. An *alim*'s educational background obtained at the end of a long period of education was crucial to his professional degree. Therefore, the madrasa in which one studied played a vital role in the determination of the positions an *alim* would hold for their whole professional life.

After receiving an education and graduating from *sibyan mektebs*, students enrolled in the madrasas to be a member of the Ilmiye class. As a result of the institutionalization movement of the nineteenth century, acceptance into a madrasa and the madrasa educational curriculum became more systematic. In this century, formal madrasas were institutions governed by certain laws, and there were criteria for enrollment in and completion of the madrasas.[15] According to statistics in the personnel records of ulema in the Meşihat Archive, students had to pass an entrance exam to start their madrasa education in the nineteenth century. This exam was an assessment of Qur'an recitation, religious information, reading, writing, and grammar of Ottoman Turkish and Arabic, mathematics (the four basic operations, calculation, fractions, and decimals), geography and history, and penmanship *(hüsn-i hat)*. The entrance exams were oral and taken before a committee.[16] Unlike in the earlier period, completing one's basic education in a primary school *(sibyan mekteb* or *taş mekteb)* or being educated by one's fathers was not enough to be accepted into and study at an Ottoman madrasa in the late nineteenth century. A candidate who wants to study at the madrasa needed to pass the madrasa entrance exam starting in the Tanzimat period.

Another necessity for a madrasa to accept a student in the late nineteenth century was the requirement of scientific maturity. Although the minimum age to begin education in the madrasa was set at fifteen and the upper limit at thirty, this could change according to the maturity of the candidates.[17] There were examples of madrasa students who were not sufficiently mature and whose educations were terminated. However, if a student came to Istanbul to study at a madrasa because there was no madrasa in the region where he lived, he would not be sent back to his home even if he was not yet fifteen and was allowed to attend courses at the madrasa by staying with his relatives such as uncles or brothers.[18]

The Ottoman madrasas were divided into two according to their purposes and services: General madrasas *(umumi medreseler)* and specialized madrasas *(ihtisas medreseleri)*. The general madrasas are those in which the Islamic sciences *(Ulum-ı İslamiyye)* and the sciences from outside the Islamic world *(Ulum-ı Dahile)* were taught in various proportions. These madrasas were established to educate kadı, *müderris*, mufti, and other Ilmiye government officials that were then spread throughout Ottoman territories even to the small villages. The specialized madrasas were those that taught one of the *Ulum-ı İslamiyye* or the *Ulum-ı Dahile*, which were required for a direct specialization in a wide variety of religious sciences. The specialized madrasas in the late nineteenth century were an important tool for the specialization and professionalization required by an institutionalized state.

In earlier periods, the Ottoman madrasas were categorized as *hariç* (exterior) and *dahil* (interior) madrasas. The fundamentals of knowledge such as Arabic and the intellectual sciences were taught at the *hariç* madrasas. There were three levels of *hariç* schools: "*ibtida-yi hariç*" schools, "*miftah*" madrasas, and "madrasas of forty or fifty". The main textbook of the *ibtida-yi hariç* was *Tecrid* and of the *miftah* madrasas was *Şerh-i Miftah*. The curriculum of the "madrasas of forty or fifty" consisted of subjects from *Mawakif* on scholastic theology and a course in jurisprudence from *Hidaye*. The *dahil* madrasas provided higher knowledge in the religious sciences. This group was also divided into three: elementary, intermediate, and advanced. The *ibtida-yi dahil* madrasas taught the *Hidaye* for elementary jurisprudence, the *Telvih* for the intermediate level, and the *Kaşşaf* for the advanced level.[19]

In our study, the personnel records of the ulema at the office of Şeyhülislam showed that the categorization of madrasas remained important until the end of the last period of the Ottoman Empire. However, during the Tanzimat period, the earlier categorization of the madrasas was changed. In this period, there were three main categories of Ottoman Madrasas: *Hariç*, *Dahil*, and Madrasas of Sixty. These madrasas were divided into two with the names *İbtida* and *Hareket*. Also, *Havamis-i Süleymaniye*, a new category, was added between the *Musıla-ı Süleymaniye* and *Süleymaniye*. With this new reorganization, in the late nineteenth century, madrasas were rearranged into twelve categories called *İbtida-i Hariç*, *Hareket-i Hariç*, *İbtida-i Dahil*, *Hareket-i Dahil*, *Musıla-i Sahn*, *Sahn-ı Seman*, *İbtida-i Altmışlı (ibtida* madrasa of sixty*)*, *Hareket-i Altmışlı (Hareket* Madrasa of sixty*)*, *Musıla-i Süleymaniye*, *Havamis-i Süleymaniye*, *Süleymaniye*, and *Dar'ül-Hadis*[20] from the bottom up. *Haşiye-i Tecrid*, *Miftah*, and *Telvih* were excluded from this ranking of madrasas.[21] Therefore, the madrasa system was a scientific structure extending from the *Hariç* Madrasas to the *Dar'ül-Hadis* in the Tanzimat period. In 1914, with the *Medaris-i İlmiye Hakkında Kanun*,[22] all the madrasas, initially those in Istanbul, were combined under the name *Dar'ül-Hilafet'ül-Aliyye*.[23] The combination of madrasas was also realized in provinces step-by-step in later periods. The education in *Dar'ül-Hilafet'ül-Aliyye* madrasas lasted a total of nine years. The first three years consisted of the preparatory class *(ihzari)*, the next three of the *ibtida-i hariç (kısm-ı evvel* / beginner level*)*, and the last three of the *ibtida-i dahil (kısm-ı sani* / secondary level*)*. Students who finished the ninth year at the madrasa could continue to the *Sahn* madrasa for a two-year period. Later, *Sahn* madrasa graduates came to Istanbul and studied for three years at *Süleymaniye* madrasas as a final step in the specialized madrasa system.[24] As is clear, after the beginning of the Tanzimat period madrasas were regulated to a degree and ranked by the government according to the courses taught, the foundation of the madrasa, and the founders' positions in the Ottoman Empire. The wealth and position of the entire official religious institution culminated with these basic criteria.

During and after the beginning of the Tanzimat period, ulema that completed a general madrasa did not have to move to a specialized madrasa. However, there was a correlation between the prestige of their graduated madrasas and their professional life. Ulema who graduated from higher-ranking specialized madrasas were promoted to the highest positions in the Ilmiye hierarchy in the late nineteenth century.[25]

Most madrasas not only had classrooms but also living quarters for students. The madrasa students were required to live in the dormitory of the madrasa outside of course hours. Fifteen of the rooms were separated out for the fifteen *danişmends* (advanced students) in the madrasa. Junior students usually shared a room with two or more colleagues. There were desks in each corner of the rooms, beds, chests, tables, and chairs.[26] All students were residents *(hücre)* in the madrasa and were not allowed to go out at night without the permission of the *müderris* except if they were married. If a student was married, he was not a resident of the madrasa, but he was required to attend the courses in the morning and evening.[27]

Paralleling the increasing number of madrasa students, especially in the nineteenth century, madrasa education began to be given in institutions outside the madrasas, as well. Educational activities were held in mosques apart from the madrasas,[28] so a close relationship was established between the mosque and the madrasa. The *müderrises* were also appointed to the mosques for educational services.[29] Mosques where madrasa courses were taught were called *Dersiye.*[30] Although *Dersiyes* were physically different from madrasas, the presence of *müderrises* appointed by the government made them educational centers.[31] Some prominent *müderrises* were chosen for the reading halls of great mosques *(Dersiyes)*, and some madrasa students took their courses in those places.[32] Apart from *Dersiyes*, some *hanigahs* (worship centers of the sects) and houses of notable people of the period were also used as educational centers because of the insufficient number of madrasas. The madrasas could not handle the number of students wanting to study in the madrasas in the late nineteenth century, so even in the last periods of the Ottoman Empire, the establishment of new madrasas was supported.[33]

Also, madrasa students took courses from madrasas other than the one in which enrolled because different courses and books were taught in different madrasas. Sometimes the appropriate courses were not offered in the madrasa in which students were enrolled; at other times, courses were taught by famous *müderrises* in other madrasas, and students chose to take these courses with those *müderrises*. Therefore, there was considerable mobility between cities for madrasa students to complement their madrasa education. The students also received an *icazet* (the license or permission to teach) for subjects they took at other madrasas.[34] The *icazets* were signed by the *müderris* who instructed madrasa students, developing and specializing their professional knowledge and skills. They were subsequently approved by the provincial mufti, *naib*, governor, or *kadı* in the name of the Şeyhülislam Office.[35] After the madrasa education was completed, candidates took their *icazets* from their *müderrises* or *dersiams* (the *müderrises* who taught in the mosques)[36] and obtained positions in the Ilmiye hierarchy such as *kadı*, *naib*, or *müderris*.

The Staff in the Madrasa

The *müderris* was the only person who had the authorization to educate students, so it can be inferred that the *müderris* was the most important element of the madrasa and the academic staff. It is useful to examine the requirements to be a *müderris* in the Ottoman Empire to explain who they were. *Müderrises* were professors of religious sciences and were in charge of the academic activities of the madrasas as the scholars in the madrasa system. The madrasas were headed by *müderrises*, and generally, only one *müderris* was appointed to each madrasa except for large madrasa complexes. *Müderrises* who taught in high-level madrasas from the *İbtida-i Hariç* to the *Dar'ül-Hadis* were known as the "*Der-i Aliyye ve Bilad-ı Selase*" and the *müderrises* who worked at the normal madrasas is known as provincial *(Taşra) müderrises*. There were twelve grades of *müderris*, the highest of which was the sole *müderris* at the *Darü'l-hadis* of *Süleymaniye* Mosque with his top-paying teaching position. In addition, this individual had the chance to assume a special judicial position known as the *mahreç mevleviyeti*.[37] Also, *müderrises* in Istanbul madrasas were usually those who had reached the top of their profession, while ulema in other cities of the empire were comprised of members of every rank. Lastly, all *müderrises* belonged to the Sunni and particularly the Hanafi school of thought.

Although the chief duty of a *müderris* was to teach, he was also responsible for other social and administrative duties in the madrasas. The main tasks of an Ottoman *müderris* were to choose students to attend the madrasa and *muid* (teaching assistant of the *müderris*), to distribute funds to students and madrasa servants, and to determine the curriculum of the madrasa, and to administrate their madrasas. In this sense, the madrasas were self-governing, autonomous institutions ruled by the *müderrises*. Despite this autonomy of madrasas and *müderrises*, they were under the strict supervision of the central government. All the madrasa *müderrises* had to consult with the mufti about any problems in the madrasa.

Furthermore, the education of the ulema was an institutionalized process performed through the madrasa. However, in this education system, the identity of the *müderris* was more important than the madrasa's institutional structure. In this respect, the process of transferring knowledge in the madrasa was a personal matter between the *müderris* and his students. The curriculum of an Ottoman madrasa was based on the compartmentalized teaching methods of the madrasa *müderrises*. The subjects and books taught in the madrasa were planned by the *müderris* himself. Also, the *müderrises* gave personal diplomas (graduation certificates) to graduates; the diplomas ratifying their *icazet* were issued by teachers, not by madrasas. Therefore, the majority of the biographies of ulema do not mention the madrasas where they studied but list their *müderrises*' names.

The *muid* was the second principal in the madrasa after the *müderris* in terms of the academic hierarchy.[38] The *muid* was selected by the madrasa *müderris* among senior madrasa students and approved by the waqf commission of the madrasa through an exam. According to the exam result, the *muid* was then appointed by the office of Şeyhülislam.[39] The duties of the madrasa *muid* were to review the lessons of the *müderris* in the mornings and afternoons, tutor the *softas* (the beginner level madrasa student) in their studies, engage them in the discussion, and maintain student discipline. In this sense, the *muid* reviewed with the *softas* what they had been taught by their *müderrises*. Students were obliged to attend both sessions of the *muid*, who was responsible for teaching from abridged and comprehensive subjects according to his ability.[40] A *muid* received a monthly salary for these services from the income of the madrasa waqf. The tenure of a *muid* was usually no less than two years.[41]

Apart from the academic staff, there was the non-academic staff that was involved in the administration of the madrasa waqf and the general work of the madrasa. This was a large number of staff members who generally worked in administrative, financial, and service sectors. A doorman *(bevvab)*, a toilet cleaner *(kennas-ı hela)*, a cleaner *(ferraş)*, a person in charge of lighting—or lamplighter *(siraci* or *kandilci)*, a librarian *(hafiz-i kütüb)*, and a scribe *(katibi kütüb)* were assigned to the madrasas. Also, each madrasa had approximately thirty collectors *(cabis)*, a building wall inspector *(nazir-i cüdran)*, a water carrier *(ibrikçi)*, and a gardener *(bağban)*, and a number of other workers for the general complex and kitchens.[42]

Furthermore, the administrative staff of madrasas included general foundation administrators *(mütevelli-i umum-u evkaf-ı)* and an administrative secretary *(mütevelli katibi)*. The whole madrasa system was overseen by a trustee *(mütevelli)*. The trustee's main duty was to check the madrasa *müderrises* and the funds allocated for madrasa expenses and students. In other words, madrasa *müderrises* were entrusted by the trustee of the madrasa. The trustees also checked the subjects to be studied by students in the madrasas.[43]

The Duration of Madrasa Education

The duration of madrasa education was set at twelve years during the Tanzimat period with a document dating of 1873.[44] However, this duration could increase or decrease according to the student's learning ability and capacity. After studying the courses required in the madrasa, students could take the exam and receive their *icazet*. Therefore, the education period could be shorter if the books they were required to read were finished early. Similarly, this period could be extended if students did not finish the books in time. It is also inevitable that the completion time for madrasa students who had to leave Istanbul to make a living was extended.

Madrasa students were in charge of religious services in various places of the empire. They met their economic needs and earned money during the three holy months—*Recep*, *Şaban*, and *Ramadan*—also known as *Suhur-i Selase*. The madrasa training was carried out in months other than these three.[45] In other words, the lectures in madrasas ended every year at the start of the three holy months of the lunar Hijri calendar. There was a period of nine months of full-time training at the madrasas in the nineteenth century. Therefore, time at the madrasa was spent efficiently, and an intensive course program was developed.[46]

A student had to be at the madrasa for the whole day.[47] The classes in the madrasas were held in Arabic, which was the language of religious study in the empire. A classic madrasa day was planned around the common prayer times. The lectures were divided into three: morning, noon, and afternoon. The first class began with the morning prayer and continued with breaks until the afternoon. Students sat in lectures for about eight hours a day. Before the class, there was a short review of the previous day.[48] In the morning, *müderrises* taught the classes, and in the afternoons, time was spent on review of the morning courses and completing exercises on the materials learned. The students were expected to study certain lines of texts before the class and to memorize and discuss important points during the class. Each student had to say his thoughts and perspective on the texts. After the class with the *müderris*, students studied with the *muid* to review the material and prepare for the next class the following day. The madrasa students attended classes five days a week in both the morning and evenings with Tuesday and Friday off.[49] The vacation period of the madrasas was the three holy months (*Receb*, *Şaban*, and *Ramadan*).[50] Moreover, some students could stop their madrasa education, but such occasions of taking leave of the madrasa voluntarily were rare. The most important reason for leaving the madrasa was health problems.[51] Ulema candidates also sometimes had to leave the madrasa to meet the needs of their families.[52]

The Curricula of the Madrasa

The Ottoman madrasa system was a classic Islamic education composed of a comprehensive education with an emphasis on the Islamic sciences. The education system of the Ilmiye candidates had strong links to the religious domain of the empire. The supporting fields of madrasa education were various, such as rhetoric, mathematics, and language. Also, the rational and religious sciences except for logic, ethics, rhetoric, and grammar were taught in the madrasas. Although madrasa education generally consisted of the Islamic sciences, they were still the centers of new facts, ideas, and discoveries.

The classical madrasa education system persisted in the nineteenth century with some regulations. A general educational method based on memorization, repetition, question, answers, and discussion was followed in the system. A madrasa student was first responsible for reading an introductory text on a subject before the lesson, then an intermediate one, and lastly an advanced text. These learning steps were respectively known as *iktisar* (abridgment, for the lower level), *iktisad* (moderation, for the middle level), and *ıstiksa* (detailed deliberation, for the upper level).[53] In the nineteenth century, the curriculum and order of courses were not random but chosen with regard to a systematic education. There were prerequisite courses before the main subjects in the madrasas. For instance, the principles of jurisprudence in the field of Sharia were the main topic of study in the madrasa besides Arabic grammar, syntax, and rhetoric, but before jurisprudence, logic was to be studied as a supporting field, and before that literature.[54] Also, decisions about the curriculum in the madrasa were determined by the *müderrises* according to their personal interests in religious texts from the fıqh, hadith, and exegesis.

Although there was no standard educational curriculum in the Ottoman madrasas, there were obligatory courses that had to be studied for graduation. After completing compulsory courses, students could choose elective courses. In this sense, madrasa students were free to choose the *müderrises* with whom they would study and the classes that they would take. For instance, Mustafa Mahfi Efendi of İzmit studied Qur'an with Mehmed Tahir Efendi, learned *kıraat* (reading) from Haci Hafiz Niyazi Efendi, *Şerh-i Akaid* from Kozulcalı İbrahim Efendi, *ilm-i usul* (a method course on the Islamic sciences and law like fiqh and Sharia) from Kangırılı İbrahim Efendi, and calligraphy *(hatt-ı talik)*, algebra *(cebir)*, geometry *(hendese)*, and geography *(coğrafya)* from Bedri Efendizade Muhtar Efendi.[55] As can be seen, a madrasa student can learn subjects from more than one *müderris* or madrasa. The syllabus of the madrasas was based on the laws of philosophy *(hikmet)*, and both religious and rational sciences were taught.[56] The madrasa students were required to read a number of texts during their education. They received a certificate from their professors stating how much of the book they had read to graduate. The first three subjects that had to be read were morphology *(sarf)*, syntax *(nahv)*, and logic *(mantık)*, respectively. The last two texts that must be read to graduate were the Hadith and the body of Qur'anic exegesis. These subjects were seen as the pinnacle of education and required a firm foundation.[57] A student could also study other texts according to their particular field of concern such as elocution *(adab-ı bahs)*, preaching, rhetoric *(belagat)*, philosophical theology *(kelam)*, philosophy *(hikmet)*, jurisprudence *(fiqh)*, inheritance law *(feraid)*, tenets of faith *(akaid)*, and methodology of Islamic *jurisprudence (usul-i fıkıh)* between the first three and last two compulsory texts.[58] Also, the mathematical and natural sciences such as arithmetic, geometry, astronomy, and physics were taught after philosophy at the Ottoman madrasas. As can be understood from the curriculum, the manner of learning in the Ottoman madrasa system was based on Islam and logic. Religion and religious education were the basis of the curricula of the madrasas. Although the natural and legal sciences were included in the curriculum, priority was given to religious sciences. The curriculum served as useful practice for a future career in teaching. These stories suggest efforts to rearrange the madrasa curriculum and the books taught in the madrasas during the Tanzimat period.

Also, a report was produced in 1873 by fourteen Ilmiye members in the office of Şeyhülislam who were interested in the madrasa education system that showed some regulations about the madrasa curriculum.[59] According to this report, madrasa education was reformulated and the common characteristics of the new education system were based on a planned, systematic structure.

Another change took place in 1910 and the content of the curriculum of the madrasa was regulated. The morning lessons, known as *Sıra Dersleri*, were to be taught for twelve years (see below Table 3.1).

Apart from the morning courses, the content of the mid-afternoon *(ikindi)* courses that started in the second year included *Halebi*, *Mülteka*, *Muhtasar Meani*, *Mir'at*, *Mutavvel*, and *Tavzih*. And courses for the holiday period were *Tefsir*, *Hadis*, *Dürrü'l-Muhtar* from *Fıqh*, *Durer*, *Vaz'iye*, *Hüseyniye* and *Velediye*, *Alaka* and *Feride*, *Hey'et* and *Hendese* from *Riyaziye*, *Hat*, and *İnşa*.[61]

The last change in the madrasa education curriculum was made in 1914 with the *Islah-ı Medaris Nizamnamesi*. This regulation resulted in the consolidation

Table 3.1 The curricula of madrasa students[60]

Years	Courses
First Year	Ilm-i sarf (Emsile, Bina, Maksud), Ta'lim-i Müte'alim, Ta'lim-i Kur'an, Tecvid, Hat, İmla, Muhtasar Hesab, Sarf-ı Osmani and Kavaid-i Farisi
Second Year	İlm-i Nahv, Meraku'l-felah from Fiqh, Talim'i Qur'an, Kavaidü'l Irab, Şuzuru'z-zeheb, Gülistan from Farisi, Hesab, İmla and Kavaid-i Osmaniye,
Third Year	Nahv, Şafiye, Mülteka from Fiqh, Vad, Hesab, Mebadi-i Hendese and İnşa,
Fourth Year	Nahv-i İkmal, Şafiye, Mülteka, Alaka, İsagoci, Muhtasar Coğrafya, Hendese, İnşa and Cezeri,
Fifth Year	Fenari, Meani, İlmü'l- Aruz ve'l- Kavafi, İlm-i Feraiz, Coğrafya, Cebir and Kitabet
Sixth Year	İlm-i Mantık, Meani, Kaside-i Bur'e, Banet Suad, Muallekat, İlm'ül-Kıraat, Hikmet, Cebir, Kitabet-i Arabiye and Usul-i Tercüme,
Seventh Year	Kutb, Şerh-i Akaid, Usul-i Fiqh, Şerh-i Menar, Şerh-i Veciz, Adab-ı Münazara, Makamat-ı Hariri, Hikmet-i Cedide, Hey'et, Kimya and Mevalid,
Eighth Year	Şerh-i Akaid, Meşarikü'l- Envar, Şerhü'l- Menar, Şerh'ül- Veciz, Usul-i Hadis, Makamat-ı Hariri, Usul-i Sak, Tarih-i İslam, Kozmografya, and Mevalid,
Ninth Year	Hikmet-i Sadiye, Mesarikü'l- Envar, Tefsir-i Beyzavi, Divan-ı Hamse, Usul-i Hadis, Siyer, Tarih-i Umumi, and Coğrafya-yi Umumi,
Tenth Year	Celal, Gelenbevi, Milel and Nihal, Muhtasar Fasıl, Tefsir-i Beyzavi, Tuhfe-i Aşeriyye, İzharü'l- Hak, Siyer, Tarih, Coğrafya,
Eleventh Year and Twelfth Year	Hidaye and Buhara or Sahih-i Müslim and Tefsir-i Beyzavi, Tarih-i Osmani and Coğrafya.

of all madrasas under the name *Darü'l-Hilafet'il-Aliyye* Madrasa and determined the curricula of the madrasas. Following the regulation, the Qur'an, *Tecvid*, *Hadis* and *Tefsir*, *İlm-i Fıqh* and *Usul-ü Fıqh*, *İlm-i Kelam*, *Sarf* and *Lügat*, *Nahiv*, *Mantık*, *Belagat-ı Arabiyye*, *Adab*, *Vaz'*, *Mükaleme*, *Kitabet-i Arabiyye*, *Siyer-i Nebevi*, *Peygamberler ve Halifeler Tarihi*, *Tarih-i İslam* and *Edyan*, *Tarih-i Umumi* and *Osmani*, *Felsefe*, *Türkçe Kıraat*, *İmla*, *Kavaid*, *Kitabet* and *Edebiyat*, *Farisi*, *Coğrafya-yı Umumi* and *Osmani*, *Riyaziyat*, *Hesap*, *Hendese*, *Cebir*, *Müsellesat*, *Mihanik*, *Hey'et*, *Usul-ü Defteri*, *Tabiiyat*, *Ziraat*, *Hikmet*, *Kimya*, *Malumat-ı Fenniye* and *Ahlakiye* and *İctimaiyye* and *Kanuniyye*, *Hıfzıssıhha*, *Elsine*, *Hutut*, *İlm-i İçtima* and *Terbiye*, *Terbiye-i Bedeniye*, *İlm-i İktisat*, *Hitabet*, and *Vaaz* started to be taught at the intermediate level *(orta kısım)*, and *Tefsir-i Şerif*, *Hadis* and *Usul-ü Hadis*, *İlm-i Fıqh*, *Tarih-i İlm-i Fıqh*, *Usul-I Fıqh*, *Hilafiyat*, *İlm-i Kelam*, *Tarih-i İlm-i Kelam*, *Felsefe*, *Hukuk*, and *Kavanin* comprised the advanced level of madrasa education.[62]

Those who completed these compulsory courses at the madrasa could graduate and receive a graduation certificate known as an *icazetname*. The *icazetname* was a document written in Arabic with the name and seal of the student's *müderris*, prominent leaders of the region, and other *müderrises* of the region apart from the student's own. It showed the courses and grades of the graduate.[63] After obtaining a graduation certificate, they became qualified and trained the Ilmiye officials in the fields of teaching or jurisprudence. Their total educational lives lasted approximately twenty years. The student's educational success was based upon individual merit and hard work.

The Life of Madrasa Students

A student just starting in a madrasa was known as a *çömez* and was obliged to serve senior madrasa students (doing things like meal preparation, making tea, washing up, and cleaning) in return for sharing a room and for tutorship in his studies.[64] A student started the madrasa at a young age and continued his education as a *çömez* for many years. After passing through the first six grades, he received the title of *softa* or *suhte* which means "one who is burned with the love of knowledge" in Persian. The introductory courses were taught in the next level of training and madrasa students who completed courses at this level were entitled to receive a certificate called a *temessuk*. In this education system, advancement from one grade to the next depended on a student's mastery of the books and subjects that they pursued.

Students starting their education in provincial areas continued their higher-level education in the madrasas of large cities. Madrasa students who proved their talent and had strong networks reached the top of the madrasa education system and continued their education in Istanbul madrasas.[65] Those who studied in Istanbul madrasas reached high levels in the Ilmiye hierarchy. However, there are a small number of exceptions to reach the top levels in this system even though they did not receive an education in Istanbul madrasas.[66] Each of the madrasas had a *müderris* to teach fifteen *danişmends* (advanced students, interns, or assistants). The *danişmends* were specialist students—equivalent to graduates. After the last six grades, students moved on to the *Sahn* madrasa and became a *danişmend.* One *danişmend* was selected by the *müderris* from among his peers as the *muid* with the approval of the office of Şeyhülislam.[67]

These increasingly sophisticated students began to teach the younger students (as tutors to *softas*) when the *muid* later turned into a *deputy müderris.* The *danişmends* and *muids* who completed the required course of study entered the teaching profession *(tarik-i tedris)* with the lowest ranking *müderris (ibtida-i hariç).* The *muids* and *deputy müderrises* were expected to teach four courses in a week. They taught courses in textual interpretation and prepared students with the knowledge of Islamic laws and jurisprudence.

After the *deputy müderris* stage, a student received permission *(icazet* or *icazetname)* from his major professor to teach some subjects of Islamic theory and earned the right to be a *müderris.* Their career life continued from the first years after receiving their *icazet* to their promotion to the top level in the madrasa hierarchy *(Süleymaniye rank).* In this hierarchical system, not every madrasa graduate who received their *icazet* had high status *in* the Ilmiye positions like full-fledged *dersiam* or *müderris.* Generally, *müderrises* having *the* highest ranks (like *Süleymaniye* rank) were appointed to the highest posts in the ulema hierarchy. Thirty or even forty years of a man's life would be consumed in reaching the top-level ranks, and only a few reached this high position.[68]

Livelihood

Even if there was no regular payment in the form of state sponsorship of madrasa students, the education in the madrasas was free.[69] At the same time, the income of the madrasa waqf was obtained by charitable persons who supported the madrasas economically.[70] Another financial resource was religious services given to the public during the Three Holy Months *(*Receb, Şaban, and Ramadan, or *Suhur-i Selase)*. The madrasa students and sometimes the madrasa *müderrises* went to provincial areas during the Three Holy Months to give religious services. This service as itinerant *imam*s or preachers to the public was known as a *cer* trip *(cerre çıkmak)*, and they earned money in exchange for their religious services.[71]

Before a student or *müderris* went on a *cer*, a recommendation letter *(tavsiyename)* was sent to the authority of the region to which the *müderris* or madrasa student would go.[72] Also, the student or *müderris* was informed about the region to be visited.[73] The documents submitted to the Ministry of Finance *(Maliye Nezareti)* showed that expenditures of madrasa students and madrasa *müderrises* traveling to provincial areas for religious services were mostly covered by the state treasury.[74] Thanks to the *cer* trips and the break in his study *(ders kesimi)*, the ulema acquired an opportunity to consolidate his scientific *(ilmi)* knowledge in addition to obtaining revenue.[75]

According to written archival documents and government laws, all costs of madrasa students such as food and shelter were to be covered by the income of the madrasa waqf. Therefore, most academic studies determined that madrasa students were not engaged in any other work to make a living other than their madrasa. However, the situation was sometimes different in practice. When the government experienced financial difficulties and in parallel with the rapidly increasing number of students in the madrasas, some madrasas, and their students, experienced economic trouble. In such periods, madrasa students requested monetary aid or salaries from the government, though this request was usually rejected by the official authorities[76] except in the cases of orphan students or students who cannot take care of themselves.[77] There are also examples of students who wanted to work to earn an income.[78] In order to make a living, students worked as debt collectors *(tahsildar)*, the receiver of tithes *(aşar)*, and in stores *(ambar)*.[79] For instance, Ali Fahreddin of Bolu worked as the scribe on the account of the repairs to in Galata Bridge while he was a young madrasa student at the Süleymaniye Dar'ül-Hadis Madrasa in 1867.[80] Another example is that of Mustafa Nuri of Ankara, who worked as a court scribe in 1886 while a madrasa student.[81] Similarly, İsmail Hakkı Efendi of Ankara began his madrasa education in 1883. By 1884, he was a member of the court and continued to be so for the remainder of his madrasa education.[82] Ahmed Raşid Efendi from Aydın also worked as a court scribe in the Sharia court while a madrasa student in Izmir in 1868 with a salary of 200 piasters.[83]

Military Service

The Ottoman conscription system first prepared after the Tanzimat Edict had many exemptions for various social groups such as certain government officials, the Ilmiye members, and the sultan's attendants.[84] Madrasa students were one of the privileged groups that were not responsible for military service in this period. However, madrasa students had to pass a "conscription examination" before a commission of officials in order to be exempted from conscription. Students to be taken into military service during this period were determined by a lottery system known in the Ottoman Empire as the *Kur'a*. Selected madrasa students who were of the age for military service and chosen as a result of the draw were subject to tests on their specific courses every year, and those who failed were taken to the army. However, if an *alim* candidate studying at the madrasa proved his proficiency in religious sciences, the lottery *(kur'a)* became invalid and he did not become a soldier.[85] This exam that determined who would become a soldier was called the *Kur'a* exam.

A student whose lot was drawn had to prove that he was a madrasa student in that region within twenty days. After proving that he was occupied with the *ilm* and a full-time madrasa student,[86] he had to prove his ability within nine months. The government appointed military officers to determine whether a madrasa student whose lot was drawn was occupied with the *ilm*. Therefore, these officers gave a competence exam and informed the central government about the madrasa students' educational ability. If the student did not sit the test to prove his license within nine months, he was taken into the military. If he proved his proficiency after nine months had expired, the test was invalid. In this sense, even though the madrasa student was exempt from military service, there were two conditions for it; it is proving that he was a madrasa student *(isbat-ı vücud)* and showing his competence in an exam. For instance, İsmail Hakkı Efendi was exempted from compulsory military service because he proved his proficiency, although his name was mentioned in two lotteries during his twelve-year madrasa education.[87] Similarly, the lot of Hasan Hüsnü Efendi of Hakkari was drawn while he was a madrasa student, but the lottery was invalidated when he proved his license at the exam.[88]

Apart from military service, the Ilmiye class was also exempt from military mobilization *(askeri seferberlik)*. During the war times, a sufficient number of students and *müderrises* in each Ilmiye institution were kept available in order to prevent harm to scientific *(ilmi)* studies.[89] In this sense, madrasa students were expected to develop their professional knowledge and skills to hold onto their jobs. If they were interested in just *ilm* and improved their scientific *(ilmi)* proficiency, they were completely exempted from military service. Students who did not want to pursue a career in the Ilmiye class, who did not work to develop their professional skills, and who did not pass the exam were identified and taken into military service. In this regard, the madrasa student who did not try to improve himself and exhibited an unethical attitude did not benefit from the privilege of being exempted from military service.

Examination and Appointment

The graduation examinations of madrasa students to receive their *icazetnames* started to be held at a regular time in the early nineteenth century. The candidates were required to deliver a lecture before the committee in addition to the written exam, and successful ones were given a written document by their own scholars.[90] Educational success was tied to students' individual efforts. These written and oral exams were generally held in the madrasa complex in the presence of *müderrises* and muftis. In the examination, the madrasa students were responsible for each subject taught to them throughout their madrasa life, such as *sarf*, *nahv*, *mantık*, *fiqh*, *kelam*, and *ahlak*.

Also, the *rüus*[91] exam was held regularly after the graduation exam to make high-ranking Ilmiye appointments in the government hierarchy. In a regulation *(nizamname)* prepared in 1877 that determined the content of the exam to be taken by the Ilmiye candidates to serve in the government hierarchy, one condition is that those participating in the *rüus* exam "must be read up until the *Hudus* part of the *Celal (*the book of Arabic grammar*)*."[92] Recalling that the *Celal* is the last book to be taught in the madrasa education, this meant that all the books have to be read and the training of the madrasa must be fully completed in order to participate in this test. With this regulation, the *rüus* exam started to be held every year under the supervision of the Şeyhülislam Office so that ulema did not have to wait long for the exam before they could be appointed to the Ilmiye positions. In this sense, the period between graduation and appointment to the Ilmiye position was shortened and candidates did not wait long before being appointed to vacant positions.

Over time, the *rüus* examination became a compulsory exam for obtaining each of the Ilmiye positions in the government hierarchy. The result of the *rüus* examination affected the candidate's whole career. All civil servant candidates were subjected to the *rüus* exam, regardless of whether they wanted to be appointed to a low or high grade Ilmiye position. Even if the ulema graduated from school and received their *icazets*, they could not start salaried work if they did not take and pass the exam.[93] This examination system designed to avoid injustice grew. For instance, bringing the sons of *müderrises* to their positions upon the *müderrises'* death became a tradition after the beginning of the Tanzimat period, and was seen as a right for these sons of the *müderrises*.[94] It was also legislated in the *Tevcih-i Cihat Hakkında Nizamname* (regulation on work conditions and appointments of religious officers) that the oldest child would be chosen if the deceased *müderris* had more than one.[95] Despite the fact that the passing of the *müderris* position from father to son became a tradition in this period, these sons were still subject to the exam. If they failed or did not take it, they were not awarded a license to teach regardless of their abilities. In this sense, it is the most important condition to prove proficiency in the Ilmiye professions for the sons of *müderris*.[96] This *rüus* examination gave them access to positions in the Şeyhülislam Office like *müderris*, kadı, and mufti.

There are also examples that the position of *müderris* did not pass from father to son. The first case in which the profession did not pass to the son concerned the son's age and maturity. When the age of the son of the *müderris* was inadequate, the task was transferred to a proxy until the son had the experience and knowledge to perform the profession *(vakt-i istidad)*.[97] In such situations, these sons were also subjected to the exam. Müderris candidates were assigned to the *rüus* exam to be appointed in the place of the madrasa *müderris* who had withdrawn from the post.[98] For instance, the sons of the *müderris* of Balıkesir madrasas belonging to the Yıldırım Beyazıt Waqf could not take up their fathers' professions because of their young age. Therefore, Müderris Edhem Efendi's son *müderris* Süleyman Efendi was assigned to this madrasa by an exam.[99] The youngest son of Hafiz Hüseyin Efendi of Isparta objected to the decision and applied for the return to his father's duty. This document suggests that the sons of the *müderrises* believed the transfer of the profession from fathers to sons was a right, even though information on the end result is not available.[100] Another situation that required a position to be given to another person was the absence of a son *(bila veled)*.[101] For example, since the Valide-i Atik Hızır Efendi Madrasa's *müderris* had no son, Mehmet Emin Efendi was appointed to this madrasa by the *rüus* exam after the death of the previous *müderris*.[102]

Furthermore, the appointment of new graduates by the office of Şeyhülislam could be done either in groups or individually with the recommendation of the grand vizier and the *berat*[103] of the sultan.[104] The names of the *ulema* to be appointed, the names of their madrasas, and the titles of their *müderrises* were prepared in a list. First, this list was presented by the Şeyhülislam to the grand vizier. The grand vizier then presented it to Sultan. The Sultan had a direct interest in all appointments of the Ilmiye members to government positions.

Before the Tanzimat era, ulema who had graduated from the madrasa were appointed as *müderris*, kadı, naib, preacher, and *imam* in the government system, and they held onto such positions during and after the Tanzimat period. They could also be appointed—especially as teachers *muallim* of religious courses—to the newly established modern schools such as the *Mekteb-i Sultani*, *Mekteb-i Tıbbiye-i Mülkiye*, and *Dersaadet Mektebi İdadisi* after the Tanzimat in this century.[105] Those ulema with an *icazet* were written in special ledgers and were expected to have the necessary qualities to be appointed to the Ilmiye positions. A *mümeyyiz* (examiner)[106] held a series of tests for madrasa graduates wanting to be a judge or a *müderris*. There was a great desire among candidates to enter the government positions in the Ilmiye hierarchy after graduating; therefore, madrasa graduates began preparations early to be on the waiting list for the *rüus* exam.[107] Appointments to the Ilmiye positions were made after the graduates who had their *icazet* passed the *rüus* exam.

The waiting period to be appointed was known as the *mülazemet* (candidacy). The *mülazemet* had a dual meaning in the Ilmiye literature. The first refers to the waiting period for reappointment to a similar position for a member of the Ilmiye class who had already worked as a civil servant in the Ilmiye hierarchy.[108]

The other meaning is the waiting period of a graduate before being appointed to an official government post. The names of candidates awaiting an appointment *(mülazım)* were printed in a book called *Matlab*.[109] Those who succeeded in the exam were given their appointments at the end of a waiting period. The duration of the *mülazemet* was shortened or extended according to the needs of the office of Şeyhülislam for staff, and this waiting process took place at the end of three to seven years of training and service.[110] After the beginning of the Tanzimat period, those waiting out their *mülazemet* undertook simple tasks such as court scribes before beginning their main assignments. In this respect, the ulema completed a kind of internship and learned his profession.[111] In this sense, the *mülazemet* was a transitional period between the internship period and public service in the Ilmiye hierarchy.

Table 3.2 shows that the duration for appointment to the Ilmiye position of ulema candidates could change. While some ulema waited for short periods like two or three years to be appointed, others waited for six and seven years. Second, this table indicates that although some ulema did not receive a salary,[113] there were ulema who gained a salary before they were appointed.[114]

Table 3.2 Waiting period (Mülazemet) for appointment to an İlmiye position[112]

Name	Duration of Mülazemet (in years)	Position during Mülazemet	Salary during Mülazemet
Ahmet Efendi	3	Officer in Fetvahane	Unknown
Halil Fehmi Efendi	6	Officer in Fetvahane	250 Piasters
Hüseyin Efendi	5	Unknown	Unknown
İsmail Hakkı Efendi	3	Court Scribe	100 Piasters
Mehmet Rüştü Efendi	5	Unknown	Unknown
Yusuf Efendi	7	Dersiam	Unknown
Hasan Tahsin Efendi	2.5	Scribe in a Sharia Court	Unknown
Mustafa Cemaleddin Efendi	4	Scribe in a Sharia Court	Unsalaried

Furthermore, the *mülazemet* system resulted in an increasing number of candidates in Istanbul because one condition of the system was that candidates remain in Istanbul. However, there are examples of ulema returning to their homes during the waiting period. Those ulema continued to be involved in science in their hometowns.[115] This waiting period caused an increase in the number of candidates for a limited number of government positions in time. In this sense, a young graduate ulema endured a long period of waiting without a salary. Even after beginning as civil servants in the Ilmiye system, their positions were not guaranteed because they had to wait for each reappointment process. Ulema candidates waiting out the *mülazemet* generally gave private courses independently of a government appointment during this waiting period in order to make a living.[116]

After the *mülazemet* period and after passing the *rüus* exam, the ulema was initially appointed to a low-ranking Ilmiye position.[117] The candidates are generally appointed by *rüus* examination after the waiting period. The appointment was made according to the results of the examination, and there was usually more than one applicant for each available Ilmiye position.[118]

Lastly, even if patronage and family background were important for appointment to the high-ranking teaching and judiciary positions, a quality madrasa education and the actual knowledge and the abilities of the ulema to be appointed to the Ilmiye position were the deciding factors. Therefore, the education process directly affected the career lives of the ulema. The ulema were chosen from among madrasa graduates who passed through certain stages in the madrasa hierarchy and passed the *rüus* exam. Most of the Ilmiye positions were decided upon based on the personal merit and knowledge of the candidates.

4

Ulema's Professional Career (1880–1920)

In the nineteenth century, *alim* candidates continued the tradition of going first to *sibyan mekteps* and then madrasas for their education. They had been educated in their hometowns by attending the primary schools run by religious scholars for an average of four years and they spent an average of fifteen years at the madrasa. At the end of madrasa training, the apprentice ulema received a graduation certificate from a master scholar who authorized them to teach. However, graduation from the madrasa was not enough to be appointed to the Ilmiye position. During the growth of the bureaucracy in the Tanzimat period, the number of staff members at state institutions expanded, and full-time salaried employees of the state transformed, affecting the Ilmiye institutions. The development of the modern form of the Ilmiye included the essential requirements to enter the institution, such as the determination of specific entrance requirements and the creation of trained career ulema.

All ulema candidates who received their *icazets* were subject to oral and written *rüus* exams, and these exams were held in front of a special commission that was assigned by the central office in both Istanbul and the provinces.[1] This commission evaluated the Islamic knowledge and intellectual capacity of the ulema candidates. Until the ulema candidates passed the *rüus* exams, they were not accepted in the Şeyhülislam Office as the Ilmiye civil servants. The office of Şeyhülislam offered all candidates certain Ilmiye positions after they passed the *rüus* exam, meaning the level of knowledge of the ulema was as important as the significance of the graduates' madrasas and their *müderrises*' fame and networks in winning positions in the Ilmiye hierarchy.

The choice of a career within the institution for an *alim* was an individual preference in the Ottoman Empire, and all the Ilmiye positions were theoretically available for all madrasa graduates. Therefore, many ulema performed active duties in various Ilmiye ranks. Those belonging to the Ilmiye class *(tarik-i the Ilmiye)* were mostly employed in two ways: education and training activities *(tarik-i tedris)* and legal affairs *(tarik-i kaza)*. After graduating from the madrasa, the *alim* would be promoted to government positions like judges, *müderrises*, other bureaucratic positions within the Ilmiye, and other government positions.

There were clear, specific criteria to hold the post of ulema in the Ottoman Empire and to be appointed to some the Ilmiye positions. Even if the criteria for ulema appointments changed according to time, place, or position, there were always basic, indispensable criteria for the selection of officials to the Ilmiye posts so that they were capable and competent *(ehliyetli ve liyakatlı)*.

Graduates who are eligible to work in the Ilmiye hierarchy chose one of the appropriate professions, in the educational and judicial fields. The ulema worked as *müderrises* or *dersiams* in the educational field and as kadıs, naibs, and muftis in the legal field. Apart from kadıs, naibs, and muftis, there were other officials working in the legal system such as the court members *(mahkeme azası)* and court scribe *(katip)*, but they were not clearly defined as part of the legal system and were in the position of assisting the judges. In addition, the Ilmiye members could be assigned to the mosques as *imam*, *müezzin*, and preacher and to other religious positions in the army such as being military regiment *imam* and mufti *(tabur imamı, alay imamı,* and *alay muftisi)*—provided they were successful in the examination or as a result of a number of outstanding achievements.[2] Furthermore, the ulema served in the palace as the teacher of the sultans' sons *(şehzade hocası)* or to the sultans' themselves, as well as the *imam* or preacher of the sultans.[3] In this respect, the career opportunities and working conditions of the Ilmiye members at the imperial and provincial levels in the context of the Ilmiye hierarchy are scrutinized.

Ulema biographies in the Meşihat Archive provide valuable information about the careers of ulema who worked as personnel in the Şeyhülislam Office between the years 1884 and 1922. With reference to the personnel records of the ulema from the Meşihat Archive, this study will present a panorama of the period, and a picture of the ulema, whose members shared common characteristics. The book's goal is not only to discuss the life of specific figures within the ulema but also to describe the institutional role of the ulema as civil servants in the government.

This part explains three main issues: First, the examination of career paths of the ulema with common origins; second, an analysis of the professional prestige and status of the ulema; and third, an exploration of the real functions of the ulema living in the provinces rather than the more popular figures from the ulema class who reached the top ranks. Although the sample does not represent the professional journeys and educations of all the ulema at the time, it does provide very important data from which arguments can be made about the general situation of the Ottoman Ilmiye class in the late nineteenth century.

The examination of career paths, teaching positions, and appointments of the Ottoman ulema presents a wide-ranging portrait and answers more detailed questions about the identities of these faceless ulema. Common major experiences, characteristics, and implications of the Ottoman ulema in the nineteenth century better explain how the ulema were adopted to the new educational and professional system and obtained new governmental positions and status.

Appointment

The qualifications required for those appointed to the office of the Ilmiye were set down in law in 1838 with the İlmiye Penal Code *(Tarik-i İlmiyeye Dair Ceza Kanunnamesi)*.[4] It made the Şeyhülislam authority the only institution legally permitted to appoint and administer the Ilmiye professions. Apart from *imam*, *müezzin*, preacher, *müderris*, and kadı appointments, the highest positions like the appointments of kazaskers were also appointed by the Şeyhülislam. Even though the Şeyhülislam Office was the foremost authority regarding the appointment of the Ilmiye officials during the nineteenth century, the local councils made the appointments directly through the examination results in some cases.

Madrasa-graduated ulema had to wait *(mülazemet)* for a time after the completion of their madrasa education in order to be appointed. Ulema candidates registered in the *matlab* book were appointed as *müderris*, mufti, kadı, and other Ilmiye positions starting at the lowest level after completing this *mülazemet* period. Most of those who studied in madrasas and could not find vacant positions in the Ilmiye hierarchy as kadı or *müderris* were first assigned as court scribes—either without waiting or at the end of a short waiting period—before later being appointed to higher-ranking government positions. In some periods, the waiting period for appointment to the Ilmiye positions was five or even seven years.[5] These long years of *mülazemet* notwithstanding, direct appointments were made with no waiting period, especially in the late nineteenth and early twentieth centuries. One of the most important reasons for the decreasing duration of *mülazemet* in this period was the need for competent people as a result of bureaucratic reforms in the empire. For instance, in 1902, it was decided that the 600 students that would graduate from Istanbul madrasas that year would be immediately employed in Istanbul madrasas for a salary of 150 piasters per month if they were willing.[6]

One of the most important requirements for ulema to be appointed to vacant Ilmiye positions was a graduation certificate. There were cases where an *alim* has lost his certificate, in which case they were subject to reexamination and expected to reprove his proficiency again. For instance, Osman Zeki Efendi of Ankara proved his proficiency with the witness of his madrasa *müderris* as he lost his graduation diploma.[7] Similarly, Mehmed Kazım Efendi of Konya was re-tested because he had lost his diploma.[8] Candidates who completed their madrasa education and had graduation certificates could solely be assigned to the Ilmiye positions if they passed the *rüus* exam.

When the government appointed ulema to the Ilmiye positions, it was considered the region in which the ulema wanted to be appointed and the candidates' exam results. Ulema who applied for vacant positions were subject to the exam,[9] and the person with the highest score from this test was appointed to the position. With respect to district appointments, the government again prioritized the preference of the ulema and the result of the exam. But if no qualified ulema applied for a vacant position in a given district of the empire, the government was led to appoint a prominent person from this region.[10]

Appointment procedures within the Ilmiye hierarchy could change according to the field of the appointment. Appointments to the administrative, judicial, and educational fields in the Ilmiye hierarchy differed from each other. One of the fields specified in the regulation of 1838 on appointment procedures in the Ilmiye system was education. According to this regulation, the appointment of *müderrises* to general *(umumi)* madrasas and the educational curricula taught by the *müderrises* in the madrasa were under the absolute control of the *Ders Vekaleti* department of Şeyhülislam Office, which was established to regulate the education and training activities of the *müderrises* in madrasas under the office of Şeyhülislam.[11] The decisions of the trustees of the madrasas and the Ministry of Waqf *(Evkaf Nezareti)* were also important for the appointment of *müderrises*, but the authority to make the final decision lay with the Şeyhülislam. Therefore, one of the most important conditions to be appointed to a madrasa was to comply with the requirements of the waqf with which the madrasa was affiliated. Madrasa trustees would choose a candidate for a *müderris* post that was vacated for any reason. These trustees would recommend the candidate to the respective local governors of the region—like the district governor, judge, or deputy judge—then to the district council *(sancak meclisi)*, and then to the Directorate of Waqf *(Evkaf Müdürü)*. As a result of *rüus* examinations performed by the

Ministry of Evkaf, and the approval of the Şeyhülislam based on the exam results, the appointment would be made.[12]

The appointments of *müderrises* to the specialized madrasa were made in a similar way to those of the *müderrises* of the general madrasa. Unlike the appointment of general madrasa *müderrises*, the appointment of *müderrises* to higher-ranking madrasas (specialized madrasas from the *ibtida-i hariç* to the *darülhadis*) was carried out directly with the approval of the sultan. A list of the names of candidate *müderrises* to be appointed to specialized madrasas, the madrasas from which they graduated, and the honorary grades *(payes)* that they had been awarded was prepared by the Şeyhülislam and sent to the Grand Vizier. The appointment of these *müderrises* was made after the grand vizier supplied this list to the sultan and received his approval. Moreover, those who wanted to be a *müderris* in Istanbul and *Bilad-ı Selase* were required to be given a test before a commission convened under the Şeyhülislam Office's commissioner of seminary education *(ders vekili)*. If they succeed, they received a certificate to teach *(Şehadetname)* and could be teaching duty at high-ranking madrasas.[13]

Another form of appointment, particularly noticeable in the appointments of *müderrises*, was a transition from father to son. If a deceased *müderris* had a son, with a madrasa education and an *icazet*, he was usually assigned to the madrasa or mosque where his father was employed. For instance, when one of the *dersiams* of Edirne, Yusuf Efendi, passed away, his elder son Mehmed Efendi was appointed to the madrasa where his father had served. After Mehmed Efendi died, Abdülkerim Efendi, one of the Karasu *dersiams*, was appointed rather than the younger son of Yusuf Efendi.[14] The important point considered was competence. When Yusuf Efendi died, his elder son Mehmed Efendi could be appointed because he was a competent *alim*. However, the appointment of a *müderris* from another family and origin was subsequently made because Yusuf Efendi's youngest son did not have this competence.

Another professional group working under the Şeyhülislam Office was muftis. The official identity of a mufti was to be the direct representative of the Şeyhülislam authority in the provinces of the Ottoman Empire. Namely, the mufti was the religious president in provincial cities working in the name of the Şeyhülislam. The mufti of each district was the head of all *imam*, *müezzin*, *vaiz*, *müderris*, and other Ilmiye officials in their regions. The muftis answered questions asked of them according to Islamic law and issued fatwas in the Ottoman Empire. In other words, the mufti was a respectable man with the authority to issue fatwas based on Islamic law. Their chief task was to find the problems that individuals encountered in their social lives in accordance with the Sharia, but the mufti also had the authority to oversee *müderrises* and the heads of mosques, *tekkes*, and *zaviye* orders as well as to supervise all religious institutions.

More importantly, the mufti had the power to dismiss or reward government officials by issuing fatwas. Muftis had a controlling role and veto power over the decisions of kadı or Sharia courts would be inappropriate to the Sharia. In this sense, muftis' fatwas justified court decisions in terms of law enforcement and legal regulations. In situations in which kadıs were hesitant, they deferred to the muftis with "the authority to give fatwa" who knew Sharia and would check the suitability of provisions to the Sharia. The kadıs also received fatwa from the mufti on ordinary subjects apart from religious matters.[15] In other words, though kadıs decided most judicial cases, they preferred to consult the muftis for their opinions, especially in cases involving Islamic jurisprudence. Therefore, it might appear as if the muftis were the more important officials than the kadıs, because they dealt with abstract theory and sacred law.[16] However, in practice, kadıs were considered the more important of the two. The education of a kadı was longer than that of a mufti, and a kadı's chances of promotion were better. Further, in theory, the highest-ranking of the Ilmiye members, the Şeyhülislam, was thought of as a promoted kadı, and he was usually chosen from among the ranks of kadıs.

One of the most important points about muftis was that they represented both the government and the office of Şeyhülislam, so they acted in accordance with the office of Şeyhülislam and general administrative rules. Therefore, their appointment was decided meticulously and carefully by the Şeyhülislam Office. The appointment of muftis was generally made by the office of Şeyhülislam without the need for an exam,[17] but they were sometimes appointed following an exam given by the office of Şeyhülislam.[18] In this regard, the exams for the selection of mufti were not always necessary in the case of the candidates that had already passed an exam for an earlier position. The muftis were generally chosen from among the qualified ulema candidates and recommended by the prominent local big-wigs of a city or province.[19] However, a recommended mufti candidate needed the approval of the Şeyhülislam Office to be appointed.[20] To select the mufti, prominent leaders first looked at the local ulema living in the region; if there was no suitable provincial ulema, they searched for a person from other regions. However, the prerequisite was the perceived competence and capability of the mufti in their region.

The position of mufti was generally given by the Şeyhülislam to a well-known *müderris*.[21] Rarely, he was chosen from among the *muallims*[22] with a high-level religious knowledge of that place. The archives show that most muftis were appointed after having been charged with the duty of *müderris*, and they fulfilled the duty of *müderris* while simultaneously holding the position of mufti.[23] Because the selected muftis often continued their teaching positions as *müderris* along with assuming the authority to issue fatwas, the position of mufti was not so different from that of *müderris*. The muftis in the Ilmiye hierarchy continued to give courses to madrasa students *(talebe-i ulum)* if they wanted. In our sample, almost all muftis maintained their teaching positions after becoming mufti. Therefore, the position of mufti was not considered a discrete official government servant. In this sense, the occupation of mufti was not thought of differently from that of *müderris*, rather, it was little more than an additional administrative duty and additional income.

Those with scientific maturity, good morals *(hüsn-i ahlak)*, and good records of service to the public *(hüsn-i hizmet)*[24] were recommended for the position of the mufti to the office of Şeyhülislam by prominent big-wigs of the region. Also, when choosing the mufti, the works the candidates had written to date were taken into consideration. In other words, the literary productivity of a candidate was important in winning mufti appointments.[25] The district's powerful figures voted the candidates who were reliable and authorized to issue fatwas by secret ballot.Then the three candidates with the most votes were reported to the office of Şeyhülislam, which determined who would be the mufti among these candidates.[26] In this sense, the recommendation letter *(tavsiyename)* of a notable of the district—such as the governor, *müderris*, *muallim*, or *imam*—could become a determinant of the appointment. The signed recommendations of leading figures affected the decisions of the Şeyhülislam Office.[27]

Even though it is known that the proposals of the notables of the region were taken into consideration in the appointment of a mufti, there were occasions when the Şeyhülislam did not take these proposals into account. For instance, when Osman Asım Efendi, who was working as mufti in the Hezargrad district, died, notables of the region tried to find a provincial mufti candidate. Because there was no suitable person with good morals and high scientific knowledge, notables recommended that the mufti of Rusçuk (Ruse), Osman Nuri Efendi, be appointed as the official mufti of Hezargrad. However, the Şeyhülislam appointed the *müderris* of Hezargrad Debbağhane Mosque as mufti.[28]

Another Ilmiye position, whose appointment method is important, is the naibs, who assist the kadis. The appointment and supervision of legal and judicial officials started to be made by the office of Şeyhülislam after regulations were decreed during the Tanzimat period. The four institutions with authority over their appointment were the governorship, the appointment office of

Şeyhülislam authority *(intihab-ı hükkam-ı şeriye)*, the kazaskers (the Anatolian kazasker over the appointment of Anatolian kadıs and naibs and Rumelia kazasker over the kadıs and naibs of Rumelia) and the Şeyhülislam.[29]

The final decision on the appointment of kadıs lay with the Şeyhülislam and the consent of the sultan. The kadıs of great cities such as Istanbul, Edirne, Sofia, Thessalonica, and Bursa—which are considered as a jurisdiction of a high-ranking Sharia judge *(mevleviyet)*—were also appointed by the Şeyhülislam with the approval of the sultan. A prospective *alim* who graduated from the madrasa would be eligible for appointment as an ordinary kadı after serving a probationary term as *mülazım* in one of the eleven ranks and entering the judicial profession.

The government attached particular importance to the appointment of kadıs and naibs who formed the basis of the justice system. The İlmiye Penal Code of 1838[30] was intended to prevent incapable and irregular kadıs and naibs. To become a kadı, professional competence became the most important condition. Therefore, it was decided to test the competence of kadıs who wanted to be reappointed to a new kadı position. The examination was carried out under the supervision of the Şeyhülislam before three or four committee members who had previously worked as kadıs. Candidates who did not pass the exam were not reappointed. In addition, ulema who were new candidates for the position of kadıs were tested, and if they failed the examination, they could continue their educations in the hopes of passing subsequent tests. Candidates had to be fully competent with respect to the fatwa, jurisprudence, and Arabic in order to be successful in the position of the kadı exam.

There were no separate madrasas to train kadıs up until the Tanzimat in the Ottoman Empire. The kadıs were chosen from among ulema who graduated from general madrasas like other staff. However, specialization began after the Tanzimat, and the *Muallimhane-i Nüvvab* was established to educate kadıs in 1858. This law school had different names at different periods such as *Mekteb-i Nüvvab* and *Mekteb-i Kuzat* and *Madrasatü'l-Kuzat* or *Madrasatü'l-Nüvvab*. After the establishment of this law school, its graduates have priority in appointments to judiciary civil service.

With new regulations made in 1873, it was decided to choose kadıs from among those who had studied the *Tasdikat*, which was a course in logic. The exams of kadı candidates were derived from a book called *Mülteka* based on the Hanafi jurisprudence, and three questions were asked for each course that they had studied.[31] In the case that candidates for a kadı position were equal, the candidate with the best calligraphy was preferred. As can be seen, appropriate regulations were made as a requirement of a bureaucratic government, and the necessary regulations were even considered in the case of equality of the candidates.

However, after the second constitutional era *(meşrutiyet)*, the kadı who headed a district administration absolutely had to have finished a judiciary madrasa apart from graduating from an Ottoman madrasa. In 1910, the Purge Law *(Tensikat Kanunu)* was released to regulate the appointments of judiciary members. According to the Purge Law, *Tensikat*, the condition of having to have graduated from a madrasa called the *Madrasat'ül Nüvvab* or *Madrasat'ül Kuzat* in order to be in the judiciary was established. Only those who graduated from *law school* could be appointed as a kadı. Those who wanted to be a kadı studied at the legal madrasa after finishing another general madrasa, or he would study at these two madrasas at the same time.

Another regulation that regulated appointments as kadı was enacted on July 30, 1914, to require the 25 years of age to assume a judiciary position in the Ottoman Ilmiye hierarchy.[32] Following this last regulation, the conditions for being in the legal or judiciary part of the Ottoman Ilmiye system were as follows: Twenty-five years old, a madrasa graduate, not having had a criminal record, and passing the exam.

Before the nineteenth century, kadı appointments were not lifelong, but in the Tanzimat period, kadı could systematically be appointed for two years. After two years he had to go to Istanbul and wait for the "*mülazemet*" (waiting period, *mülazemette beklemek)* without a salary. This means that a person who has served thirty years in the judiciary has had a ten-year *mülazemet* period.

Because kadıs could not leave the courts and had to physically remain in the courtrooms, the Şeyhülislam Office assigned naibs to do discovery work, especially in provincial regions on behalf of the kadıs. The naibs carried out some legal work on the kadıs' behalf and possessed all of the authority of the kadıs. In this sense, the naibs were substitute judges in small towns. Undoubtedly, the naibs were one of the largest, most important groups in the bureaucracy with hundreds of members, and their power reached all the Ottoman provinces. With the centralization of the bureaucracy, the number of naibs continued to grow in every province and were well-accepted, government-approved positions in society.

The naibs were separated from the kadıs in the Tanzimat period by reforms made in the judicial field. In 1855, Sharia judges started to be named as naib regardless of their rank in the five-grade system. As mentioned before, in this system, members of the judiciary were divided into five ranks. These ranks were given to judges and other judicial posts according to the importance and size of the district or region in which they were assigned (central big cities comprised the first and second grades, and provincial regions the third, fourth, and fifth), their fame, their exam results, and their competence as Sharia judges. Therefore, naibs were no longer subservient to the kadıs, and for the first time, they were recognized as a professional group. One of the most important conditions to be appointed as a naib during the Tanzimat period was to have the *icazetname*. Naibs who did not have the *icazetname* were reexamined by the Sharia court or by provincial councils. They could be appointed as a naib when they proved their competence. For instance, Halil Hulusi Efendi of Adana, who worked as a naib despite lacking an *icazetname*, was reexamined by a commission on 29 November 1910, and given an *icazetname* for him to be re-appointed as a naib in Kozan.[33] Another point concerning naib appointments was the *mülazemet* period. Madrasa graduates had to wait a long time before being appointed to a judiciary the Ilmiye position. For instance, Ahmet Efendi of Antakya waited three years to become a naib[34]and Halil Fehmi Efendi of Benghazi waited for six.[35] However, newly graduated ulema were sometimes allowed to serve as naib at the Sharia court without waiting due to the need for qualified persons given the bureaucratic reforms in the empire.[36]

The naibs were appointed to districts of different ranks as a result of their ranks, reputation, and exam results. Also, the authority to appoint naibs belonged to the Şeyhülislam by taking persons recommended by the provincial administration's council into consideration. The appointment was made absolute by the Şeyhülislam with the approval of the sultan.

Furthermore, while *müderris* and mufti for a district were generally selected from among ulema living there, naibs were generally appointed to districts other than the ones where they originated. Again, in another contrast from *müderrises* or muftis, the naibs were tested every two years and assigned to new places according to their exam results.[37]

Madrasa students who wanted to guarantee to hold the judicial post as kadı or naib began to enroll in the *Madrasat'ül Kuzat* or *Madrasat'ül Nüvvab* during their education in the madrasa or after graduating. These schools helped to facilitate their professional careers. For instance, Halil Fahri Efendi of Erzurum took the exam to be accepted to the *Madrasat'ül Nüvvab* after having graduated from Horhor Madrasa in the Fatih district, and he graduated from the *Madrasat'ül Nüvvab* in 1888. After one year, he was appointed as a naib in the Tortum district of Erzurum when he was twenty-seven years old.[38] Similarly, Halil İbrahim Efendi of Antalya was appointed as a naib after graduating from the *Madrasat'ül*

Nüvvab. He attended the *Madrasat'ül Nüvvab* while studying in the madrasa to become a member of the judiciary part of the Ottoman Ilmiye class.[39]

After 1910, all kadıs and naibs who had not graduated from the *Madrasat'ül Nüvvab* were removed from their positions in the Ilmiye hierarchy. But there were examples of ulema who objected to this decision. For instance, Said Efendi was a kadı who had graduated from *Madrasat'ül Nüvvab* and was also at the rank of *sınıf-ı ulya*, which is the top tier in the Ilmiye system. Said Efendi did not enter the *Madrasat'ül Nüvvab* examination after the law was passed due to his graduation certificate from this madrasa. However, he was terminated from his position for refusing to take the new test. Said Efendi applied to the office of Şeyhülislam informing the institution that he had been a victim of misconduct, submitting a document that showed his proficiency and rank in the Ilmiye system. Because he had only passed the old exam, his old exam result was considered incomplete and inadequate by the office of Şeyhülislam. Said Efendi was informed that if he renewed his competence in the new courses, he would be appointed again.[40]

Another official position in the Ilmiye hierarchy was the *nakibü'l-eşraf*. The position of the Prophet Muhammad's family, close relatives, and descendants *(sayyits* and *sheriffs)* were considered exceptional before the Muslims who always showed them respect. Therefore, the government appointed staff to carry out services related to them such as registering the works of *sheriffs*, registering their births and deaths, and protecting their rights. Thus, over time, the position of "*nakibü'l-eşraf*", which was also called "*nakib*", "*nakibü'l-eşraf*," and "*nakibün-nükaba*", emerged.[41] The *nakibü'l-eşraf* was generally appointed from among the descendants of the Prophet Muhammad.[42] There were also those who were appointed from the kazasker and Şeyhülislam.

The other officials in the Ilmiye hierarchy who carried out religious duties were the *imams*, *müezzins*, and preachers. Records obtained about the educational status of preachers, *müezzins*, and *imams* indicate that few had more than basic religious information and that they were not educated systematically. Most of the religious education required for this work was received within the family because the office of an *imam* was usually transferred from father to son. In order to be assigned to the Ilmiye positions such as *imam*, *vaiz*, or *müezzin*, a candidate did not need to be a madrasa graduate, but they were still subject to a test. For instance, Mehmed Efendi who wanted to be appointed as *imam* to the El Hac Ali Mosque was tested to prove his competence. The mufti, waqf officer *(evkaf memuru)*, and three court members gathered under the chairmanship of the region's kadı and tested the religious competence of Mehmet Efendi with a five-question exam. His appropriateness for reciting the Qur'an, recitation rules of the Quran *(tecvid)*, and the suitability of his voices for reciting the Qur'an and adhan are rated by this committee. He could be appointed by the committee after receiving enough grades from the exam.[43] The region's kadı, mufti, and the official of orphans waqf *(eytam* and *evkaf memuru)* were decision-making mechanisms for the appointment of provincial ulema to work as *imam*, *müezzin*, or preacher.[44]

The important point to note while studying the professional career patterns of the Ottoman ulema is the mobility that individuals possessed—that is, their movement from city to city. Even if the positions of *dersiam* and *müderris* were more fixed and the civil servants served longer terms compared to judicial officials such as kadıs or naibs, re-appointments to new districts applied to all professional groups. In other words, despite differences in the duration and frequency of changes, reappointments to other places were typical in each professional group in the Ilmiye.

Importance was always placed on the demands of provincial people in the reappointment process. The request by a region's notables that the Ilmiye members' duty be prolonged was important for extending the period of the duty of this civil servant. For instance, upon the request of locals, *müderris* Ahmet Hilmi Efendi was appointed by the government to the Mardin Kasımiye Madrasa with a salary of 500 piasters in January 1872, indicating that the requests of locals were significant in the appointment process.[45] Similarly, Halil Fehmi Efendi of Hüdavendigar was appointed to Mecca as a naib for two years; after the two years passed, his tenure was extended in accordance with the desire of the people of the region.[46] The other point to be mentioned in the re-assignment process is the examination system. Examinations of ulema continued even after the appointment of an *alim* to the Ilmiye position within the government hierarchy. The *alim* who wanted to be reappointed had to participate and pass the examination that was given by the institution to which he wanted to be appointed. Exchanges of the places of duty of educational and judiciary people (such as promotion or exile) were made by the Şeyhülislam Office.

Furthermore, many academic works assume that every person who received a madrasa education became *müderrises*, muftis, or kadıs or that they generally held religious posts in the Ilmiye hierarchy. However, they actually took on broad governmental functions in the new Tanzimat ministries and institutions, as well. There were many other professions available to the ulema, especially in the last quarter of the nineteenth century. Even though most ulema in government service generally worked under the office of Şeyhülislam within the Ilmiye hierarchy, some madrasa graduates did not work for the Şeyhülislam Office. Assignments of madrasa graduates could be made to vacant positions of various government institutions as needed. Our sample provides evidence of these varied career paths because it includes ulema working in administrative positions after graduating from madrasas. For instance, Mesud Efendi of Diyarbakır graduated from Kasımpaşa Madrasa in Mardin and then served as a tax collector in Mardin under the Ministry of Finance in 1888.[47]Similarly, after Musa Kazım Efendi of Denizli served in Izmir as a naib, he served as a collector of the tithe, a debt enforcer, and then a building contractor in 1870, 1880, and 1886, respectively. After he finished these tasks, he returned to the naib in 1890.[48] On the other hand, Hacı Hasan Efendi of Batum who graduated from the Fatih Tetimme-i Hamse Madrasa was appointed as a teacher *(muallim)* in Düzce under the Maarif Nezareti.[49] Similarly, Şeyh Rüstem Efendizade from among the respected ulema of Sivas was appointed to the Aziziye district as a police commissioner under the Interior Ministry.[50] If madrasa graduates wanted to be part of the Ilmiye system, they could later continue their careers in the Ilmiye posts such as *müderris*, kadı, or mufti.

Lastly, the government permitted the opportunity for ulema to pass proper positions among the Ilmiye cadres. Since ulema assigned to the Ilmiye professions in the educational and judicial fields were of madrasa origin and received a similar education, the Ilmiye professions like *müderris* and kadı were not separated by precise lines. Therefore, transfers among professional groups with differing hierarchies were possible, and it was possible for ulema to shift between service in the field of education and service in the field of justice within the Ilmiye professions. For instance, the scholar Abdüllatif Efendi who taught in 1902 at Beyazıt Madrasa where he earned 1500 piasters later preferred to assume a judicial position. After he passed an exam to enter the judicial profession and became the kadı of Galata, Abdüllatif Efendi's monthly income increased and reached 3000 piasters.[51] In another example, Şakir Efendi began his career as a *muid* and then successfully continued as a *dersiam* in Kasımpaşa Mosque and finally became a mufti of Mardin.[52] Another example is Mustafa Asım Efendi of Trabzon. He first became a preacher and then transferred to the position of *dersiam*.[53]

There are also examples of ulema in the Ilmiye positions who were transferred to the Ministry of Education *(Maarif Nezareti)*. For instance, İsmail Hakkı Efendi of Kastamonu was an *imam* in Bursa, and then became a member of the Ministry of Education as a teacher.[54] By contrast, there are also examples of ulema switching from the Education Ministry to the Ilmiye staff. For instance,

Hafiz İzzet Efendi was working as a teacher in Çanakkale at the Education Ministry when he was appointed as a naib in the Ilmiye hierarchy to a district of Adana.[55]

In sum, even though transitions from one occupational group to another were allowed, there are only a few examples who changed their occupational field. These usually did involve moving between the judiciary and educational positions.

Promotion

Graduates of the madrasa started off as official servants like *müderris*, naib, *imam*, preacher, and kadı at the lowest level in the Ilmiye hierarchy after having finished their waiting period known as the *mülazemet*—or sometimes without waiting. With time, ulema were promoted and moved up the ranks in the Ilmiye hierarchy. Higher ranks and promotions were given to the Ilmiye servants taking into consideration their good service *(hüsni hizmet)*, their good performance *(hüsni hal)*, their honor *(namuslu)*, and their mastery of their jobs *(işinin ehli)*. Personal merit, the prestige and fame of the ulema family, and the recommendations of supervisors also affected the position of an *alim* and his promotion within the Ilmiye ranks. Almost every ulema candidate moved step by step from the bottom toward the top in this system. This regularity of the Ilmiye system continued until the end of the empire. It took an average of 20 to 30 years for ulema to reach the highest ranks in the Ilmiye hierarchy.[56]

However, it was easier for children coming from famous, recognized Ilmiye families to move up in the Ilmiye hierarchy. Because ulema were excellent benefactors for their own sons, the sons of ulema were fortunate. The candidates belonging to these ulema families started in higher-level Ilmiye positions due to the privilege given to them by the government. Therefore, some ulema figures reached the highest ranks in the Ilmiye hierarchy—that could normally be reached only at an advanced age—at a young age.[57] However, this method of appointing ulema was infrequently implemented. To be promoted in the Ilmiye hierarchy required a long stay in low-level positions. For instance, naibs reached the level of kadı or *müderris* only at the end of a long duration of service as a naib. Most remained as a naib and retired without having become a kadı.

The promotions of the ulema were carried out by Şeyhülislam. They were transferred to more important cities than where they were currently serving and given a higher degree *(payes)* than their current position.[58] It was expected that promotions would be financially beneficial, and they were generally accompanied by increases in wages. Wages were raised immediately after promotion. For instance, the salary of Dersiam Hüseyin Avni Efendi of Ankara increased to 250 piasters after he received the *paye* of Istanbul Rüusu in 1877.[59]

The nature of promotion in the Ilmiye hierarchy could change between different professional groups. Judicial civil servants were promoted as a result of their achievements in their professions. Kadıs and naibs were promoted to different places from the one in which they currently served, and their salaries increased according to their rank. Naibs underwent the most change in the Ilmiye system. They were promoted to a higher rank every two years on average if they did their duty well. However, for a naib to reach the position of kadı took a long time. Their promotions were generally to more important regions, but again as a naib. They generally did not become a kadı.

The condition for promotion among educational staff was a similar hierarchical process like the judiciary system. If an *alim* who was newly graduated from a madrasa wanted to gain a higher-position rank like the *müderris* of an Istanbul madrasa, it was necessary to continue in the madrasa to specialize in the field and then win promotion step by step in accordance with the conventional madrasa hierarchy. For instance, if a *müderris* wanted to move up from *İbtida-i Dahil* to *Hareket-i Altmışlı*, it was necessary to complete the ranks of *Hareket-i Dahil, Musıla-i Sahn, Sahn* and *İbtida-i Altmışlı*.[60] The ordering of madrasas extending from *İbtida-i Haric* to *Darülhadis* continued to be used for the promotion of *müderrises* in the Ilmiye hierarchy in the Tanzimat period. Few ulema who lived on the periphery of the Ottoman Empire completed studies in the highest-ranking madrasas, so few ulema of Anatolian origin were appointed to higher-ranking madrasas. The ulema within the Ilmiye system could reach the highest-ranking *müderris* position after serving twenty-one to twenty-seven years after having graduated from the madrasa (see Table 4.1).

Salary

In the Ottoman Empire up until the Tanzimat, officials had an income, but it was not a systematic salary for government officials in the contemporary sense. The government allocated income by providing financial resources equivalent to salary to most of the public servants in the empire rather than giving cash salaries. For instance, one of the incomes of the Ilmiye members was provided from an allocated stipend known as "*arpalık*"[62] up until the Tanzimat period.

Table 4.1 Years of education in specialized madrasas *(Madrasa-i Mütehassisin)*[61]

Ranks of Madrasa	Mehmed Tevfik Efendi	Mehmed Kamil Efendi	Mehmed Emin Efendi	Osman Nuri Efendi
İbtida-yı Hariç	½	1	1	1
Hareket-i Hariç	½	7	7	3
İbtida-yı Dahil	1	3	7	7
Hareket-i Dahil	3	1	2	1
Musula-i Sahn	5	2	2	4
Sahn	7	5	1	1
İbtida-yı Altmışlı	1	1	1	1
Hareket-i Altmışlı	1	1	2	1
Musıla-i Süleymaniye	2	1	2	1
Hamise-i Süleymaniye	Unknown	2	2	1
Total	21	24	27	21

However, *arpalık* was subjected to wide abuse and was not suitable for a modern state structure. It was necessary to pay regular salaries to oversee the civil servants given the centralized government policy. Therefore, on March 28, 1838, it was decided to pay salaries to all civil servants.[63] In this way, the central government sought to prevent officials from resorting to corruption such as taking bribes to make a living. Therefore, a regular salary system for the ulema began in 1838, and the Ilmiye members became salaried members of the Ottoman State's bureaucratic staff in the Tanzimat era. However, the government could not initially pay salaries to all members of the Ilmiye. The salary system first covered the Ilmiye staff working in Istanbul.

Then other Ilmiye members in the provinces were brought into the system during the reign of Sultan Abdülhamid II. (This took place via an imperial decree issued by the Sultan in 1882 that provided a monthly salary of 100 piasters to all newcomers to the teaching profession and to those already teaching but without a salary. This decree also raised the wages of those officials already allocated salaries.) Requests for increases in wages made by the Ilmiye members to the Prime Ministry Office *(Sadaret)* were transmitted to the office of Şeyhülislam, and they were given a salary if it was deemed appropriate by the office of Şeyhülislam. İlmiye members who wrote books were also rewarded with salaries.[64] In addition, the *arpalık* salary was completely abandoned and replaced by a system of regular salaries after 1838. Some ulema continued to receive their salaries as *arpalık*.[65]

The salaries of the Ilmiye members differed from one occupational group to the other—that is, from the educational, judicial, and administrative fields. Also, the salaries of the Ilmiye servants could change according to the place to which they were assigned. For instance, an officer in the center usually earned much more income than a provincial officer did. This was a categorization based on the five-grade system.[66] There were also significant differences in the salary among officers in the provinces.

For instance, Tables 4.2, 4.3 and 4.4 show the wage distribution of the Ilmiye members with respect to their place of work—Ankara (an example of a province), the Gediz District of Kütahya, and the Karamürsel District of Kastamonu (as examples of districts)—between the years 1914 and 1916.

Furthermore, the ulema assigned temporarily to vacant positions received half the regular salary. For instance, Müderris Yusuf Ziya Efendi of Bitlis was appointed as a temporary naib in a district of Bitlis on April 26, 1902, and

Table 4.2 Wage distribution in Ankara province in 1914[67]

Duty and Name	Monthly Salary (in Piasters)
Kadı Mehmed Rıza Efendi	4500
Baş Katip Nasibzade Arif Hikmet Efendi	800
Baş Katip Muavini Abidin Efendi	500
Mukayyid Müftüzade İbrahim Efendi	400
Zabıt Katibi Hacı Ömer Efendi	300
Eytam Müdürü İsmail Efendi	750
Mufti Refet Efendi	1000
Müderris Refet Efendi	255
Müderris Tahir Efendi	300
Muhzır Ali Ağa	200
Odacı Halil Ağa	150
Mufti Müsevvidi Hacı Süleyman Efendi	300

Table 4.3 Wage distribution in the Gediz District in 1916[68]

Duty and Name	Monthly Salary (in Piasters)
Mufti Süleyman Şakir Efendi	400
Müderris Ali Vasfi Efendi	200
Baş Kâtip Hafız Süleyman Sıdkı	400
Eytam Müdürü Mehmed Reşad	250

Table 4.4 Wage distribution in the Karamürsel District in 1916[69]

Duty and Name	Monthly Salary (in Piasters)
Mufti Hacı Ahmed Hamdi Efendi	400
Müderris Hacı Mustafa Efendi	200
Baş Kâtip Hafız İsmail Efendi	400
Eytam Müdürü Hasan Hilmi Efendi	250
Muhzır İbrahim Efendi	150

received a half salary of 200 piasters during his period of duty.[70] Another situation that resulted in a half-salary was an appointment as a civil servant who was not a tenured officer. For instance, Abdülkadir Efendi of Trabzon was appointed as a naib in the Akra district in 1882 and took a 250 piasters monthly salary, half of the regular salary. Shortly afterward, he became a tenured civil servant and began to receive 500 piasters.[71] Similarly, while Ömer Faruk Efendi of Kütahya worked as a teacher for a half salary of 75 piasters per month at Uşak Madrasa, his salary rose to 150 piasters after becoming a tenured civil servant.[72] Only tenured officials who sent their curricula vitae to the Şeyhülislam Office received a full salary.[73]

Apart from this, there were ulema who were, for some reason, terminated professionally. For instance, some of the regulations removed certain departments of existing institutions or the district that was dutied of the Ilmiye members could be removed with the regulations. In this case, civil servants had to be removed from their occupations in the government. Under such conditions, the civil servants were paid a *mazuliyet* salary.[74]

In terms of the incomes of those in the Ilmiye hierarchy, madrasa teachers *(müderrises* and *dersiams)* comprised the middle layer as opposed to ulema in the positions like kadı or mufti. However, the salaries of *müderrises* and *dersiams* who taught at the highest-ranking institutions in the empire were always higher than others. For instance, the Süleymaniye *müderris* was the top-paying teaching position in the empire. To reach this level, the *müderris* was required to complete the twelve grades of the madrasa system.[75] The salaries of ulema who taught at the madrasas or worked as *dersiam* were strictly controlled by the government, which took their qualifications and job performance into account. For instance, if a higher-quality *müderris* or *dersiam* was assigned to a lower-ranking madrasa then he should be given his education (due to the absence of a vacant position in a higher-level madrasa, for instance), he would receive a higher payment for his service. In this sense, he was treated as if he had been assigned to a high-grade madrasa. If the qualifications of a teaching person were lower than usually needed for the madrasa or mosque to which he was assigned, he received only the money allocated for his usual pay bracket; the remainder reverted back to the waqf.

The expenses and needs of a madrasa, the *müderris*, the students, and the other staff were met by the income of the madrasa's waqf. Also, the salaries of the Ilmiye members were met by the waqf, and if the income of the waqf was inadequate, it was supplemented by the government treasury. Thanks to the economic support of the madrasas and *müderrises* by the waqfs, they did not suffer economic difficulties until the centralization of waqf incomes. With the establishment of the Ministry of Pious Foundations *(Evkaf Nezareti)*, the administration of almost all waqfs was tied to the Ministry of Pious Foundations, and new sanctions emerged that aimed to limit the incomes of madrasas.[76] In the years of the Tanzimat, all income of the waqfs was transferred to the finance treasury *(maliye hazinesi)*. Every month, a certain amount of money was transferred to the Ministry of Pious Foundations to be spent on the expenses of the waqfs. However, there was little left to be spent on waqf institutions because their incomes were used to overcome general budget deficits caused by economic turmoil.[77] These distorted economic conditions led *müderrises* and students to carry on their activities in difficult financial conditions.

Before the Tanzimat, there was generally no separate salary for the services of the mufti. Since muftis were generally chosen from among salaried *müderrises* of the government, they continued to receive their salaries as *müderris*; nevertheless, a certain fee was generally to the mufti by those who asked for fatwas. These muftis, who had not received a prescribed salary up until the Tanzimat period, started to receive salaries together with the Tanzimat. After the Tanzimat, they sometimes received a separate salary for their position of mufti apart from their additional *müderris* salaries.[78] However, this was generally a low salary. Even if an *alim* was only a mufti, did not hold a teaching position, and had no income from other positions, the salary given to him was small. A document from the governor of Manastır sent to the Ministry of Internal Affairs in 1908 is proof of the low salaries. The governor stated that the muftis received a maximum monthly 360 piasters salary or worked without a salary. In this document, the governor demanded that muftis be paid at least as much as naibs.[79] Even if a mufti did not receive a separate salary,[80] he could at least receive a certain amount of money for the fatwas he issued. However, there are examples of some muftis working without salaries.[81]

The salaries of some important ulema were increased when they asked the sultan or Sadaret to increase their salary. For example, the salary of Mustafa Safvet Efendi of Ermenek, one of the Beyazıt Dersiams, was increased with the permission of the sultan due to his request for a raise.[82] The salaries of civil servants who remained in the same position for a long time were also regularly increased. However, this increase in the salaries of the ulema was not available to all the Ilmiye officials. For instance, İbrahim Ethem Efendi of Aydın first started work as a naib in the Düzce district for 900 piasters monthly in 1874. Although he worked in the Taşlıca district for 1800 piasters in 1878, he later served as a naib in the İnyos district for only 1650 piasters in 1883. This irregular salary system continued in other naib positions in different regions until 1902.[83]

The salaries and the annual rate of increases were determined by the waqf of a madrasa according to the needs and requests of the *müderrises* and *dersiams*. Therefore, each madrasa had a different budget. The salaries of people working in the educational area were determined by looking at the ranks of the madrasas in which they worked. The payment for each *müderris*, madrasa student, and madrasa worker and the overall financial plan of the madrasas differed from each other.

Moreover, the salaries of naibs did not increase so long as their place of service did not change, irrespective of the number of years they served—even when the duration exceeded two or three years.[84] In this sense, the salaries of the naibs were determined solely according to the region in which they served.

Furthermore, after a madrasa student's graduation, an appointment was not always guaranteed by the government. Some graduate ulema were not government employees and the government did not pay these ulema. For instance, Halil Hulusi Efendi of Adana indicated in his personnel record that he did not receive a salary from the government treasury throughout his twenty-one-year service as naib.[85] Similarly, Mehmet Şakir Efendi of Adana did not receive a salary from the government for approximately three years while on duty as a preacher in Adana.[86] Furthermore, for calculation of his retirement age and year, Ali Rıza Efendi, stated in his personnel registry files that he worked for a total of twenty-seven years, six of which were without a salary.[87] In a document dated 1900, İsmail Efendi, Hafiz Osman, Mehmed Ali Efendi, and Hafiz Murat who had been educated in Dersaadet madrasas, and had begun to work as in the provinces demanded a regular salary from the central government. However, the government rejected their request and told them that only *müderrises* working in Istanbul were paid.[88] In such conditions, the needs of ulema in the Ilmiye system who were not government officials were met by provincial residents, donations, and gifts. Also, some ulema had personnel endeavors and occupied themselves in different economic areas to make a living. For instance, they engaged in commerce like merchants.[89] The ulema were involved in the commercial activity because kadıs authorized every form of commerce like sales, purchases, and transfers of property.[90] However, the economic participation of the ulema were not limited to trade. Also, a few of the ulema were part-time farmers.[91]

Another important source of the wealth of the ulema was the revenues of waqfs. The ulema class administrated the waqfs and received a fee for this service. The ulema's financial situation was strengthened if their supervision and administration of the waqf were also strong. Religious endowments provided additional support for the ulema in addition to their assigned salaries.

The ulema could also bequeath their waqf and its income to heirs upon their deaths. The right to bequeath ulema's wealth and positions to their sons, which had the purpose of maintaining the continuity of social and educational life in the madrasa differed from the situation of most of the other officials in the Ottoman Empire.[92] For instance, Süleyman Şakir Efendi of Kütahya took over the administration and income of his father's waqf and he started to work as *müderris* and mufti in the Gediz district of Kütahya in his father's madrasa after his father's death in 1909.[93] They guaranteed both their own and their descendant's privilege with the right to bequeath.

In addition, the ulema enjoyed generous grants and lavish gifts from the Sultan and his households.[94] The Sultan and those around him did not hesitate to reward ulema in return for their services or their help in the government. Apart from the gifts of sultans and their households, charitable donations in cash or property were another source of their wealth.

Additionally, there was special treatment for the ulema with respect to taxation. As employees of the state, the Ilmiye members often enjoyed important economic opportunities such as tax exemptions and reduced fees. For instance, they were exempt from the property tax *(tarik mükellefiyeti)*[95] and profit taxation *(temettü)*.[96] Also, they were exempt from drudgery like work on public road construction and from paying for it.[97] Taxation privileges reinforced the ulema's presence on the economic scene. They were considered members of the ruling class, but unlike other ruling classes, they were exempt from all forms of taxation and forced loans. These economic privileges accompanied the social elite status of being ulema. Apart from their services as members of the Ilmiye staff, as judges in the courts, and as the providers of training for students at the *mektebs* and madrasas, their private estates, commercial investments, religious endowments, and economic privileges were the sources of their income.

Social Security Rights and Retirement

No planned and inclusive regulations were made for the social and economic security of all the Ilmiye members and their families until the end of the Tanzimat period. At that time, social assistance, which had been carried out through traditional institutions, started to be fulfilled by the central government.[98] As part of the central government's social assistance service, which began in 1872, a charity fund was established to help the Ilmiye members and their families who needed it, but it was not put into practice until 1874. The first step forward on the issue was in 1874 when the "Charity Fund of the Council of Orphans" *(İdare-yi Emval Eytam Meclisi Yardımlaşma Sandığı")* was established. The capital required for the establishment of the "this fund" was obtained from members of the Ilmiye class. One month's salary of each person belonging to the Ilmiye was seized in accordance with the "Regulation on Orphans and Widows" *(İnfak-i Muhtacin-i Eytam ve Eramil-i İlmiye Nizamnamesi)*. It was decided in this regulation to distribute the collected income to the widows and orphans of the Ilmiye members who passed away leaving them no property and no income.[99]

In addition, before the nineteenth century, some of the Ilmiye posts were lifetime appointments,[100] not limited to a certain period. They only lost their posts if they resigned.[101] They often continued their duty until their deaths. After the Tanzimat, all civil servants were provided with the opportunity to retire, and retirement laws were enacted to regulate retirements. Also, a monthly retirement salary was allocated to retired Ilmiye members who had served for thirty years starting in their twenties. They were entitled to retirement following the enactment of the *Memurin-i Mülkiyye Terakki ve Tekaüd Kararnamesi* in 1879.[102] In 1881, a regulation in the *Memurin-i Mülkiye Terakki ve Tekaüd Kanunnamesi*[103] was made concerning the retirement of the Ilmiye officers; if the Ilmiye members wanted to retire, they would receive retirement pay. In order to create a retirement fund, 5 percent was deducted from every employee's salary, and the income from this deduction was transferred to this fund. Also, half of the first salary of any officer assigned to a new task or assigned to service for the first time as well as the first installments of the increase in the salaries of civil servants receiving a promotion or raise was allocated for this fund. Retirement for the Ilmiye servants was the result of efforts to integrate the social government systems, which gained importance with the Tanzimat reforms, into the bureaucratic system. With the *Memurin-i Mülkiye Terakki ve Tekaüd Kanunnamesi*, retirement became a social security right. Civil servants who completed thirty years of service and who wanted to retire could apply to the Nezaret and retire.

İlmiye members had the right to retire without completing the thirty-year civil service period, especially due to reasons like health problems, physical weakness, or family reasons.[104] Also, the service duration of ulema during the war was calculated as twice as long as in the Ilmiye service during peace.[105] Therefore, the thirty years to be completed when calculating the retirement age of Ilmiye members was reduced if they served during the war.

Even if civil servants changed jobs or filled more than one job at the same time, they were given a pension (not separately) based on their total salary over the previous ten years.[106] However, if average earnings in the last decade were lower than earnings in the first twenty years, the average salary in the earlier periods was reflected in the pension, and the salary was increased.[107]

In the case of a government official's criminal conviction or death, the retirement salary was transferred to the wife and children of the ulema officer as their social security right.[108] This regulation tried to prevent the families of the Ilmiye members from falling into a miserable situation after an ulema's death and to meet the needs of their children and wives. If the Ilmiye officer had a boy, the child could receive this salary until the age of twenty. However, if he was occupied with science in a madrasa, this salary would continue throughout his madrasa life. If the ulema had a girl, this salary continued until the girl got married.[109] The retirement salary was a minimum of 40 piasters for each individual. If the salary to be shared was less than 40 piasters per individual, the remainder was compensated by the government.[110] Although not all retirees in the Ilmiye positions were able to receive regular pensions in the beginning, their pensions were made more regular with the arrangements made in the following years.[111]

After 25 August 1909, 65-year-old civil servants were retired irrespective of their wishes with the Purge Law.[112] In this sense, after 1909, many civil servants including the Ilmiye members were excluded from the government because they were more than sixty-five years old. The Purge Law commissions were established in each province of the empire to monitor the ages of the Ilmiye members in this context. In such conditions, retirement was tantamount to the dismissal of government servants, not a social security right. However, the government made use of this law to dismiss supporters of the old regime from the Ilmiye class, strengthening its authority in the provinces. In this sense, this regulation was a political tool. Following the regulation, a significant number of ulema were removed from the Ilmiye staff. Also, the Purge Law restructured the central organization of the Şeyhülislam Office. The Purge Law Commission also evaluated the skills and knowledge level of the ulema, and the government dismissed ulema who, according to the commission, did not have the required skills.

On the other hand, some ulema had not yet reached the age of 65 but were retired or terminated from their positions in the Ilmiye hierarchy. Naib İsmail Efendi's personnel record indicates that he was retired in 1911 before he reached the age of sixty-five.[113] In such a case, the central state applied the law flexibly and dismissed those it wanted to be terminated from the profession with reference to the Purge Law as an excuse.

While some ulema were dismissed, others were barred from carrying out their additional duties and allowed to continue their initial duties. For instance, Ali Efendi of Bolu started in the profession of *imams* in 1902 in addition to his ongoing duty of twenty-one years as a preacher. Ali Efendi held these two positions for three years. After the Purge Law, in 1905, his additional task was terminated and he continued as just a preacher.[114] Although some of those with more than one duty were relieved of their duties with the Purge Law, in other cases ulema appointed to vacant positions were given more than one task. For instance, when mufti Ahmet Efendi was appointed as naib of Nusaybin in 1899, he began work as both mufti and naib, despite the Purge Law.[115]

Even though the duration of service of officials in the Ilmiye institution was given an upper limit of 65 in the Purge Law, there were many exemptions to this age limit decision for members of the Ilmiye staff of the Empire.[116] Some officers who were not terminated from their profession were protected by government authorities who left them out of the Purge Law. For instance, Ali Rıza Efendi of Erzurum, who worked as a *fetva müsevvidi* (a clerk who made a fair copy of fatwas given by muftis), states that he was removed from the Ilmiye staff because he had passed 65 years of age, but that this law did not cover everyone. He said that some ulema who were over 65 years old were still working in their Ilmiye positions as a result of the favoritism of Şeyhülislam Musa Kazım.[117] On the other hand, Mehmed Efendi of Aydın was expelled from the duty of *müderris* in 1907 for being over 65 years of age on the basis of the Purge Law. However, provincial people of the region applied to the government for the reinstatement of Mehmed Efendi. And he returned to his position of *müderris* in 1908.[118]

Other Ilmiye officers continued in their posts after the age of sixty-five because of a decision by the Ottoman Assembly of Deputies *(Meclis-i Mahsus-u Vükela)*, which decided the state would benefit from their experience, but their salaries would remain constant[119] because the government did not want their experience to be wasted. Although a mandatory retirement age was determined by the regulation, an important Ilmiye position that was largely exempt from compulsory retirement was that of the office of the mufti. There were many public appeals to the office of Şeyhülislam to exempt many muftis from this age limit.[120] Therefore, most muftis were able to continue their profession upon the insistence of the public—for another three years in the case of the aforementioned mufti who was reelected by the provincial people irrespective of his age.[121] Another example of a person who continued work in line with the wishes of the people despite being of retirement age was Mehmet Efendi from Aydın. Mehmet Efendi was at first retired because of the age limitation for civil servants, but he was later recruited once again upon the intense demand of the people.[122] Also, the retirement of mufti Emin Efendi, whose memory and strength were intact, was postponed in order to benefit from his experience.[123] Another interesting case was the decision about the retirement of Mustafa Efendi, the mufti of İzmit. When Mustafa Efendi reached retirement age in 1898, the governor of the İzmit sent a letter to the Grand Vizier requesting an exemption for Mustafa Efendi. According to the letter, Mustafa Efendi had a strong body and strong memory, and was loved by the provincial people. As a result, the office of Şeyhülislam postponed the retirement of Mustafa Efendi.[124]

It is important to note that the only occupational group which the age of 65 has strictly adhered was naibship. Naibs were certainly retired at the age of 65.[125] İsmail Efendi of Kütahya was forced to retire when he reached 65 in 1913 irrespective of whether he wanted to.[126]

Lastly, according to the personnel registry files, some ulema entered into the Ilmiye positions at very young ages—as young as twenty-three—after graduating from the madrasa. However, the average age of recruitment for the Ilmiye positions was thirty-five. After it was decided to limit the length of service to the age of sixty-five, the average service duration of Ottoman state cadres after the Tanzimat was thirty years.[127]

Reward and Punishment

The most effective way for the government to lead the civil service and to ensure the obedience of the ulema was to punish and reward them. Apart from the central government, the Şeyhülislam was able to distribute rewards and punishments for all the Ilmiye members. If the ulema obeyed the rules of the government, the government rewarded the ulema with high ranks and promotions. The government also did not refrain from punishing the ulema if they did not comply with the wishes of the government. The government punished ulema with imprisonment, exile, and even dismissal from the Ilmiye service.

Trustworthy ulema with higher education who worked in the interests of the government and successfully carried out their Ilmiye professions were rewarded with higher salaries and promotions. The personnel registry files allow for an examination of ulema rewards. All these awards were symbols that show that the government placed importance on ulema as a group and formally recognized them. The ulema were motivated, felt the need to develop, and were highly satisfied due to these rewards. The ulema's self-esteem and the public's respect for them also increased as a result of the rewards given to them.

Ranks and promotions were important rewards for the Ilmiye members. Rank in the Ottoman Empire is a degree that refers to titles given to the people or officials. Higher ranks *(payes and nişans)* were mostly given to ulema due to their excellent educational careers. For this reason, graduates from specialized madrasa could generally reach high-level positions in the Ilmiye hierarchy.

One way to reach high-level status within the Ilmiye system was to be trusted by the government. The government's trust in the ulema was made possible by the ulema fulfilling a service when the government demanded it of them and providing those services in accordance with the interests of the government. One of the most important circumstances which caused the government to trust the ulema was their taking part on the side of the government in times of social unrest and rebellion and helping to solve the problem in favor of the government. For instance, Sheikh Mehmed Efendi was rewarded with a monthly wage and a higher rank due to his mediatory role in the conflict and the social unrest between the Nesturis and the Kurds in 1888. His mediation role made a contribution to regional peace. [128]

Another reason for the ulema to be rewarded was a success in their professions. For instance, Şemseddin Efendi was rewarded with the rank of *müderris* as a result of his achievement and competence in his profession while he was a military regiment mufti.[129] The other situation that resulted in a reward was good service and loyalty to the government in times of war. For example, Hüseyin Avni Efendi participated in the Russian–Turkish War (1877–1878) and was rewarded with the Order of the Medjide, 4th class because of his services in the war.[130]

Ulema who consistently carried out their duty and fulfilled orders and assigned obligations were also gratified with increasing ranks *(paye)*, higher salaries, and certificates of achievement *(nişan)* by the central government.[131] The ulema were given higher ranks at the same time they received promotions in their office. For instance, Mustafa Efendi, who started teaching as a *müderris* in Fatih Mosque in 1897, was promoted in 1907 and gained a higher degree due to his competence in his profession. This high rank was also accompanied by a rise in his salary, which increased from 95 piasters a month to 600 piasters in 1908.[132]

Successful Ilmiye officers were also granted higher ranks, *nişans* in some special cases. In these cases, the government rewarded the ulema to honor them in return for outstanding success and service in the Ilmiye hierarchy. The activities of Mehmed Nuri Efendi, a *müderris* in Bursa, benefited the government which awarded him with the Order of the Medjide, 4th class which was created in 1852, for his good service and loyalty.[133]

Even though the ulema did not directly intervene in government politics, they had to be careful about expressing their political thoughts before society while preaching and doing public speaking; they were not only officials of the central government but also spokesmen of the government due to their role of representing both the office of Şeyhülislam and sultan. Despite the ulema's distinctiveness and their autonomous activities, the political administration closely followed their political tendencies, and if necessary, their power and financial resources could be taken away and they could even be dismissed from their professions.[134] Therefore, they had to be careful about whether their speeches and actions fulfilled their political and religious obligations to the government so as not to be dismissed from their occupations in the Ilmiye hierarchy.

The ulema were put under the control of the government to prevent various forms of corruption such as taking bribes or adopting attitudes against the central government with the İlmiye Penal Code *(Tarik-i İlmiyeye Dair Ceza Kanunnamesi)* of 1838. If the central government uncovered irregularities, members of the ulema were punished with exile, temporary dismissal from the profession, or even expulsion from the profession. Therefore, the government even controlled the content of the ulema's fatwas and khutbas. The ulema were not free to determine the content of their khutbas at the Friday sermons. The contents of the sermons were limited to one religious interpretation: The *Sunni* tradition and *Hanafi* jurisprudence. The *imams* and preachers were obliged to mention political topics that benefited the government in their sermons. They also had to support government and provincial administrations with respect to security and order in the cities in their fatwas and khutbas.[135] The subjects of these sermons were strictly controlled by the muftis and Şeyhülislam, and if a preacher diverged from the outlined topics, he faced the danger of being expelled from his profession.[136]

The central government could punish the ulema with imprisonment, exile, and dismissal from the ranks of the Ilmiye staff for inappropriate behavior after

Table 4.5 Crimes and punishments[137]

Name	Profession	Crime	Punishment
Abdullah Şevket Efendi	Naib	Opposition to the central government	Forty days in prison
Yusuf Efendi	Mufti	Being a member of the Committee of Union and Progress	Four months in prison
Ahmed Hamdi Efendi	*Baş Katib*	Taking an excessive fee	Dismissal
Rüşdü Efendi	Mufti	Complaint from district's provincial governor	Dismissal
Abdüllatif Lütfi Efendi	*Dersiam*	Political opposition	Dismissal
Abdünnafi Efendi	Ulema	Disorder	Exile
Mehmet Ali Efendi	Beyazıt *Dersiam*	Improper sermon	Exile
Hasan Efendi	Ulema	Corruption	Warning

starting with the Tanzimat period. The ulema was frequently removed from their duties and strictly punished for reasons such as disagreement with provincial administrators, the inadequacy of their scientific knowledge, negligence in duties, or their opposition to government authority. Also, the ulema had to avoid movements that would cause any suspicion, such as making trade, borrowing money, accepting gifts, or hosting public banquets. If they were concerned with such activities, it was a reason for their dismissal from their occupations.

There are many documents about the ulema's dismissal at the Prime Ministry Ottoman Archives and in the personnel registry files of Ottoman Ulema at the Meşihat Archives. The table indicates some examples of crimes committed by the ulema. Ulema who committed crimes were punished because they were deemed neither loyal to Islam nor the government; they were only interested in their own selfish benefit.

One of the most important punishments for ulema was dismissal from their position. There were many reasons for the dismissal of ulema, such as political opposition, levying of excessive fees, and complaints from prominent leaders of the region in which these government officials worked. For instance, Abdüllatif Lütfi Efendi of Mamuratülaziz was dismissed from his position as a member of the court due to his ideas that opposed the government, and he returned to his position after the second constitutional era *(meşrutiyet)*.[138] The ulema's professional performance was under the absolute control of the government. Not only were their political opinions monitored, but so were the fees they charged. Ahmed Hamdi Efendi of Adana was dismissed from his profession as head court scribe on March 22, 1909, due to a complaint about suspicions of his taking excessive fees. However, the investigation into Ahmed showed that the claims were unfounded, and Ahmed returned to the Ilmiye office on November 6, 1909. Ahmed continued to thrive in his position after returning to his duty, and on July 20, 1912, he was awarded with the position of naib. On October 16, 1912, in addition to his duty as naib, he was also given the *imam* duty.[139] The important point here is that being removed from civil service was not an obstacle to moving up the hierarchy once an *alim* returned to duty. He experienced no exclusion in the social and political scene, and *alim* who proved his innocence and paid for his crime was still rewarded for good service in their profession.

Sometimes, the complaint of a provincial manager was a valid reason for dismissal from the profession. For instance, as a result of hostilities between Rüşdü Efendi of Mamuratülaziz and provincial governor Asım Efendi, the district governor complained about the mufti Rüşdü Efendi. As a result of this complaint, mufti Rüşdü Efendi was dismissed in 1889. When the innocence of Rüşdü Efendi was realized in 1890, he returned to his profession.[140]

Another government punishment was imprisonment. Political opposition was a significant reason for imprisonment. For instance, Mufti Yusuf Efendi spent four months in a prison in Beşiktaş in 1894 due to his being a member of the Committee of Union and Progress. Yusuf Efendi returned to his homeland as a civil servant after four months in prison.[141] Despite having been in prison in 1894, he was rewarded with a higher rank in 1895. Yusuf Efendi returned to Konya his hometown as a basic civil servant, probably as a clerk, but within a short time was appointed to Athens as an *ibtida-i hariç müderris*. Another case was the imprisonment of naib Abdullah Şevket Efendi of Konya. Abdullah Şevket spent 40 days in prison in 1908 due to the central government's suspicions that he was a member of the political opposition. Mutasarrıf Musa Kazım asserted that Abdullah Şevket Efendi supported Şehzade Mehmed Reşad when he assumed the naibship of Konya and informed Sultan Abdülhamid. Therefore, Abdullah Efendi was dismissed, and he was held in detention for 40 days at the Beşiktaş police station. Once Abdullah Efendi was cleared at the end of the trial in 1910, he was reemployed as a naib in the district of Bandırma with a 1250 piaster salary.[142]

The last kind of punishment was exile. The central government exiled ulema if they disturbed the public peace with their attitudes and speeches. For instance, Abdünnafi Efendi was exiled to Sinop due to his inappropriate speeches against the central government.[143] Similarly, Mehmed Ali Efendi was exiled to Mamuratülaziz because of his speeches about the central administration.[144]

The punishment of the ulema was largely the result of complaints or the reports of informants. There are many complaint letters about the Ilmiye members written to the office of Şeyhülislam by provincial people and notables of the provinces, as well as telegrams requesting the appointment of the new ulema. Many complaints about the ulema's inappropriate behaviors were sent to the *Şeyhülislam* Office. Local institutions were in close contact with the center by this point, and in a short time, they have written documents on many subjects and there was continuous traffic of related documents between the center and the province. For example, the Prime Ministry was informed in a complaint letter about the incompetence of the mufti of the Biga district. This letter claimed that the mufti did not even have an *icazet.*[145] Similarly, the center was informed about the Yanya mufti in another complaint letter that examined Fuat Efendi's unqualified character and his cooperation with Christians.[146] Another example complaint came from Tokat. Muallim Ahmet Efendi of Tokat complained to the Ministry of Education that the Mufti Abdülkadir Efendi of Reşadiye cultivated the land instead of reading the Qur'an. His Quran lessons were as short as 20 minutes instead of one hour. For this reason, Muallim Ahmed requested that the Ministry of Education change the mufti of Reşadiye, and he suggested Tokadi Çelebi Efendizade Mehmed Efendi who was living in Dersaadet to replace mufti Abdülkadir Efendi.[147] Abdüllatif Efendi of Mamuratülaziz was dismissed from the duty of the sharia court as a result of the reports of informants *(Jurnal)* of Uryanizade Afidi Cemil Bey. He received 500 piasters a month of unemployment pay *(tarik maaşı)*[148] until he returned to his profession.[149]

Complaints about the ulema in the empire could be made by single individuals as well as by the subjects *(reaya)* of a provincial district or by the provincial administration. The government intervened in this religious group's behavior and sometimes dismissed them as a result of the complaints about the ulema by the districts' notables to the office of Şeyhülislam. Furthermore, most ulema were dismissed from their duty during the prosecution process *(tahkikat süreci)* until their innocence was proven. For instance, it is reported that on June 10, 1889, Ömer Lütfi wrote a complaint that the activities of Beyazıt Mufti Mehmed Dursun Efendi were not befitting a mufti and that a new mufti had replaced him immediately.[150] Therefore, Mehmed Dursun Efendi was dismissed from his duty, and he could return to duty only after his innocence was proven.

Lastly, it should be noted that the ulema in the sample were dismissed but were actually not guilty and returned to their professions after their innocence was proven. The ulema who were guilty could not return to their professions, so they have no personnel registry files. But these examples are important because they identify what was considered a crime and a reason for punishment.

Resignation

Each Ilmiye member had the right to leave the Ilmiye service and resign on request. They also had the right to be re-appointed to the Ilmiye or any other institution after resigning. The possible reasons for resignation were varied: failing to get used to living conditions away from their hometowns, frequent rotation (generally once in two years), problems adapting to new places of duty, the necessity of making a living for their families in their hometowns because of reasons like a fathers' death and finding a more advantageous position.

One important reason for resignation from the Ilmiye profession was health problems. For instance, Musa Kazım Hacı Bahri of Aydın resigned due to illness in 1885.[151] Similarly, Ahmet Sami of Konya resigned due to the earthquake and health problems in 1913 when he was in Burdur.[152]

Another reason for the resignation was the educational desires of the candidates. For instance, Hocazade Mustafa Efendi of Burdur was appointed as a court member in 1831 while continuing his education, but he resigned that same year worrying that his learning would be harmed due to the heavy workload of his duty in the Ilmiye system.[153] Similarly, Hafız İsmail Hakkı of Kastamonu resigned from the teacher *(muallim)* position on the grounds that it could interfere with the courses he was taking in Hagia Sophia Mosque.[154] Mehmed Sadık of Adana also resigned because of his wish to learn more science, and be transferred to various positions in the Ilmiye hierarchy that required more knowledge.[155]

Some ulema resigned because they could not adapt to the climate of the region in which they were appointed. For instance, Mehmet Rüştü of Konya resigned in 1845 because he could not get used to the weather in his appointed district, and he had to wait for reappointment for around five years after his resignation.[156]

Furthermore, there are examples of those who resign from their profession and switch to other Ilmiye positions or who switch from one madrasa, school, or court to another within the same professional group.[157] For instance, Mustafa Efendi of Bitlis wanted to be assigned as *müderris* to the madrasa in which his father worked. While working as a *müderris* of a madrasa in the district of Haki, he resigned in order to be appointed to his father's madrasa after his father passed away.[158]

There are also examples of those who assumed more than one duty in the Ilmiye system, and then chose one of these duties and resigned from the other. Nadir Cemil Efendi of Adana was one of them. After Nadir Cemil became a mufti, he resigned from his position as a member of the court on 31 January 1911.[159] However, he continued as *müderris* after he became a mufti.

Multiple Duties of the Ulema

The ulema especially in the provincial regions were assigned many other official duties in addition to their own responsibilities in the Ilmiye hierarchy because of the scarcity of qualified government personnel in such regions. They could be assigned to vacant teaching, security, and bureaucratic positions either temporarily or permanently. Many ulema worked in more than one position at the same time. For instance, Ali Fahreddin Efendi of Bolu was appointed as *imam* to Şeyhülislam Office, *Bab-ı Meşihat* in 1901 while working as a preacher, which he had done since 1884. He carried out these two tasks together until 1904.[160] Similarly, Ali Efendi of Hüdavendigar worked in two positions at the same time in the Ilmiye system. He served as a court scribe in the sharia court; in 1903, he became a member of the sharia court *(mahkeme bidayet azası)*.[161] Mufti Abdülhamid Efendi of Trabzon also worked as a naib besides being a mufti.[162]

There are also examples of ulema who take positions other than the Ilmiye positions in addition to those working more than one duty within the Ilmiye hierarchy at the same time. In other words, some ulema worked in another field outside the Ilmiye hierarchy and assumed two tasks at the same time. For instance, the Naib of Baghdad, Aziz Efendi was both a naib and a commissioner.[163] Similarly, Şeyh Rüstem Efendizade of Sivas was appointed to the position of the commissioner to resolve security deficiencies given his beneficial religious service in the Ilmiye hierarchy.[164] Also, while Halil Efendi of Adana was in charge of self-employment *(hizmet-i hususiye)*, he began to serve in the government as a naib in the Ilmiye hierarchy starting on November 29, 1910, and he carried out these two tasks at the same time.[165] Mufti Ahmet Hilmi Efendi of Diyarbakır was also charged with the inspection construction and repair of the Istanbul Posta Caddesi.[166] İsmail Efendi of Ankara was assigned as a warehouse officer *(ambar memuru)* while a naib.[167] Furthermore, there are examples of ulema teaching in both traditional and modern schools at the same time. For instance, Mustafa Asım Efendi was both *müderris* in Fatih Madrasa and teacher *(ulum-u ahlakiye ve islamiye muallimi)* at the high school of Mekatib-i Aliye.[168]

Apart from provincial regions, there were many ulema throughout the empire working additional duties and newly established institutions that accompanied the Tanzimat reforms. Even though there was a great expansion in the bureaucracy as part of the effort to centralize the government, the number of expert personnel available for new government positions in the empire was limited.[169] To reinforce and develop bureaucratic structures throughout the empire, the central government needed qualified civil servants. The result of the development of the new administrative and educational apparatus of the state in the countryside was the integration of the ulema with the new state apparatus, so the ulema improved the infrastructural capacity of the government. For the Ilmiye members, it did not take long to get along with this bureaucratic system. As the Şeyhülislam institution was reorganized in the late nineteenth century through regulations and laws enacted by the government, the careers assigned to ulema in the empire were redefined and new positions and spaces were available for ulema in administrative fields. The ulema often held positions especially in provincial administrations in addition to their Ilmiye positions. In this regard, ulema had opportunities to get new jobs. For example, Mehmed Sadık Efendi of Adana[170] and Müderris Mahmud Celaleddin Efendi of Adana[171] served on the administrative council of the province of Adana. Mufti Nadir Cemil Efendi served on the district council of Mut.[172] Naib Refet Efendi served on the administrative council of Ankara.[173]

At the same time, ulema helped fill the positions in the new educational centers (the *Mekteb-i Mülkiye, Rüşdiye, Mekteb-i Sultani, Mekteb-i Tıbbiye Mülkiye, Dersaadet Mekteb-i İdadisi,* and *İdadi schools*). This led to the incorporation of ulema into new modern schools as teachers.[174]Religion and Arabic and Persian language courses were taught by madrasa graduates in the new schools. For instance, while Süleyman Sırrı Efendi of Konya was working as Arabic *müderris* at the Beşiktaş School in 1877 he took an additional Ilmiye position and was appointed as *müderris* to a law school *(Mekteb-i Hukuk)* in 1899.[175]

In some cases, ulema were able to work more than two duties at the same time. For instance, After Ali Efendi was appointed as the manager of orphans (eytam müdürü) in 1889, he started two more duties at the same time as a judge *(Mahkeme-i Bidayet Azası)* in 1902 and a member of the provincial council *(Meclis-i İdare Azalığı)* in 1903.[177] Also, Ahmet Efendi of Mardin worked as mufti, naib, and *müderris*.[178]

Table 4.6 Additional duties[176]

Name	Existing duty	Additional duty
Süleyman Sırrı Efendi	Beyazıt Dersiamı	Mekteb-i Hukuk Muallimi
Mehmet Fevzi Efendi	Beyazıt Dersiamı	Müderris
Mustafa Efendi	Mut Müderrisi	Vaiz
Mehmet Şaban Efendi	Tercan Müderrisi	Müderris
Halit Efendi	Müderris	Vaiz
Mehmet Emin Efendi	Kastamonu Müderris	Vaiz
Osman Fevzi Efendi	Kastamonu Müderris	Vaiz
İsmail Hakkı Efendi	Ayasofya Dersiamı	Muallim
Musa Bahri Efendi	İneabad Naibi	İcra Memuru
Mustafa Hulusi Efendi	Bergama Müftüsü	Rüşdiye Muallimi
Mehmet Tevfik Efendi	Meclisi Meşayih Nazırı	Tetkik-i Müellefat Encümeni
Osman Zeki Efendi	Arabsun Naibi	Müderris
Mehmet Sabri Efendi	Görele Naibi	Mahkeme-i Adliye
Ali Kemal Efendi	Atranos Eytam Müdürü	Mahkeme-i Bidayet
Süleyman Şakir Efendi	Gediz Müftüsü	Müderris
Mesud Efendi	Lice Naibi	Müstantik
İbrahim Efendi	Diyarbakır Müftüsü	Muallim
Mustafa Efendi	İspir Müftüsü	Müderris
Nadir Cemil Efendi	Mut Müftüsü	Mahkeme-i Bidayet Azası
Mustafa Efendi	Kozan Müderris	Mebusan Azası
Ömer Faruk Efendi	Diyadin Müftüsü	Müderris

Furthermore, the Salary Decree, *Maaşat Kararnamesi* which came into force in 1880 stipulated that officers who served in more than one office in the government hierarchy, for whatever reason, could not receive two or more salaries. However, this decree was not always applied in practice, and some of the Ilmiye officials working more than one official duty earned an extra salary. For instance, Halid of Kastamonu was appointed as a preacher in October 1910 in addition to his duty as *müderris*. He received an additional salary of 150 piasters a month for his service.[179] Osman Nuri of Sivas also performed the duties of teaching and healing through prayer at the same time. He taught tafsir on one hand and prayed healing prayers for those who came to him for prayer once a week on the other. He received an extra salary for his additional teaching service.[180] Another example was *müderris* Mustafa Efendi of Adana. While teaching between 1878 and 1912, he was a member of the council for two years and seven months in 1878. A further monthly salary of 5000 piasters was paid in addition to the *müderris* salary given his council membership, which was the secondary duty behind that of *müderris*. In addition, 5000 piasters' subsistence *(harcırah)* was paid in addition to the additional salary.[181] Similarly, İsmail Hakkı Efendi from Hagia Sophia *dersiam* served as both an *imam* and a *müderris*. In 1908, İsmail Hakkı Efendi worked for a salary of 400 piasters as a *müderris*. He was made head *imam* of Hagia Sophia in 1911, and an extra monthly salary of 200 piasters was given to him.[182] Ali Kemal Efendi was appointed as manager of orphans *(eytam müdürü)* in 1889 with a monthly salary of 350 piasters. As an additional duty, he began to serve as a judge *(mahkeme-i bidayet azası)* in 1902 for an additional 200 piasters a month. His total salary reached 550 piasters.[183] While Hasan Hüsnü Efendi of Van served as an *imam* in Van Katırcı Mosque in 1888 for 100 piasters monthly, he was appointed as the Ottoman Turkish teacher in the İbtidai and Armenian schools and received an additional salary of 200 piasters each month.[184]

On the other hand, some ulema assigned to a second position chose not to receive a salary for their newly appointed position. For instance, Muallim Ahmet Naci Efendi of Konya was appointed as mufti because there was no other ulema in the region. Ahmet Naci Efendi declared that he would accept this position; but he did not want an extra salary for the service. He added that a very low salary would be sufficient.[185] Also, as mentioned, muftis were usually selected from among the *müderrises* in the region. Thus, the professions of *müderris* and mufti were performed by the same person in provincial districts; they held two duties at the same time, and they generally did not receive a separate salary for their position as mufti.[186]

It was essential for officials who fulfilled more than one profession at the same time to be credible and honorable. The criterion of reliability varied at different times. Some written documents during the constitutional period *(meşrutiyet)* emphasized the commitment of the ulema who carry out two professions at the same time to the Constitutional regime.[187]

Conclusion

With the regulations brought about by the Tanzimat, a regular, comprehensive policy vis-à-vis all civil servants including all the Ilmiye members was applied. In the nineteenth century, these regulations were made within the Ottoman

Ilmiye hierarchy, through promotion and retirement laws, the compensation system, full-time, salaried, and professional officials who were hierarchical organized, and formalized record-keeping.

A professionalization policy of the government towards the Ilmiye members emerged in the late nineteenth century. Contrary to the premises of conventional Ottoman historiography, which denied that the ulema had power in the modernization reforms of the government during the Tanzimat, the transformation of the professional identity of the Ilmiye members and their integration into the bureaucratic administration in the nineteenth century occurred.

The institutionalization of the Şeyhülislam Office and the implementation of professional principles for the Ilmiye members went hand in hand. After ulema candidates graduated from a madrasa, they became actively involved in the Ottoman Ilmiye system and were appointed by the central government to ranked positions such as *müderris (eytam müdürü)*. Also, other important administrative services were open to them, such as being teachers, provincial council members, and inspectors.

As a result of the process of the professionalization of the Ilmiye class of the Ottoman Empire, the differences among the educational, judicial, and administrative fields became more apparent and graduates had the right to be appointed to the Ilmiye positions under the Şeyhülislam Office in accordance with their interests, but before taking up a duty, they had to complete a waiting period called the mülazemet before receiving an appointment. İlmiye members gradually ascended the ranks after their appointment. Reaching high-ranking posts was closely correlated to their educational background, capabilities, and competence throughout their careers. Furthermore, in a period when new, modern institutions were being established, well-educated men were needed. This need for qualified people increased the importance of the ulema who were the only educated group of the period. In this sense, it was explained why most ulema had more than one duty, especially in the last quarter of the nineteenth century.

The average duration of service in the Ottoman Ilmiye hierarchy was thirty years once it became an obligation for the civil servants to retire at the age of 65. Nevertheless, some of the Ilmiye members had the right to resign from their positions without completing the thirty-year period of service in the Ilmiye hierarchy due to reasons such as problems adapting to the place in which they were appointed, and health problems, and some family problems. There were also examples of some ulema who were dismissed from their professions prior to their retirement for reasons such as incompetence, poor job performance, or inappropriate behavior and speeches against the central administration.

5

Social Profile of the Ulema: A Prosopographical Study

The number of people working at the Şeyhülislam Office grew rapidly, which necessitated adding service staff to accommodate the needs of the increasingly institutionalized Şeyhülislam Office in the nineteenth century. The personnel records of the ulema in the Meşihat Archive of the Istanbul Mufti's Office covering this period shows that the increasing number of ulema was related to the growing importance of institutionalization for the government. After the central administration permitted the Şeyhülislam Office to develop its own networks and its own allies in the provinces of the empire, recruiting qualified personnel became one of the government's most important goals. The exact number of ulema in the Şeyhülislam Office is uncertain, but thanks to the biographies in the Mesihat Archive, we know the number of ulema under the command of the Şeyhülislam Office was approximately 5 thousand between 1884 and 1922. It is also known that there was continuous expansion in the number of people working in the office throughout the nineteenth century.

In this part, the research method known as prosopography[1] is used in order to understand the institutional and professional transformation of the Ilmiye, and the place and function of the ulema in the nineteenth century. The focal points of this study are the ulema's social origins, career paths, intellectual capacities, training, and career locations and destinations. The prosopographic method provides the opportunity to answer questions such as what were the family backgrounds of the ulema, who formed the Ilmiye class, and whether ulema candidates in peripheral regions had the same opportunities as students studying in Istanbul to ascend in high-level madrasa education.

It was made descriptive and explanatory generalizations about the Şeyhülislam Office and its officials with reference to empirical data gathered from the personnel records of ulema in the Archives of the Meşihat. There are abundant, systematic archival data giving a clearer picture of the ulema during the nineteenth century. These archival documents provide background information about the ulema working under the office of Şeyhülislam between 1884 and 1922. The number of the last file between those years in the Meşihat Archive is 5,692.[2] In the personnel registers of the ulema, there is only information about the scholars of the Ilmiye class, who worked officially in the Ottoman Şeyhülislam office, that is, worked as civil servants.

These personnel records, which include educational and professional biographies, were written by staff engaged in the Ilmiye at the request of the government. Keeping personnel records was necessary for a modern government both for making new assignments to government positions and for promotion procedures in the government hierarchy. Therefore, the office of Şeyhülislam asked its employees to prepare their curricula vitae and to keep them in the government archive for use when needed. These registers resulted from a centralized government mechanism to compile ulema biographies and create a regular system of information regarding a large number of the ulema. The biographies of the ulema in the Meşihat Archive are significant because they offer rare clues about the professional and educational career of the ulema.

This chapter focuses on provincial ulema coming from ordinary origins, which explains the nature of the ulema from a provincial perspective. The biographies of ulema in Anatolia constituted 45 percent (2,743) of the total ulema in Ottoman territories according to their personnel records. The number of ulema from Anatolian regions is selected in accordance with their proportional distribution according to their hometowns. Since the personnel records of ulema are plenty in number, this study focuses on a part of the whole to see the overall picture. It has been limited to 200 examples chosen from Anatolian provinces of the empire according to the distribution of ulema in the respective provinces. In this chapter, I focus on the Anatolian ulema working at the Şeyhülislam's Office between the years 1880 to 1920. In this respect, this chapter aims to explore the educational and professional careers of ulema who graduated from madrasa beginning with a survey of the diverse background and posts held by the ulema. The career paths of ulema were examined in a prosopographical study for identifying their crucial characteristics.

These biographies also include basic information such as physical and social descriptions[3] of members of the ulema (like their eye and skin color and their average size), their residential addresses in different periods of their lives, and the number of their wives. Apart from that, the biographies also provide information like their names, their fathers' names and professions, their hometowns and birthdates, where they were educated, the list of madrasas they attended, their *icazets* (graduation certificates), the languages they spoke, the books and other materials they wrote, the date of their entry into the Ilmiye service and their age at the time, whether they started their service as salaried or unpaid civil servants *(mülazemeten)*, the various professions they held at different times in their careers, what salary they received in each position, their ranks and titles at different times, how many years they were in the Ilmiye office, whether they were dismissed from their positions, the reasons for dismissals, any accusations against them, and whether they were found guilty. If a member of the ulema belonged to an ulema family, this was also indicated in the biographies. It is possible to obtain accurate information concerning the personal lives and career trajectories of the ulema from these biographical works thanks to notations ranging from their geographic origins and social backgrounds to their educational and professional lives. In other words, studying these registers is the most valuable way to identify the ulema's geographical origins, career patterns, intellectual capacities, educational mobility, their *icazets*, their appointments, their ranks, and all other aspects of the Ilmiye life. These parts of the biographies in the personnel records of ulema are the focus of the study.

The biographical archive is a crucial source for exploring the career patterns of the ulema. To develop an understanding of ulema careers, the personnel records of ulema are the best source for looking at the ulema's educational and professional life in the context of the Ilmiye history. Therefore, the personnel records of ulema constituted the most vital source of information. The use of the Meşihat Archive provides reliable data for this inquiry, but of course, there are obstacles. Much material in the Meşihat Archive has been lost or damaged over the years. Also, these files only contain information on ulema who worked for the government, but many ulema worked privately without dependents in the government. It is not possible to access information about these ulema.[4] Another difficulty of studying ulema records is that they generally use nicknames rather than the real names of the ulema. Therefore, it can be difficult to access the desired biography. However, in this study, biographies were chosen randomly rather than focusing on certain figures.

A listing of ulema from the registers of the late nineteenth century provided new information about ulema like kadıs, *müderrises*, muftis, and scholars who held those offices. These registers also include an identity card, graduation diploma, exam results, and recommendation letters from prominent figures in the region for ulema who worked as civil servants in the Ilmiye hierarchy.[5] Therefore, the aim was to suggest new interpretations of the ulema's professional identity by interpreting the criteria to become an Ilmiye member.

Relying on archival documents of the period, this section also discusses the educational and professional functions carried out by the ulema after the centralization of the Şeyhülislam Office. It provides an overview of the career paths of the ulema from their madrasa education to their retirement and discusses the departments in which they worked and the roles they played in the office of Şeyhülislam.

In addition, this study argues whether the quantitative assessment of the social, cultural, and educational backgrounds and career trajectories of the nineteenth-century Ottoman ulema in the capital is also valid for provincial ulema *(taşra uleması)*. In other words, the differences and similarities between central and provincial ulema are presented. Portraits of nineteenth-century Ottoman ulema in Anatolia are also painted, and general rules that can be applied to their educational or professional histories are examined.

The Anatolian ulema constituted nearly half of those in the empire, numbering 2,743 (about 45 percent of the total).[6] The sample for this study consists of 200 ulema, approximately 4 percent of the total number of ulema, and approximately 8 percent of the Anatolian ulema in the personnel records. By selecting these 200 ulema from the Anatolian region and focusing on the history of provincial ulema, the aim was to localize the history of the Ottoman ulema and religious affairs. This chapter also pays specific attention to showing the progression of the Ilmiye careers of each of the figures by focusing on the biographies of ulema with various educational and professional backgrounds from the Anatolian provinces of the empire.

Place of Birth

The period covered in the personnel records of ulema from 1884 to 1922 includes 5,692 autobiographical records of the ulema. The ulema registered in the personnel records came from all over the Ottoman Empire. Of the 5,692 registered ulema, 2,743 (44.4 percent) were born in Anatolia, 822 (13.3 percent) were born in Rumelia, and 528 (8.5 percent) were born in the capital, Istanbul. These were followed by 340 (6.6 percent) born in Syria, 325 (5.2 percent) born in Iraq, and 120 (2 percent) born in Central Asia. Of the remaining numbers, 118 (1.9 percent) were born in Yemen, 57 (0.9 percent) were born in Jerusalem, 53 (0.85 percent) were born in an African country such as Egypt, Tunisia, Algeria, or Libya, 40 (0.6 percent) were born in Cezayir-i Bahr-i Sefid, 22 (0.3 percent) were born in Arabia-Hicaz, and three (0.04 percent) were born in Iran. There are 995 (16.1 percent) ulema about whom no information regarding their places of origin or family backgrounds is given in the biographical collection.[7] The Anatolian ulema, who constituted the largest number of the Ottoman ulema, are the subject of this section.

One of the most important distinctions concerning the status of ulema in the Ilmiye hierarchy is the birthplace. All ulema in this sample came from provincial areas. Although the examples have been chosen randomly, the number of ulema selected from each province was determined according to the distribution of ulema in those provinces. Of the 2,743 ulema from Anatolia, 425 were from Konya, 418 from Trabzon, 219 from Kastamonu, 217 from Aydın, 200 from Ankara, 191 from Hüdavendigar, 185 from Sivas, 164 from Mameratülaziz, 138 from Diyarbakır, 130 from Erzurum, 107 from Bitlis, 92 from Adana, 50 from Maraş, 49 from Van-Hakkari, 47 from İzmit, 26 from Bolu, and 85 from other Anatolian cities.[8]

According to this distribution, I chose 30 ulema from Konya, 29 from Trabzon, 16 from Kastamonu, and 16 from Aydın. These were followed by 15 ulema from Ankara, 14 from Hüdavendigar, 14 from Sivas, 12 from Mamuratülaziz, 11 from Diyarbakır, 10 from Erzurum, eight from Bitlis, seven from Adana, four from Maraş, four from Van-Hakkari, three from Bolu, three from İzmit, and three from Urfa.

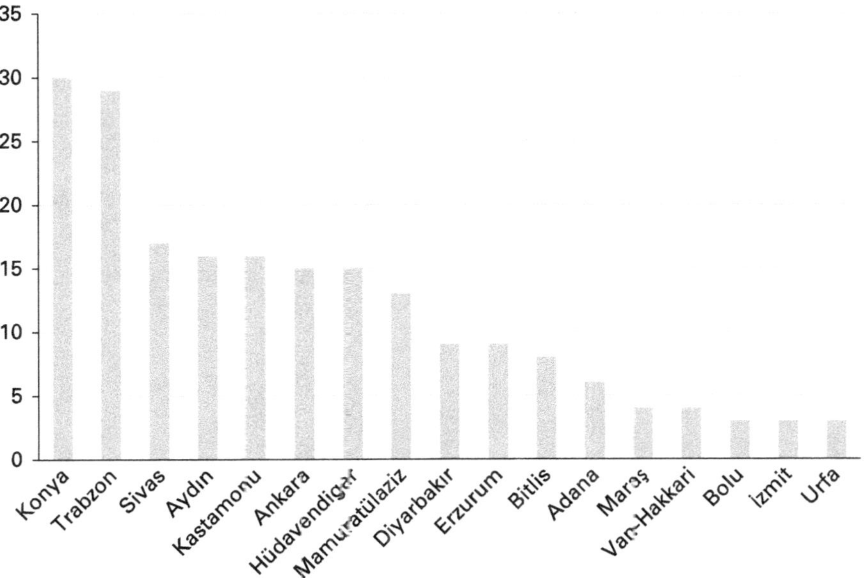

Figure 5.1 Distribution of the hometowns of 200 selected ulema.

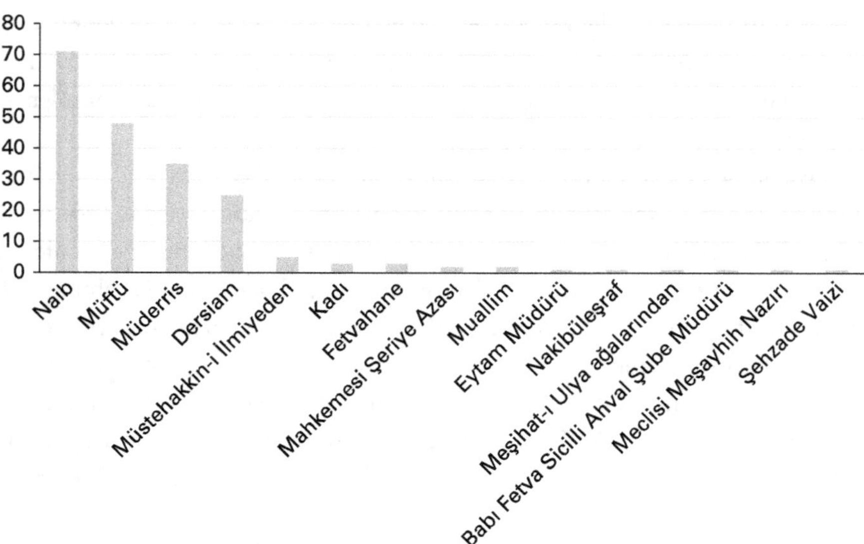

Figure 5.2 Professional distribution of 200 selected ulema.

Judges were of two main types: the kadıs, who officiated in the Sharia courts, and naibs, who were the heads of the secular *(nizamiye)* courts. In our sample, there were 71 (36 percent) ulema who filled the position of naib, and three (2 percent) served as kadıs. It can be shown, therefore, that more naib positions were available than kadı positions. In this sample, 48 (24 percent) of ulema held the position of muftis. Furthermore, 35 (18 percent) held the position of müderris in a madrasa and 25 (12.5 percent) were *dersiams*. Five were religious officials *(müstehakkin-i the Ilmiye)*, three officers were in the *fetvahane*, two were court members in the sharia court, two were teachers, one was a manager of the orphanage *(eytam müdürü)*, one was the chief of the prophet's descendants *(nakibüleşraf)*, two were officers in the *Şeyhülislam Office* and one was a minister at the council of şeyhs *(meclisi meşayıh)*, and one was a preacher for the Sultan's sons (*şehzade* preacher).

Effect of Family Background

An important mechanism for examining the ways in which the ulema's social origins shed light on their place among the privileged elite is their career patterns. Therefore, the career trajectories of the sample ulema and their professional prestige within the Ilmiye class are examined in terms of their social origins. The ulema's access to government power, which affected their social and economic positions within society, was also mostly a result of their social origins. In other words, the most important factors affecting the power of a member of the ulema were their family background and their personnel connections, another being his academic career in both the religious and non-religious sciences.

Famous scholars were clearly role models for the candidate ulema, not only to be admired for their knowledge but also to be improved for future career opportunities. The career development of Ilmiye members in the traditional Ottoman bureaucracy was sometimes shaped by his association with patrons in various echelons of government.[9] To get in a famous *alim*'s good graces and to be loved by one's *müderris* meant a bright future for a madrasa student. The ulema's professional contacts with famous scholars and their family backgrounds played a vital role in their professional advancement. For instance, Musa Kazım studied at the Konya and Balıkesir madrasas after he had completed his initial education in Erzurum, where he was born. Then, he took his graduation diploma from Hoca Şakir Efendi, a famous nineteenth-century *müderris* in Istanbul, and he had the chance to establish relations with palace bureaucrats as a scholar, despite having come from the periphery of the empire. Musa Kazım was one of the most capable and popular scholars of his time. He rose to the rank of Dersiam of Fatih and Müderris of Süleymaniye and finally became Şeyhülislam, which was the highest authority in the Ilmiye hierarchy. His promotions were achieved thanks to connections he had established with government bureaucrats through his *müderris*, Şakir Efendi.[10] Being close to the sultan or the current Şeyhülislam was an important tool in reaching high-level positions in the Ilmiye hierarchy.[11]

Furthermore, in terms of their educational opportunities and their chances of appointment to the civil services, it was an advantage to come from the Sayyid and Sheriff families (descendants of the Prophet Muhammad), from sheikhs, or families already serving in positions within the Ilmiye. First, ulema candidates from *alim* families grew up seeking Islamic knowledge from a young age and received their initial education from their fathers. A successful *alim* was an excellent mentor for his own son. Therefore, to be born the son of an *alim* was a significant advantage in terms of advancing the *alim* candidate's educational career. Ulema candidates from ulema families generally received better religious educations. Secondly, they were more successful in securing appointments because children born and raised in such families had an exceptional reputation before the government due to their education. Once the sons of the ulema finished their primary educations from or in proximity to their fathers and then received madrasa educations, they easily obtained available positions in the Ilmiye hierarchy.

Another factor that facilitated their finding good positions in the Ilmiye system was their fathers' connections. These connections helped move the sons of ulema within the government system, which meant that they served in a variety of posts in the Ottoman Ilmiye system. In this context, an *alim* family's previous service and connections were effective in the establishment of direct relationships. However, personal connections were certainly not enough to ascend this hierarchy; the educational background of an *alim* always took priority in promotions in the Ilmiye system. For instance, Mehmet Kamil Efendi of Bursa was the son of a high-ranking *alim* with the rank *(paye)* of Istanbul. He rose to high-ranking positions in the Ilmiye hierarchy like the ranks of Istanbul and Haremeyn-i Muhteremeyn.[12] However, Mehmet Kamil was at the forefront with his education rather than his father's position in the Ilmiye. He graduated from twelve high-ranking, specialized madrasas *(medrese-i mütehassisin)*. Of course, the connections of his father were instrumental in this fabulous education of Mehmet Kamil. The number of examples like Mehmet Kamil is quite excessive. One such person was Mehmed Tevfik Efendi of Ankara. In 1834, Sultan Mahmud II granted the Istanbul *rüus* (one of the highest ranks in the Ilmiye hierarchy) to Mehmed Tevfik Efendi due to his reverence for Mehmed Tevfik's father, Sayyid Sheikh Osman Efendi. Mehmed Tevfik Efendi completed his education at the Süleymaniye Madrasa at the highest level of the Ilmiye education system and received his license to work *(icazetname)* in 1847 from the famous Istanbul scholars Kangirili Ahmed Efendi, Vidinli Mustafa Efendi, and Hafız Seyyid Efendi.[13] After graduation, he became the naib of Bursa in 1855 and received the rank of Halep *Mevleviyet* (one of the highest ranks in the Ilmiye hierarchy) in 1857. Later, in 1858, he became the naib of Kayseri, then the naib of Bursa in 1861, and the naib of Balıkesir in 1866. He also received the rank of Mısır *Mevleviyet* (one of the highest ranks in the Ilmiye hierarchy) in 1867 and Medine-i Münevvere *Mevleviyet* (one of the highest ranks in the Ilmiye hierarchy) in 1871. After serving in naib positions in different regions and receiving these great ranks, he became a member of parliament. In 1882, he became president of the court of the first instance *(bidayet mahkemesi ceza* reisi*)* and in the same year, he was awarded with the rank of Istanbul (one of the highest ranks in the Ilmiye hierarchy). He then immediately became an important figure in the political arena as minister of the Meclis-i Meşayih *(Meclis-i Meşayih Nazırı)*. Mehmed Tevfik Efendi was also awarded with the rank of kazasker of Anatolia (one of the highest ranks in the Ilmiye hierarchy) in 1889 and the rank of kazasker of Rumelia in 1890. This privileged position was foremost the result of his superior education (he successfully graduated from the twelve grades of a high-ranking madrasa degree, from *ibtida-yi hariç* to *musıla-ı Süleymaniye*) apart from the social network he built during his studies and from his *alim* father's connections.[14]

Ulema families encouraged their sons to enter the Ilmiye professions and raised them with the science *(ilm)*, which given the importance of science and the ulema to the Ottomans, was one reason the ulema profession never died out. Therefore, the social networks of ulema fathers eased children into the ulema profession, and a scholarly environment impelled the sons of ulema to choose that career path. In other words, the ulema encouraged their sons to prepare for a career in the Ilmiye ranks. In this regard, the ulema remained strong and family influence and connections assured ulema families' estimable reputations in society and government authority.

Since the ulema sons were in positions to protect their status within the religious field of the empire thanks to their family backgrounds and connections, some of the Ilmiye positions passed within the same family. There were also examples of the Ilmiye professions being passed directly from father to son. For instance, Murad Zühdü, who was born on January 25, 1880, in Kastamonu, was appointed to the madrasa where his father worked as a *müderris*, and he served there until his father's death on February 27, 1906.[15] Similarly, Mustafa Efendi of Bitlis was appointed as *müderris* to replace his father when his father passed away.[16] In these examples, it appears that family relationships had priority in the appointments, but to be assigned to important positions, it was not enough just to be a close relative of a person in a certain Ilmiye position. Murad Zühdü and Mustafa Efendi studied the classes they needed to prepare for their positions, completed their madrasa educations, received their graduation diploma, and worked in various posts before being appointed to their fathers' offices. The valuable inheritance passed from father to son was only achieved if the son had the necessary scientific *(ilmi)* qualifications to assume the father's position in the Ilmiye hierarchy.

The phenomenon of sons and grandsons taking up the occupations of their fathers and grandfathers began in the early Ottoman Empire, but this tendency for the sons of the ulema to follow in their fathers' footsteps grew. The statistical study of ulema biographies shows a continuity of occupations among the ulema over two and three generations.[17] In other words, many ulema were born into ulema families and rose up in the ranks of the ulema as their fathers had. Therefore, many of the great scholars were of one of the ulema families. Also, a few ulema came from Sayyid, Sheriff, and sheikh families.

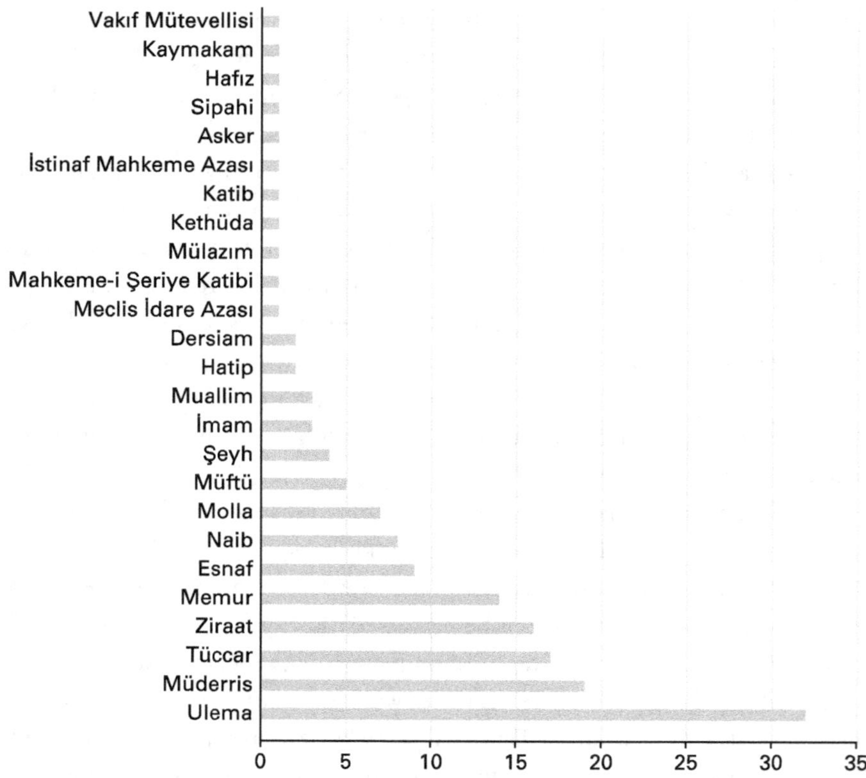

Figure 5.3 Professions of the fathers of 200 sample ulema.

When compared with the sons of ulema, the sons of farmers, merchants, and artisans enjoyed less success in the government hierarchy. They tended to serve in modest Ilmiye positions rather than receive high administrative appointments. For instance, of the madrasa graduates with modest backgrounds, Mehmet Ruşen Efendi[18] and Ali Vehbi Efendi[19] assumed modest posts.

The graph above provides significant information with respect to the origins of the sample ulema. Their fathers' occupations can be divided into four categories: the Ilmiye servants, farmers, artisans, and administrative workers. There is a large number of members from the Ilmiye families (of ulema origin). The professions of the fathers of these Ilmiye included *müderris,* kadı, kadıasker, Şeyhülislam, mufti, and *imam*. Of the 200 ulema listed in Figure 5. 3, 91 (46%) had fathers that were part of the Ottoman Ilmiye class. That is, 91 of their fathers were themselves members of the religious establishment, and these 91 ulema thus came from families already represented in the Ilmiye. This data shows that almost half of the ulema who occupied the Ilmiye positions came from ulema families.

There were also ulema with other kinds of family backgrounds. For instance, of the 200 ulema in the sample, 19 belonged to families in administrative positions and two had fathers who were military men. In other words, 21 ulema, or 11 percent of the total, were the sons of men who occupied administrative or military posts. The fathers of 17 (9 percent) ulema were merchants. 16 were the sons of men who earned their livelihoods in agriculture, cultivating their own land. Nine ulema were the sons of artisans. There were 46 whose fathers' professions are unidentified, but most were likely members of the Ilmiye.[20] Most of these remaining ulema identified their fathers as having performed religious functions, but their precise occupations could not be ascertained.

Although the great majority of biographies do not mention the grandfathers' professions, it is probable that the ulema whose fathers were *alim* also had ulema grandfathers. There are examples where the grandfather's profession is recorded as being in the ulema, along with the father's.[21] Therefore, a three-generational continuity can be identified in the social backgrounds of these ulema.

Early Education

Education at home was a popular way of teaching ulema before madrasa. These children initially studied with their fathers and other scholars, and they were considered to have received a better education. A child whose father was from a profession other than the Ilmiye did not grow up receiving a religious education from his father. Ahmet Hulusi of Ankara, for example, learned basic Islamic knowledge like the Qur'an, *tecvid*, and *ilmihal* from his *alim* father,[22] while Nadir Cemil of Adana learned Turkish grammar and punctuation from his father, a member of the council administration.[23]

After their educations at home, many families sent their sons to *sibyan mektebs* to prepare for Ilmiye's career. Hafız İzzet, born in Kastamonu in 1827, gained his first religious knowledge from his father, Abdullah Yakup. He also learned Arabic grammar from him and went to Istanbul only after his father's death in 1858. Hafız İzzet continued to study in Istanbul with the Müderris of Beyazıt Mosque Ahmet Nüzhet Efendi.[24] Similarly, Mustafa Ahmet Hulusi Efendi first studied with his father, Haci Ali Efendi, and learned *Tecvid, İlmihal, Sarf,* and *Nahv* in his hometown before being sent to Istanbul and earning his graduation diploma from Abdullah Rüşdi Efendi.[25]

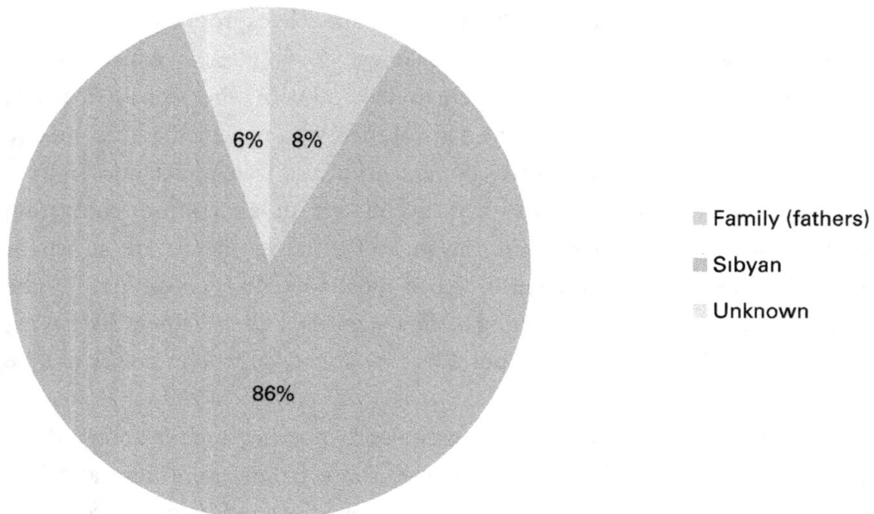

Figure 5.4 Early education of 200 sample ulema.

In our sample, 8 percent (17) of the *alim* received their initial education from their *alim* fathers, and 86 percent (172) went to *sibyan mektebs*. SIX percent (11) of them did not remark on where they received their initial education.

Istanbul as an Educational Center

The social backgrounds of provincial Ottoman ulema always differed from those of the central ulema. The conditions in provincial regions were a disadvantage for provincial candidates in terms of accessing education and becoming qualified *alim*. Because opportunities in the provinces were limited, it took time to gain the necessary knowledge. Therefore, an *alim* who grew up in a village, after receiving his initial education somewhere near his village, would be advised to proceed to a higher madrasa with the reference of his scholar *(hoca)*. Although there were madrasas in most regions of the empire, Istanbul always had a privileged position in terms of science, careers, and networks, and it protected its status as the science center. It attracted students from all over the empire wishing to pursue a quality education.[26]

A large number of students in Istanbul was foremost the result of the quality of most Istanbul madrasas. One of the most prominent features of the Istanbul madrasa system that attracted students was the upper-level education they offered that differed from the provincial madrasa education. Another reason, almost as important as the first that explains why ulema chose a particular or famous madrasa, especially when in Istanbul, was those career opportunities in the bureaucratic positions of the Ottoman government system after graduation were greater. Receiving an education in Istanbul provided many job opportunities for career seekers; Istanbul was the purpose of many madrasa students who wished to acquire an advanced madrasa education and career opportunities. Therefore, many ulema candidates living in the countryside left their hometowns to gain admittance to a madrasa in Istanbul.

The madrasas in Istanbul were not just institutions for training students for religious service, but they also provided the necessary training for administrative and judicial personnel required by the government. Students who graduated from Istanbul madrasas generally embarked on careers in the imperial administration as kadıs, muftis, or *müderrises* at the central places.

Students who first started their educations in provincial areas could continue in madrasas in large cities if they proved their talent, but personal connections also played a vital role for ulema candidates with provincial origins in gaining admittance to Istanbul madrasas.[27] It was difficult for a student from a provincial district who studied at a central madrasa to succeed without connections to an influential person in Istanbul. On the other hand, opportunities like receiving training from famous *müderrises* and ease of access to information were easier for a central madrasa student to access. Whether students came to the Istanbul madrasas with the purpose of gaining knowledge for their own sake or with the goal of pursuing a high-ranking post in the government, those who studied in the Istanbul madrasas reached higher levels in the Ilmiye hierarchy. There were only a small number of ulema who reached the top levels of this system without having been educated in Istanbul madrasas.[28]

The number of ulema in the empire's various regions corresponded to their populations. For instance, the male population of Anatolia was about 4,270,000 and of Rumelia 1,007,005, according to Ottoman population records from 1881 to 1893.[29] During the same period, the number of Anatolian ulema with 2743 was almost four times larger than the number of those in Rumelia of 822.[30] However, the number of ulema in the capital, Istanbul, did not correspond with its population. While the Muslim male population of Istanbul was about 223,500, the city was overrepresented among ulema with 528.[31] The reason for the discrepancy in the number of ulema with Istanbul's population is that Istanbul provided many opportunities for an *alim*. An *alim* born or educated in Istanbul received more appointments and promotions than ulema from the provinces.

The status and privilege of the ulema who graduated from provincial madrasas and the ulema who graduated from those in Istanbul were not the same. Ulema who graduated from the Istanbul-based madrasas worked as kadıs, kazaskers, Şeyhülislam, and *müderrises*, which were important administrative, teaching, and judicial positions that received higher wages. Provincial madrasa graduates did not have the same opportunities. The opportunity of reaching high-ranking status in the Ilmiye institution was more limited than for Istanbul graduates. Therefore, the city and madrasa where ulema were educated were more important predictors of government appointments than their birthplaces.

Provincial madrasa graduates with obscure family origins were less successful in the Ottoman Ilmiye hierarchy, and few madrasa graduates from provincial centers achieved top administrative posts if they did not have a close relationship with someone in the bureaucracy. For instance, Süleyman Şakir Efendi from Gediz remained a district mufti in Gediz for the whole of his career due to his lack of connections with the famous ulema.[32]

According to Figure 5.5, 124 (62 percent) of the sample ulema trained in the provinces, while 76 (38 percent) of these candidates went to Istanbul for training. Our sample shows why ulema went to Istanbul or remained in their hometown for their education. Many students preferred to go to Istanbul due to the fact that its educational opportunities were better, and graduates of the Istanbul madrasas achieved more important positions in the Ilmiye hierarchy than the provincial

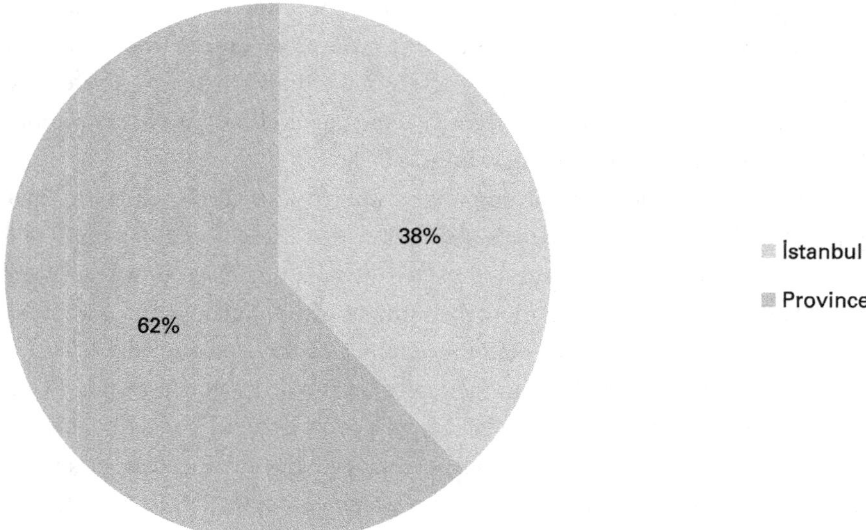

Figure 5.5 Regional preferences for education of 200 sample ulema.

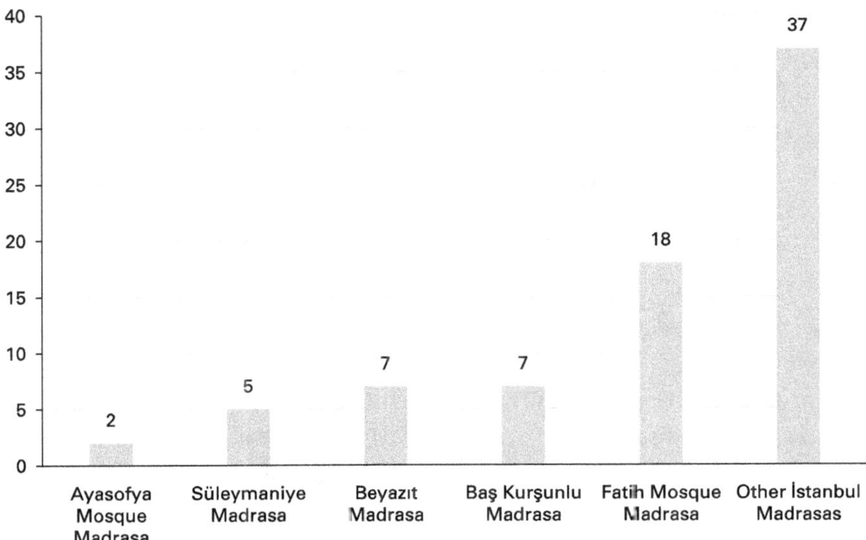

Figure 5.6 Preferences for Madrasa Education of 200 Sample Ulema in Istanbul.

madrasa graduated ulema. There were many reasons, one of the most important of which was that students without good connections in the Ilmiye in Istanbul found it difficult to be accepted into a madrasa there.

Among the sample ulema, 53 (70 percent) of the 76 students who studied in Istanbul madrasas went to Istanbul directly after finishing the *sibyan mekteb* in their hometowns. 23 (30 percent) studied at a madrasa in or near their hometowns before going to Istanbul for further madrasa education.

According to Figure 5.6, 76 (38 percent) ulema studied in one of the great Istanbul madrasas such as *Fatih*, *Bayezit*, *Süleymaniye*, and others—either exclusively or partially—due to the importance of an Istanbul education for moving up the Ilmiye hierarchy. Considering the total number of students studying at Istanbul madrasas, the fact that 38 percent of this sample taken from the personnel registry files proves that madrasa education in Istanbul was essential for the education of provincial students. The personnel registry files indicate that the connections made by *alim* candidates affected their educational careers. Most of the time, students who went to Istanbul for their educations sought out a *müderris* from their hometowns and studied at the madrasas where they taught.[33]

The sample indicates that madrasas in Istanbul like Fatih, Beyazıt, and Süleymaniye continued to be popular education centers in the nineteenth century. The most important difference between central and provincial madrasa students was that students in Istanbul had the opportunity to receive an education from diverse *müderrises* and well-known instructors. They also studied in modern law schools such as the *Mekteb-i Nüvvab* and *Mekteb-i Kuzat*. Although often obtaining sophisticated educations and social contacts by attending the highest madrasas of Süleymaniye, Fatih, and Beyazıt, others completed these wide-ranging backgrounds at provincial madrasas.

Modern School Education

During the late Ottoman Empire, two types of educational training existed: the traditional Qur'an school and a new style of school that reflected the reform movements of the nineteenth century. The new schools of the late nineteenth century (the 1870s) had a new method of teaching known as *usul-i cedid*. Despite the new style, the curriculum was still mainly religious. In other words, the new schools of the Tanzimat *(Mekteb-i Maarif-i Adliye, Muallimhane-i Nüvvab,*[34] and *Darülmuallimin*) combined Islamic education and a modern educational system.

In our sample, a significant number of ulema encountered this new, more modern curriculum in the newly established schools. According to Figure 5.7, of the 200 sample ulema, 72 *(*36 percent*)* studied at modern schools like *Darülfünün*

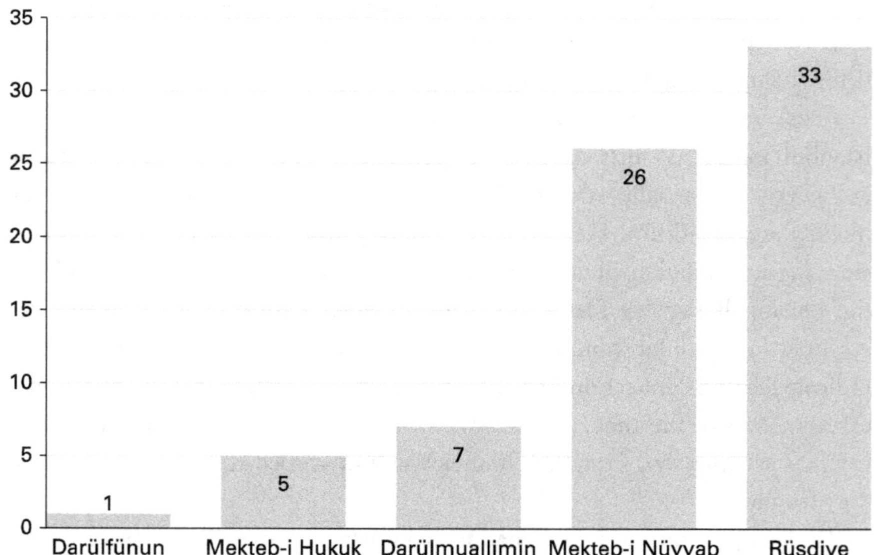

Figure 5.7 Number of ulema who attended modern schools among 200 sample ulema.

(the university), *Mekteb-i Hukuk* (law school), *Darülmuallimin* (teacher's training school), *Mekteb-i Nüvvab* (the school for judges), and *Rüşdiye* (secondary school), 33 (16.5 percent) in our sample studied in *rüşdiye* schools, which were the upper elementary division of the new education system. In addition, 26 (13 percent) ulema attended a *Mekteb-i Nüvvab*. Seven (3.5 percent) ulema studied in one of the teachers' colleges *(Darülmuallimin)* and earned the right to teach in government schools. Five ulema (2.5 percent) studied in law schools (*Mekteb-i Hukuk*, later the Law Faculty), and one (0.5 percent) went to *Darülfünun*. However, importantly, those who received modern school educations either first studied at a madrasa or studied at a madrasa and a modern school at the same time.[35]

In modern schools, some new courses on specialized field topics were taught apart from religious courses. Given the new educational system, the staff, and their disciplinary principles, these schools can be seen as reformed madrasas rather than as strictly secular schools.[36] The ulema also learned many languages at these new modern schools.

According to the personnel records of the ulema, the language knowledge of the ulema was extensive. They primarily spoke the classical literary languages: Turkish, Arabic, and Persian. Many from multilingual areas could also speak Kurdish and Greek. The madrasa education in both Eastern and Western Anatolia was the same, although Persian was more prevalent in madrasas in Kurdish-speaking areas due to the similarity between the languages. There are many examples of ulema with traditional madrasa educations who could read and write Arabic and Persian as well as Turkish and Kurdish in Eastern Anatolia.

Figure 5.8 shows the vast majority of the Ottoman ulema was multilingual. In our sample, 197 ulema knew both Turkish and Arabic. According to this figure, most ulema were fluent in Arabic along with Ottoman Turkish and were writing in this tongue. It is also noted that all ulema, even from Kurdish-speaking areas such as Bitlis, Van, and Diyarbakır, knew and wrote in the official language, Ottoman Turkish. Although the rest of the 197 ulema of the 200 did not specify the languages they know, it was compulsory to know Turkish and Arabic for education at the madrasa. Also, in the sample of 200 ulema, 165 knew Persian and 21 ulema knew Kurdish. Knowledge of these languages was mostly correlated to ethnic origin and the regions in which they lived. In addition, two could speak French, one Armenian, one Greek, and one German. The personnel registry files also showed that the ulema who learned these languages learned them in modern schools.

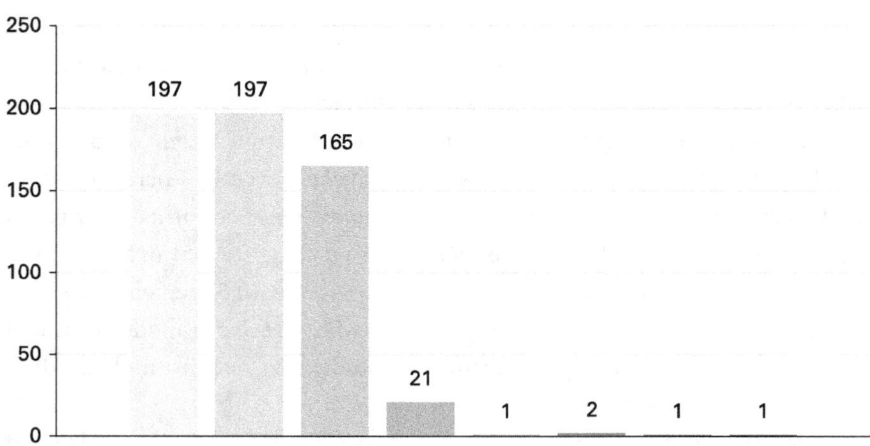

Figure 5.8 Language knowledge of 200 sample ulema.

Recruitment

The Şeyhülislam Office encompassed all religious fields, including the appointment of religious officers in the Ottoman Empire. The Şeyhülislam Office was the only religious authority that could nominate religious staff and receive the approval of the sultan. The Şeyhülislam presented candidates for vacant Ilmiye positions first to the grand vizier and then the sultan.

Since the Şeyhülislam Office was the only authority for both appointments and promotions, a career in the Ilmiye required powerful connections in the capital's Şeyhülislam Office. Although the Şeyhülislam was the final decision maker and was generally not personally involved in the politics of the nomination process, he did intervene directly in some cases. For instance, regarding the appointment of Hoca Ruşen Efendi as *müderris* of Trabzon, Şeyhülislam Mehmed Cemaleddin Efendi intervened during the first stage of the assignment.[37] Normally, the Şeyhülislam gave his approval of the person to be appointed at the last stage, but in this case, the Şeyhülislam was engaged from the beginning. It appears that there was a relationship between the Şeyhülislam and Hoca Ruşen Efendi.

Figure 5.9 indicates that of the 200 sample ulema who served in the Ilmiye hierarchy, 62 were recruited between the ages of 29 and 35. Four were recruited between the ages of 11 and 17, while two were recruited at a late stage, between the ages of 64 and 70. This shows there was no upper or lower age limit to be

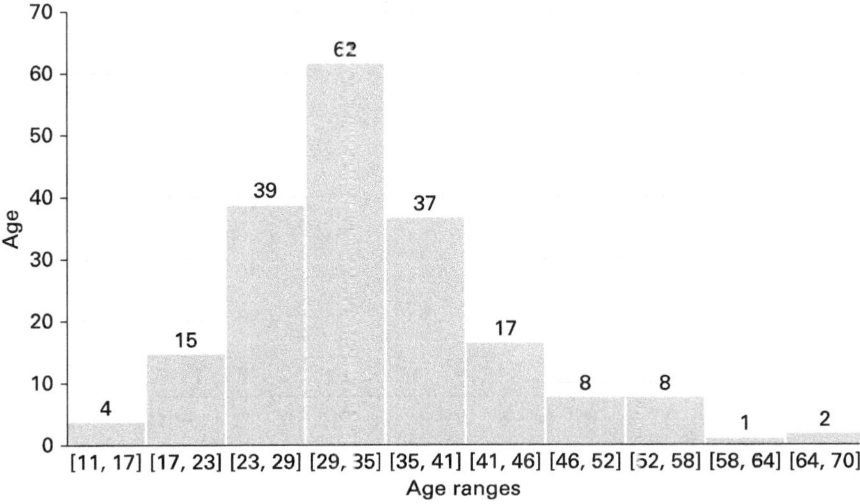

Figure 5.9 Recruitment age distribution of 200 sample ulema.

appointed as a civil servant in the Ilmiye hierarchy. For example, Abdülhalim Efendi, the son of a farmer from Kastamonu, was accepted into an Istanbul madrasa in 1873 when he was 56. After he took his graduation diploma, *icazet*, at the age of 66, he was placed in the Ilmiye hierarchy in 1883.[38] Similarly, Haci Hasan Tahsin Efendi of Sivas was born in 1830 and was appointed as teacher to *rüşdiye mektep* in 1878, although he did not enter the Ilmiye hierarchy until the age of 48.[39] On the other hand, Ahmed Cemil Efendi of Diyarbakır became a scribe in 1889 when he was just 11.[40] A statistical analysis of the sample ulema indicates that their average age of recruitment was 33. Although there are few old recruits in our examples, there are plenty who started work in the Ilmiye positions at a young age. The reason for the appointment at the young ages of ulema was the demand for knowledgeable and literate people in the bureaucratic hierarchy, especially after the Tanzimat. Therefore, the ulema candidates started to work at young ages without having finished their education.

Madrasa graduates took their graduation diplomas and entered traditional professions within the Ilmiye hierarchy. While Figure 5.10 illustrates that the time to find a job varied from less than a year to 18 years, it is clear that most ulema settled into the Ilmiye position without waiting. Twelve of the selected 200 ulema began work in the Ilmiye position without having graduated. Furthermore, those who had to wait for an appointment generally waited a maximum of one or two years. The average recruitment age in this period was one and a half years. The waiting period for graduates to be assigned to the

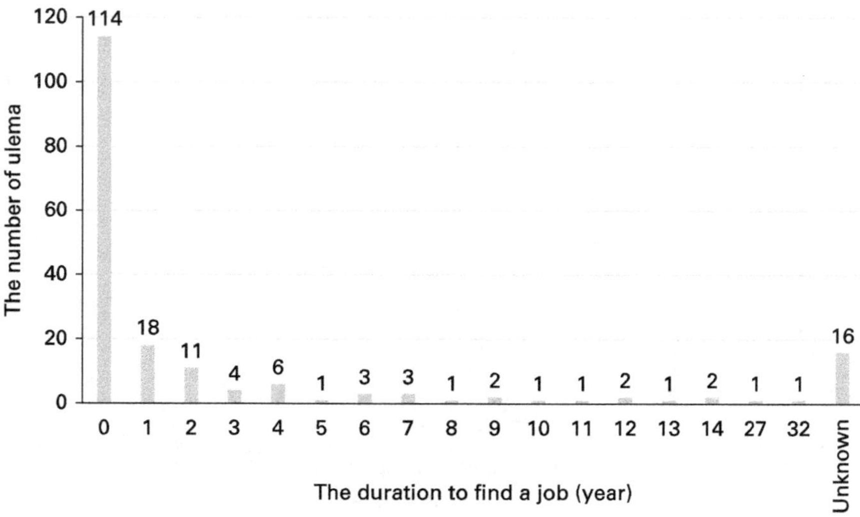

Figure 5.10 Waiting period for 200 sample ulema to enter the Ilmiye service.

Ilmiye position was shortened in more recent periods. The waiting period in the earlier time frame was seven to eight years but was shortened to as little as five or six months. Centralization caused the bureaucracy to grow, leading to greater demand for qualified civil servants. In this sense, the Ilmiye professions were very popular even at the end of the nineteenth century and were the positions in which madrasa graduates were employed as soon as they graduated.

Figure 5.11 shows that 100 ulema (50 percent) in our sample started their positions in a city other than their hometown, while the other 100 started working in their cities of birth. Most of the time, newly recruited ulema were immediately appointed to positions in their places of birth.

There was an occasional request that ulema stay in their hometowns after graduation from the madrasas. One of the most important reasons why ulema chose to work in their hometowns or neighboring provinces was better advancement opportunities. In this sense, one reason ulema would return after the completion of their education in Istanbul was their father's or family's position in their hometown. Therefore, members of the ulema also sometimes wanted to live near their families.

There are also examples of ulema who returned home, opened madrasas there, and were then appointed to these madrasas after completing their education.[41] On the other hand, there was considerable mobility from city to city for ulema serving in the government.

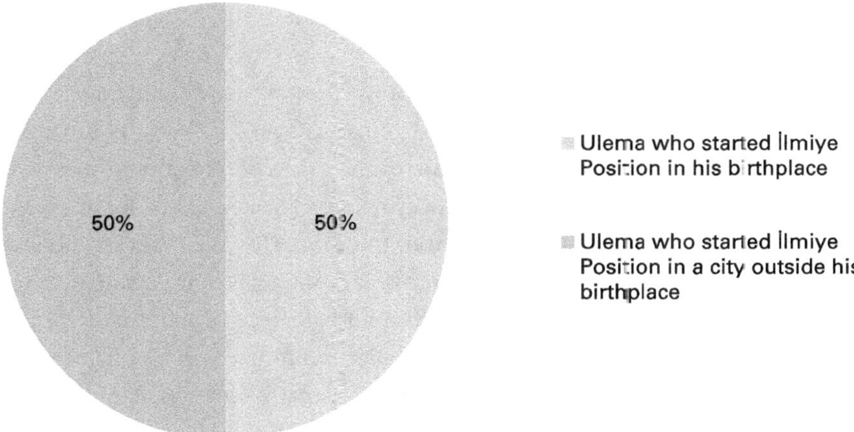

Figure 5.11 Location of the first appointments of 200 sample ulema vis-à-vis their birthplaces.

At the time of preparing the *personnel registry files*, the number of sample ulema assigned to their places of birth increased to 105 and the number of those working in a city other than of their hometowns was reduced to 95. In this sense, the places where the ulema last served did not change from their first places of appointment. As seen in Figures 5.11 and 5.12, a few ulema ended up serving in their hometowns after having served in other provinces.

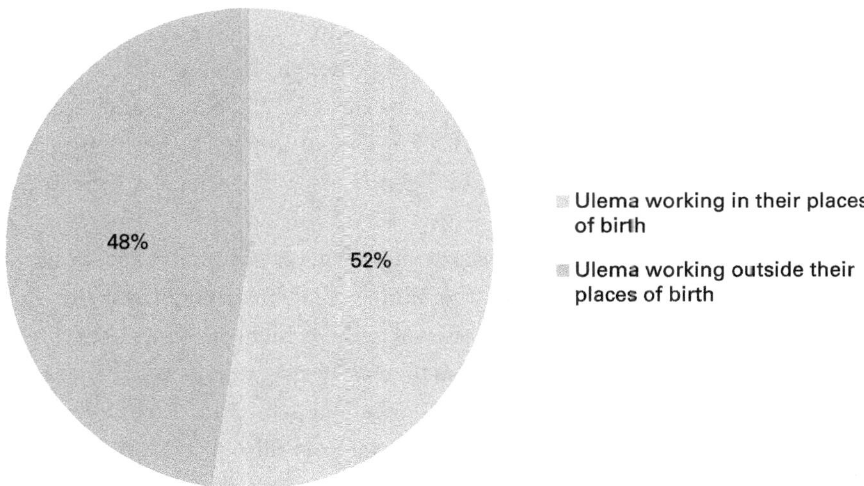

Figure 5.12 Location of the last working assignment of 200 sample ulema.

Income of the Ulema

The sources of the ulema's income were various. The first source of income of the ulema was the *arpalık* (an allowance for Ottoman officials).[42] Until the Tanzimat period, Ottoman officials did not receive a regular salary because the government budget was inefficient. Instead, the government allocated them lands called *arpalık*, and the ulema made a living from this land. However, this system was misused, so the government tried to remove it in the eighteenth century. But it was not fully removed, and the ulema continued to receive the *arpalık* in the nineteenth century. After the Tanzimat, regular monthly payments called *tarik maaşı* or *rütbe maaşı* were given to the Ilmiye members. These regular payments to the Ilmiye members along with other bureaucrats of the *seyfiye* and *kalemiye* meant that they also began earning pensions.[43] In this sense, the ulema underwent a transformation from voluntary staff to salaried civil servants of the government after the Tanzimat.[44] However, these salaries were not provided to all the Ilmiye officials, due to the insufficiency of the government treasury—until the Constitutional Era, when regular monthly payments and retirement benefits were given to all the Ilmiye officials. The Ilmiye class, like other classes, received salaries from the government treasury for their services according to the rate and amount specified by the government.

Furthermore, there was a hierarchical order among the Ilmiye members reflected in the number of their salaries. Therefore, it is necessary to indicate what their salaries were and how the hierarchical order of the Ilmiye civil servants affected these salaries. Figure 5.13 shows the upper and lower salaries of our sample ulema working as civil servants in the Ilmiye system between 1884 and 1922. It shows that kadıs and naibs earned the highest salaries.

Between 1884 and 1922, on average, kadıs earned 3,750 piasters, followed by naibs with 2,150 piasters. Müderrises, who held an important position in the Ilmiye hierarchy, earned an average of 795 piasters, and teachers at the *rüşdiye schools* earned 625 piasters.

Another observation is that the salary rates of ulema groups did not regularly increase. Despite long service in the Ilmiye hierarchy, members were not necessarily promoted and did not always receive higher salaries. There are even examples of ulema earning more in their early assignments and then taking pay cuts in later appointments. For instance, Halil İbrahim Efendi received a 1,000 piasters salary in 1868 as a naib in the Karakilise district of Erzurum, but in 1895, he was appointed as a naib in the Karaağaç district of Aydın with a salary of 750 piasters.[45]

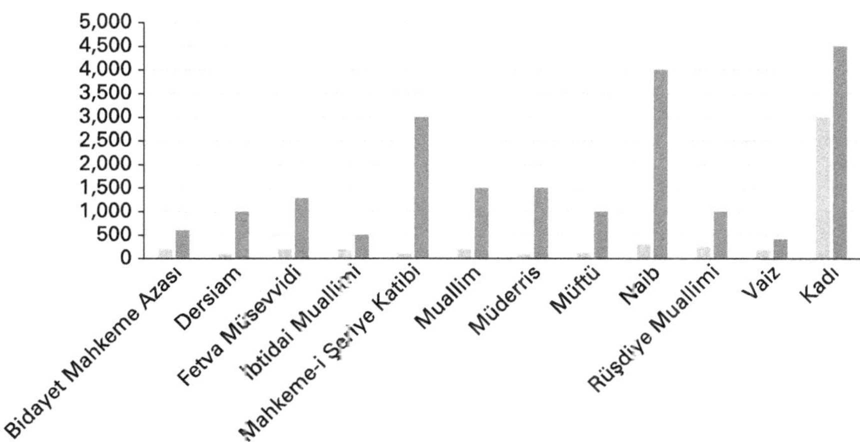

Figure 5.13 Lower and upper limits of the salaries of 200 sample ulema according to their rank (in piasters).

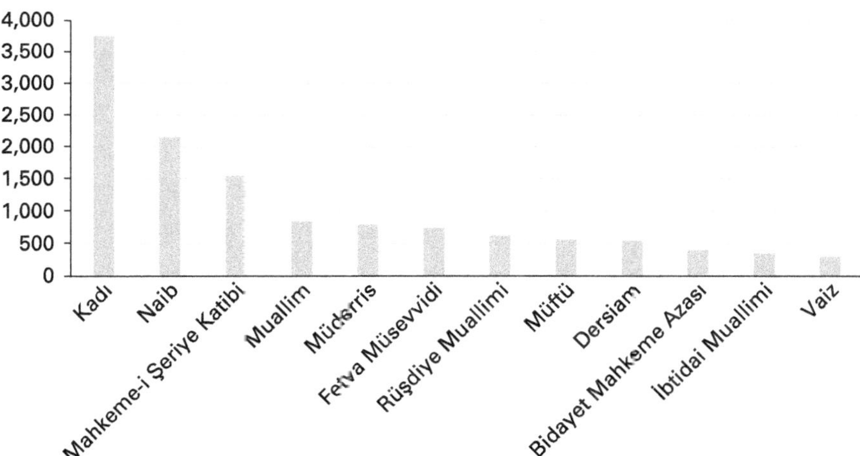

Figure 5.14 Average salaries of 200 sample ulema according to their professions.

Apart from salaried Ilmiye members, there were also unsalaried Ilmiye officials in government positions. Although the government appointed the *müderrises*, muftis, and *imams* of mosques, it could not always pay them salaries. There are plenty of examples of ulema working without any salary for a part of their career. For instance, Mehmet Hamdi Efendi of Kütahya was appointed as mufti of Söğüt district on July 15, 1909, without a salary.[45] Another example is that of Ahmed Hamdi of Kastamonu. He worked for two years at a madrasa in the Karasu district and then worked as a mufti in the same region, both without taking a salary.[47] Similarly, Hafiz Mehmed Necib Efendi of Sivas worked as a mufti without a salary in Divriği in Sivas.[48] Ahmet Efendi of Mardin earned a 400 piaster salary in 1910 as a mufti after having worked in the same job without earning a wage for the previous 10 years.[49] Another resident of Mardin, Mehmet Tahir Efendi, worked as a *fetva müsevvid* without a wage from 1911 until 1914.[50] İlyas Efendi from Batum worked in 1911 without receiving a salary after being appointed as a *müderris* at the Fatih Mosque, but his time working without a wage was luckily short, and six months later he began to be paid a salary.[51]

Marital Status

The marital status of the ulema is another point to be examined in the curricula vitae of the ulema. Most academic works suppose that the vast majority of ulema were polygamous; however, the statistical data showed the opposite.

Most biographies did not include information on marital status. Of the 200 ulema examined, information on the marital status of 85 was provided in the official biographies. Of those, 81 (95 percent) were monogamous, 3 (4 percent) were bigamous, and 1 (1 percent) was trigamist. The remaining 115 biographies in the personnel records did not give information about the number of their wives. The fact that 81 of 85 ulema for whom the number of wives was indicated

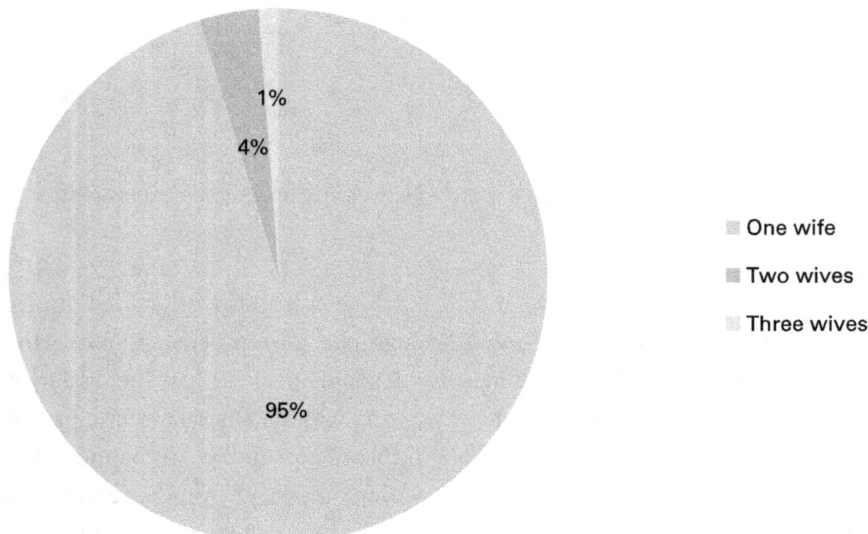

Figure 5.15 Number of wives of 200 sample ulema.

were monogamous, suggests that the majority of the remaining ulema who did not mention the number of wives was also monogamous.

No information is provided concerning the mothers and wives of the ulema, but the available evidence suggests that most ulema married daughters of ulema. There were strong alliances among the ulema. Intermarrying among ulema families and the resulting familial connections were mutually beneficial. These interrelationships through marriage resulted in the distribution of wealth and prestige in the same family lines. Important ulema dynasties were interrelated both with one another as well as with other families with considerable economic and political status.

Conclusion

The biographical registers at the Meşihat Archive known as the *Sicill-i Ahval* are essential sources for revealing the nineteenth-century Ottoman ulema's role in society and explaining their educational and professional history. Even though some crucial questions about the ulema as personnel of the Şeyhülislam Office remain unanswered, the ulema's biographical information provides information on leading ulema's family backgrounds and places of origin, their intellectual capacities, their training, and their career locations, answering such questions as What were the top education centers (madrasas) for ulema candidates, how did popular madrasas open doors in terms of career opportunities after graduation, and what was the impact of the *müderris* on the ulema candidate? In this sense, the biographies in the office of Şeyhülislam discuss the career histories of ulema from their first educational history *(sibyan mektebs)* to specialized madrasas to their retirement from the Ilmiye hierarchy. In this part, I focused on Anatolian ulema, who constituted the majority of ulema in the Ottoman Empire, in order to clarify the provincial history. I have analyzed 200 ulema spread across the different regions of Anatolia in proportion to the number in each region according to their social, educational, and professional backgrounds.

One of the mechanisms that affected the career life of the ulema was their social background. The first matter investigated was the question of the family origins of the sample ulema. In this analysis of 200 ulema biographies, even though they came from similar regions of Anatolia, the families were varied; some were religious, some farmers, some merchants, and some military servants. The sons of ulema were more fortunate in terms of their rise up the Ilmiye hierarchy because of their fathers' connections to the government system and their superior education. It was also realized that most ulema families encouraged their children to enter the Ilmiye professions. The passing of the Ilmiye profession from father to son was not unconditional; the sons took their fathers as a model and grew with science. In our sample, 91 of 200 sample ulema came from families with Ilmiye origins, and this shows that almost half were from ulema families. In other words, they were the sons of men in the Ilmiye posts, like kadıs, naibs, and *müderrises*. The remainder were the sons of farmers, artisans, and administrative civil servants. In our sample, fathers in other professions included 19 government officials, 17 merchants, 16 farmers, nine artisans, and two military men.

The second important situation that influenced the ulema's career path was their educational background. One popular way of teaching ulema was for their ulema fathers to educate them at home. If candidates had ulema fathers, they were generally first educated by their fathers. After this training with their fathers, they enrolled in the *sibyan mektebs*. Finishing a *sibyan mekteb* was a prerequisite for enrolling in a madrasa. Of the 200 sample ulema, 124, or 62 percent, received higher education in their hometowns or places near their hometowns, and 76, or 38 percent, went to Istanbul for their education. No doubt, the higher quality of education in Istanbul madrasas attracted madrasa students. Many provincial students who wanted to be qualified *alim* studied in Istanbul if they had the opportunity to go to Istanbul. In this sense, the general student population of Istanbul was from all over the empire. Since Istanbul provided many opportunities to students, the number of students studying in Istanbul was high in every period. Also, the ulema who graduated from Istanbul-based madrasas worked in high-level Ilmiye positions such as Şeyhülislam or kadı, while provincial madrasa graduates did not.

An important number of ulema candidates studied at modern schools either instead of or after attending traditional madrasas. However, the educational curricula of the new modern schools were not so different from that of traditional madrasas. In these new schools, languages like French, and German and some new courses on specialized field topics were taught in addition to courses taught at traditional madrasas. This part also illustrated that the ulema from Anatolian regions of the empire spoke Turkish, including ulema whose mother tongue was Kurdish. They could also read and write Arabic, Persian, and other languages.

Thirdly, the appointment procedures for the Ilmiye members, their recruitment ages, and their recruitment places were expressed with the statistical data. The appointment of the Ilmiye members from among madrasa graduates who had received a graduation diploma was made by the Şeyhülislam and approved by the sultan. Despite there being no upper or lower age limit for being a civil servant in the Ilmiye system, the average recruitment age was 33. Furthermore, some madrasa graduates were immediately appointed to the Ilmiye profession after receiving their diploma *(icazets)*, while other graduates waited for years. However, the average duration that an *alim* graduate had to wait was one and a half years. The increase in the demand for quality civil servants as a requirement of institutionalization shortened the waiting time for employment after graduation. After finishing their studies, 50 percent of the sample ulema chose to work in their hometowns and remained there throughout their careers. The other 50 percent worked in cities other than their hometowns.

All biographies indicate that there is a relationship between ulema appointments to the Ilmiye positions and their social origins and family backgrounds. The probability of reaching the Ilmiye positions was high for the sons of *alim* fathers. The *ulema* families constituted a privileged social group and their privileges, social status, power, and knowledge could pass to their sons. Ulema positions were often maintained from generation to generation within the same family.

Instead of the *arpalık*, the government started to pay a regular salary to the Ilmiye members in this century. The ulema received salaries from the government treasury on a monthly basis. However, this salary was not given to all the Ilmiye officials due to the limited government budget. Some of the Ilmiye members worked long years without taking a salary. There was a hierarchy among the Ilmiye members according to their salaries. While high-paid kadıs, naibs, or *müderrises* held a higher position in the hierarchy of the Ilmiye, low-paid preachers, *imams*, and scribes were in a lower position.

Ulema marriages were also examined. Even if the marital status of most of the ulema are not indicated, the majority of those whose marital status is mentioned were monogamous. Of the sample of 200 ulema, the number of wives is reported for 85, of which 81 were monogamous. Among the sample ulema whose marital statuses were known, 95 percent had one wife. Contrary to the current literature, which claims that the Ottoman Empire was characterized by polygamy, the ulema were generally monogamous. In addition, our sample biography records showed that ulema were usually married to women who had *alim* fathers.

To conclude, this section was not merely a biography of the sample ulema but a prosopographical study that sheds light on several trends about the nature of and career paths in the ulema profession. In this respect, it contributed to a further understanding of the social, educational, and professional characteristics of the ulema with a special focus on those holding official Ilmiye posts in the nineteenth century.

6

Ulema in the Context of Everyday Social Life[1]

There were different groups that undertook the role of mediator between the rulers and the ruled at diverse times and under diverse conditions in the Ottoman Empire. These intermediary elites were great potential allies of the rulers and were placed in centers of political and social power, especially in provincial areas of the empire. These intermediary elites fulfilled important functions in providing public order in the Ottoman Empire. According to Albert Hourani, three groups in the nineteenth century undertook the role of mediation to maintain public order and provide the obedience of subjects to the center.[2] The first were leaders of local garrisons. Since they had direct contact with the armed forces, the government needed them greatly. These leaders acted on the direct orders of the government. They served as both military bodies and organizations of provincial stabilization, defending the central government's interests. If the number of battalions was inadequate, the second and third groups of mediators working on behalf of the government came into the political spectrum as part of traditional actors. The second was secular notables known as *ayan*, *aghas*, or *amirs* who had their own autonomy and official, semi-governmental character. The power of these individuals and families came from political and military tradition or, for some big families, from control over the agricultural production, the possession of *malikanes*, or the supervision of the waqfs. The third group was the ulema whose power was derived from their religious position. They were well-educated scholars, muftis, and jurists and were the only group that could confer legitimacy to the government thanks to their divine knowledge and Quranic discourse.[3] In other words, the ulema's leadership did not come from the military force in contrast with the members of other ruling-class institutions. Their power rested upon just religion, which provided them with general recognition and respect.[4] In the realm of mediation, these three groups played certain roles—as leaders and intermediaries - in closing the gap between the government and the rest of the society at different times. The central government directly maintained interaction with these groups and persisted with the help of these different kinds of local, notable groups. These groups continued their legacies in administrative areas in the empire throughout the nineteenth century as a result of their mediatory function. The fundamental, rising role of the ulema as an intermediary in dispute resolutions was accompanied by the increasing reliance of government on alternatives to military force in the nineteenth century.

The maintenance of order became more significant because it played a crucial role in the imperial decision-making process of the centralized government. This process was more complex and multidimensional than the standard narratives of Ottoman historiography. This part emphasizes the Ottoman ulema's active role in maintaining order and in preserving the feeling of imperial unity during the nineteenth century. In this regard, examining the ulema and their networks provides an opportunity to understand the complexities of the relations between the state and ulema.

Undoubtedly, religion was one of the most effective factors in preserving imperial unity during the nineteenth century as in almost every period. The religious leaders were also generally one of the most influential groups in government that could affect society and had the power to mobilize the people in defense of the government. The central government continued to use the power of religion, religious leaders, and religious institutions to provide public security in provincial areas in the nineteenth century. Religious leaders and institutions contributed to public security with the following three methods: The adjudication and mediation of disputes, the building of social ties that bound society, and the establishment of common civic values.[5] Especially in the nineteenth century, the central government benefited from the support of the ulema to create togetherness among Muslims and to effectively apply its centralized administrative policies. The effect of religion that builds loyalty guided Muslim subjects to act on behalf of common interests. In this sense, the ulema class played an effective mediation role and they were a channel to reach beyond a particular, limited locality in this century. The Ottoman government used this group's powerful support to legislate its politics. The central government became more visible in the provinces thanks to the fact that the ulema provided security, order, and religious and political togetherness and played a mediatory role between the rulers and the ruled.

Although there is limited knowledge of the ulema's personal life, it is known that the ulema's responsibilities in the public sphere spanned a large area and included preaching, dispute resolution, supervising pious endowments, and providing certificates of marriage and divorce as well as acting as mediators.

These were carried out voluntarily, apart from their primary tasks relating to the educational and judicial systems. The Ottoman ulema provided public order and security especially in provincial districts with two methods. The first was acting as a mediatory power between the government and the public—that is to say, between the rulers and the ruled, in cases of public discontent with the government, as well as explaining the government's practices to the public. The second one was acting as an arbitrator between the government and provincial powers in situations when society was dissatisfied with the administration of provincial governors.

The ulema's religious prestige and the respect they commanded allowed them to provide final resolutions to conflicts in many uprisings. Therefore, the ulema was used as a government mechanism to consolidate social and religious order, especially in the peripheral territories of the empire in the nineteenth century. This significant role of the ulema in enhancing government capacity in provincial regions of the empire describes the relations between the center, provincial administrative systems, and society. The examination of the ulema's role in conflict resolution better explains the ulema at the peripheral level, especially in the late nineteenth century.

In addition, most studies about state and province relations in the Ottoman Empire describe the Ottoman central state as the most powerful authority and every province depends on the central state. Many historians agree with this classical understanding and ignore other social groups and peripheral forces in the Ottoman Empire exclusively. Until recently, previous mainstream studies have not, with a few exceptions, provided data in terms of multiple agencies and power relations between the central government and regional actors. But in the past decade, new approaches of Ottoman historians to state and province aim to criticize this understanding of state power and the position of other provincial networks. They focus on provincial society by asking new questions about the nature of the central state and the regional alliance network of the state in the Ottoman provinces. These historians enable us to study critically new insights and deeper understanding of Ottoman provincial history.[6] For instance, Abdulhamid Kırmızı is asking new questions about the relationship of capital to province and how governors actually practiced in the provinces of the Ottoman Empire. The power struggle between provincial governors and the central government was defined by Kırmızı as one of the most significant developments of the nineteenth-century Ottoman Empire. Kırmızı also arrives at a conclusion that the central government could strengthen its authority in the provinces thanks to close contact and cooperation with local powers.[7] Similarly, John Bragg asserts that the central government needed the notables' support in order to reach its provinces and consolidate state power, so the central elite strategically incorporated the notables into new institutions of the provincial government.[8] In this regard, our study aims to make new interpretations of state and society relations by uncovering broader patterns of Ottoman ulema.

Ulema as the Voice of Public

The Ottoman Empire intended to make provincial areas more accessible to the center in the context of centralization by using the support of the regional and religious powers. To extend Ottoman central authority and control over provinces, the government needed to replace limited, regional, autonomous groups with a strong, accessible government system. Therefore, long-term relationships between ruling elites and powerful provincial powers who were recognized by the central body were enhanced. For instance, the central government could not always take measures to prevent or eliminate provincial problems because it had inadequate knowledge of them.[9] The government was obliged to form alliances with provincial, respected ulema who were well-known for their mediatory performance in the provinces. In such conditions, the central government mostly relied on provincial ulema to rule the provincial centers.[10] The government consulted the ulema for access to knowledge and to provide social order. In this sense, the ulema served as a channel assuring public order. The existence of the ulema as a source of authority to reach and govern the provinces helped to increase the government's power and prestige in the countryside.

There was a constant dialogue and ongoing negotiations between administrators and religious actors because of their common interests. Government authorities directly collaborated with the ulema as a strategic partner to mobilize people, and the ulema commonly worked together as part of a larger structure of ruling elites and were involved in the processes of provincial administration in the provinces as a result of this collaboration. They served the political interests of the government, functioning as a channel of religious and political propaganda that provided security and order in Ottoman society. This mediatory role of the ulema facilitated to build up trust and close networks between the center and periphery. This mutual bargaining and cooperation between the government and the ulema continued so long as the interests of the ulema did not contradict the government's politics. If the ulema served in accordance with the government's interests or when the ulema's attitudes overlapped the government's policy, the government protected the ulema and promoted their position.[11] Namely, the ulema's power depended on adapting to and complying with the central government, particularly with respect to supporting the government and its legitimacy. In this sense, the relationship between the ulema and political rulers provided a stable community life in rural regions.[12]

The Ottoman ulema were an effective channel for delivering public complaints to the central government in the nineteenth century. The ulema became the representatives of public opinion and spokesmen of communities before the center, and they informed the central government about important social and political events occurring in their regions in this century. As an important mediatory power, the ulema expressed the needs of the society to the government, and they enhanced the voices of the empire's subjects. The region's order and discipline, the maintenance of provincial life in political matters, and the fulfillment of social obligations were provided by the ulema. The central government expected them to report on the general situation of the region, on the wishes of society, and on the activities of provincial officials in their provinces. Therefore, they kept records of citizens' wishes and complaints vis-à-vis provincial rulers and sometimes made recommendations with respect to the administrative rules. In this regard, they were a voice of the people on many social and political subjects and shaped the movement and thought of the government. Letters sent by the ulema to the center were taken into account by the government more so than the letters of ordinary people.[13] In other words, the ulema's wishes and recommendations were more powerful than those of other institutions and officers of government when it came to the fulfillment of the public's requests from government authorities.

Ulema were often used as mediators by provincial individuals and the central government in two respects. First, the requests of the people on the government and those of the government on the people were conveyed with the help of the ulema. For instance, the central government sometimes met with the ulema and gave them information on government policies in order that they inform the public about government politics. In addition, the government received information about provincial problems and the demands of the community at these meetings. For instance, Kazasker Yusuf Efendi gathered together the respected ulema of Kosova in a government office in 1903, and he relayed information on the current political and ideological thinking of the central government to the ulema.[14] In another meeting between the ulema and central government officials, the ulema delivered a demand of society about the need to establish modern schools (*İdadi*, *Rüşdiye*, and *İbtidai*). The individuals of the

Erzincan district of the empire needed modern schools and news of their desire reached the central government via the ulema. In the end, the government started to establish modern schools in Erzincan in 1896.[15] In this respect, the ulema was used to convey the messages of the central authority to provincial people and the messages of provincial people to the government in the nineteenth century. This relation constituted the network of the center with peripheral regions. Thanks to this mediatory role between provincial people and central government, the ulema increased their influence over society.

Second, the ulema mediated with provincial administrators and private individuals to solve the problems society had with the provincial administrators. They contributed to providing suitable relations among subjects and to protecting the image of the government from bad politics and habits of provincial administrators. In this sense, the Ottoman ulema were responsible for investigating oppression, corruption, and irregularities made by provincial officials in the provinces in which they lived. The ulema reported to the center about bad conditions on the periphery and acted in opposition to problems in the peripheral administration. Although there was not a sufficient bureaucratic government mechanism to supervise government officials' activities, especially in provincial areas, the provincial ulema acted as the government's eyes, controlling those officials' behaviors and enhancing the bureaucratic structure. For instance, the ulema wrote a complaint to the Aydın governor on behalf of some merchants who sought to buy cheap figs from provincial producers but were excessively taxed. Therefore, provincial farmers suffered great economic losses. The ulema of Aydın expected immediate help from the Aydın governor to resolve this issue.[16] Similarly, Mufti Abdüllatif Efendi informed the central government about the high taxation implemented by local officials in the Basra district. After the mufti's letter reached Istanbul, the officials who were forcibly collecting these high taxes were dismissed by the central government. Another similar example concerning the ulema's role as an inspector in public affairs came from the ulema of Palestine which complained to the Interior Ministry that government officials Rıfat and his brother Süleyman Efendi were persecuting the provincial people and acting illegally.[17] In a similar example, the Isparta *müderris* complained to the Ministry of Justice about the hateful words of Sedad Efendi, the chief justice of the criminal courts of Isparta that disturbed the peace in the region.[18] In another example, the ulema from Damascus complained to the Bab-ı Ali about consular agents of the Persian government that had attempted to attack the purity of the honorable women of Damascus and had brought prostitutes from Iran to Damascus.[19]

Another example was a compliant letter of provincial ulema about the governor of Mecca and Medina who had violated order and stability. The respected ulema in Mecca and Medina (Kadı, İmam, Müezzin, and Mufti) complained to the palace about the maladministration of the governor, Şevket Paşa. The crimes of Şevket Paşa were that he beat people and did not pay the salaries of officers. The ulema also informed the center that Şevket Paşa had imprisoned people in spite of having no such legal right. Also, he did not publicly announce the auctions of goods belonging to the waqfs and he gave tenders to people of his choosing. The prices set by Şevket Paşa on real estate and households belonging to the foundations were too exorbitant. Therefore, the ulema urgently requested a solution from the government.[20] Another complaint by the ulema concerned of Halid Paşa who was a provincial administrator in Medina. The Medina ulema complained of Halid Paşa's impotence in the administration of the city. This letter of complaint mentioned that Halid Paşa reached old age and was only interested in praying all day and night instead of administering the city. The gap in the administration of Medina was managed by the major of the city Ahmed Medini, scribe Ali Musa, and commander Abdülaziz Efendi, a former Arab bandit. These three officers persecuted the provincial people. Therefore, the ulema demanded of the grand vizier that these three persecutors and Halid Paşa be dismissed immediately.[21] Although there was continuous traffic of related documents between the center and the Medina province about these cases, the archival documents do not address what happened at the final stage. However, the archival sources in the Medina event show that this case apparently reflects the need for ulema in the mediatory events of provincial life.

Social Dispute, Conflict Resolution, and Ulema

The ulema were enthusiastic advocates of the straight path *(sirat al-mustakim)* and acted as a guide to subjects under government rule. This role of the ulema was even more important in times of growing political instability and resistance. Therefore, the central government sometimes undertook initiatives to increase the number of the ulema in the provinces because the effectiveness of the ulema's words over subjects was crucial for maintaining government subject relations and creating a loyal, proper society. For this reason, the government selected highly educated *müderrises*, preachers, naibs, and muftis and sent them to every region of the empire.[22]

In fact, the Ottoman government elite adopted two strategies in response to broad, and provincial tensions. They first tried to solve these serious problems through the use of military force in areas of rebellion or conflict. The ruling elite preferred to order soldiers to suppress the opposition rather than tolerate it. However, this first plan of the Ottoman central government required adequate military and economic capacity to solve or prevent a crisis.[23] Further, military power was a coercive solution to squashing rebellions to ensure order, but this method brought about deeper moral questions among subjects. In this sense, the government did not generally use military power, both because of the bloody characteristic of military solutions and due to the inadequacy of military power. In such conditions, the government was obliged to resort to the second strategy of using intermediaries who had direct influence over the rebels to persuade rebellions. Therefore, the central government created a committee composed mostly of ulema, and they mostly suppressed the uprisings in rural regions.

There is much correspondence and written evidence of the need for the government or ulema's mediation in resolving the problems of or controlling the provinces. For instance, in one telegram sent from the Governor of Sivas, Halil Paşa, to the Grand Vizierate, he asked for immediate permission to use the ulema as arbitrators instead of using military force against the Kurdish uprising in the town of Gürün. He did not want large numbers of people to die in a conflict between rebels and military forces. Although Halil Paşa did not request troops from the central government, the government sent fifty soldiers to the region to suppress the rebellion. Moreover, the number of soldiers in the town of Gürün thus reached two hundred. The town was surrounded by fifty soldiers stationed in the mountains. With this action, the government tried to prevent Kurds living in the mountain from coming to the town and supporting the rebellion. However, Halil Paşa reported in correspondence sent to Istanbul that the ulema had the power to exercise control over the insurgents and restrain their dangerous uprisings; he proposed to suppress the revolt with the help of comprehensive networks of ulema before using the military force in the region. Halil Paşa negotiated with respected ulema and requested that they resolve the rebellion by talking with the Kurdish leaders who had initiated the rebellion. Halil Paşa insisted in his correspondence that the rebels would not listen and that if the rebellion could not be suppressed, the military force could be applied to stop the rebellion. In the end, the ulema stopped the rebellions without the need to use military power by advising rebellious Kurdish leaders.[24]

The other crucial example was an event in Kumanova district, Macedonia. According to correspondence written by the provincial governor, Ferik Şemsi Paşa, rebels in Kumanova demanded that the central government reorganize provincial administration policies. The rebels in Kumanova objected to the new administration and system of rule that accompanied the Tanzimat. The central government first thought to use military enforcement to ease the crisis but changed course and decided to use the ulema's mediation efforts to overcome the crisis in Kumanova. Military force was ineffective in this incident. In fact, the resolution of the crisis through negotiation and dialogue with the rebel groups via the ulema was a second but better option for both the government and the protestors: It meant a resolution without killing, imprisonments, and deportations. Governor Ferik Paşa requested that the ulema expedite the resolution process. The advice given to the protestors by respected ulema finished the conflict, and more dangerous uprisings in the city were prevented.[25]

In another example, the governor of Van, Tahir Paşa, informed the Interior Ministry on 7 January 1904 about crises among a group of soldiers in the Van district. According to his telegram, a group of soldiers had surrounded the house of a battalion commander at eleven thirty because of the arrest of a lieutenant. The soldiers also stated that they had been starving for two days. Tahir Paşa negotiated with Said Efendi of the ulema before events among the soldiers got worse, and Said Efendi convinced the rebel soldiers to stop the rebellion. After the soldiers took their ablutions, they retreated from the battalion commander's home and swore that they would never again make such a move. They said, "Live long my sultan!" three times and then went to their barracks.[26]

Similarly, Governor Cevdet Paşa referred to the significant mediation role of ulema in the Trablusşam event in a telegram sent to the Sublime Porte. Governor Cevdet Paşa informed the center that approximately two thousand protestors had attacked the Sharia court and then gathered in the square in front of the provincial governor's office on March 6, 1909, with the demand that the district governor *(kaymakam)* be dismissed from duty. Cevdet Paşa immediately sent a telegram to the Sublime Porte during the protests and warned Istanbul of the anger of the public. Cevdet Paşa asked for an immediate solution for suppressing the protests against the district governor. Also, he requested that military force be used to suppress this rebellion. In fact, the Sublime Porte intended to use military force to suppress the revolt rather than to meet the protestor's demands. However, the military center stated that neither infantry nor cavalry soldiers were available due to their being in training. Also, there was no gendarmerie in the town[27] because they were on duty in the provincial areas to collect taxes and track bandits. Therefore, Cevdet Paşa addressed the ulema, especially the mufti, as mediators to end the uprising, and respected ulema were invited to give advice to the protestors. In this example, the ulema had a politically conscious leadership and agreed to become a mediator between the protestors and the government and perform the reconciliation mission. Thanks to the ulema's arbitration, the protestors were persuaded and the ulema promised to deliver their requests to the Sublime Porte. Later, the ulema recommended the dismissal of the provincial governor from duty because people were filled with hatred against him. The center dismissed the provincial governor from duty, following the ulema's advice.[28]

Apart from the ulema's mediatory role in political uprisings that generally derived from discontent with provincial administrators, they also acted as mediators for problems between tribes and different groups. For instance, a commonality in telegrams sent by governors of regions in the east of the empire in those same years to the Sadaret concerned the problems of tribes living in the region, such as their not paying taxes, there not being an established order, and their continuously causing problems. For instance, the Sadaret was informed in a telegram sent by commander Said Efendi that the Peşdor tribe living near the Iranian border, in the Alan district, had established an armed force independent of the central government, which was composed of 1,500 people, and they had attacked the Ocak tribe in an attempt to destroy them. The militia of the Peşdor tribe had also captured 100 Ottoman soldiers who had gone to intervene in the events in the region. Two soldiers were killed and four were injured as a result of the conflict between soldiers and the militia of the Peşdor. The Peşdor and Ocak tribes engaged in a bloody struggle and dozens from both tribes died. After the military force of the government was suppressed by the Peşdor tribe, the Mosul governor asked an *alim*, Said Efendi of Süleymaniye, for advice on how to stop the events in the Alan region. Sheikh Said Efendi accepted the governor's request, went to Alan, and negotiated with the leader of the Peşdor tribe. As a result of the negotiation, the Peşdors ended their struggle with the Ocaks and within a few days released the soldiers that had been sent by the central government to suppress the conflict between the two tribes.[29]

In another telegram sent from Van province to the *Sadaret* in 1889, the central government was informed about the general situation of tribes in Van and the surrounding districts. According to this telegram, there were close to 4 million Persians in the provinces of Van, Hakkari, Bitlis, Mosul, Diyarbakir, Erzurum, Mamüratülaziz, and Iraq. However, the exact number of Iranians living in those regions was uncertain. Since they did not pay taxes, their population could not be calculated. Some lived in tents, dealt only with animal husbandry, and were not involved in agriculture. These people lived in the Mosul and Mardin deserts in the winter months and the Hakkari region in summer. Similarly, the Nesturis, which was one tribe in the eastern region of the empire that lived in the towns of Tiyar and Tahob in Hakkari, had not paid a tax of 260,000 piasters over thirty years. They never obeyed the rules of the government and only followed their own religious leaders. These Persian tribes had difficulties maintaining a livelihood and constantly clashed with each other.[30]

In the same region, Kurdish tribes often led disturbances and escaped to Iran to avoid punishment by the government for their improper actions. The governor warned the central government that these groups need to be settled, should be required to cultivate the land, and should pay taxes in a telegram dated 1888. The governor also recommended that the central government construct military units to prevent their escape to Iran. Because the tribes were generally good at horsemanship and marksmanship, a few battalions of troops that were more skilled than these tribes were needed in the region.[31]

Another official letter sent by Hakkari District Governor Kenan Paşa and Commander *(Orduyu Hümayun Erkanlarından Mirliva Ağası)* Abdurrahman Paşa to the Zabtiye Nezareti in 1888 informed the center about disturbance between the Nesturis and the Kurdish tribes in the Hakkari district. The Kurdish Aşuta tribe began to kill Nesturis and plunder their animals. Even though Governor Kenan Paşa had met with the leaders of these two tribes individually to end the conflict, they continued to struggle with each other. There was a possibility that the past hostilities of various tribes, would turn into violent conflict. The governor thus informed the Sadaret that central soldiers needed to be placed in this area immediately.[32]

In 1888, another document sent to the Ministry of Internal Affairs concerned the urgency of ending the disturbance between the Kurdish people and the Tiyaris. Kenan Paşa warned the ministry about hostilities between them and informed the ministry that if the conflict among the tribes in Van and its surroundings were not ended within fifteen or twenty days, the roads would close due to rainy and snowy weather in the region that would start in October. It would then be difficult to deploy soldiers.[33] Since the conflict between the Nesturis, the Tiyaris, the Kurdish people, and other tribes did not come to an end, the central government sent the Commander of the Fourth Army *(4. Orduyu Hümayun Müşiri),* Mehmed Zeki Paşa, to Hakkari from Van.[34]

Similarly, the central government used military force in a conflict during the collection of the cattle tax in the Hakkari district. The military unit was put under the order of the Hakkari district governor, Mehmed Bey because the number of Tiyarids had reached 7000 and the cattle tax for 300 animals had not been paid to the government. However, in armed conflicts between soldiers and some members of the Tiyarids, fifteen Kurds *(ekrad)* were killed and two soldiers were wounded.[35]

The common characteristic of these telegrams was the importance of providing order among the Kurdish tribes for the purpose of protecting the government. Even though governors in the regions demanded military power from the central government to suppress the conflicts in their regions, it was generally not possible. There was an insufficient number of soldiers and using the military to suppress the conflict could also lead to the death of people. Therefore, the Ottoman central elite and regional governors wanted to use religious leaders and the ulema to overcome crises among tribes and individual members of society. For instance, as the crisis grew, Sheikh Muhammad Efendi from among respected ulema in Van province was asked to mediate the conflict on July 6, 1888. According to the report, the only person who could preserve the peace without conflict was Muhammad Efendi.[36] This shows the importance of the ulema for making it possible to resolve an unending conflict without recourse to military power.

According to a report of the district governor of Zöhre in 1888, the Kurds, Christians, Tiyarids, and Nesturis in the region were armed and a battle was imminent. Another letter sent from Van province to the *Sadaret* noted that there was no public order in the Hakkari district because of problems between the Kurds and the Nesturis. The governor demanded that the central government severely punish those who were opposed to peace. The government asked for two officials to provide order. Therewith, Van governor Halil Bey went to Amediye and appealed to Sheikh Mehmed Efendi from among the ulema to suppress the crisis. Similarly, the governor of Mosul, Faik Paşa, met with Sheikh Nurullah Efendi. It was requested that Sheikh Mehmed Efendi and Sheikh Nurullah Efendi suppress the conflict between the tribes. Therefore, the sheikhs informed the Kurdish tribes that whatever happens, they should not join the war.[37] The crisis was ended with the intervention of Sheikh Mehmed Efendi and Sheikh Nurullah Efendi, and the conflict between the Tiyarids and Nesturis was quietly concluded.[38] At the end of the conflict, Mosul Governor Faik Paşa requested that the government reward the respected ulema Sheikh Mehmed Efendi and Nurullah Efendi, granting them certificates of achievement for carrying out his mediation service in Van province.[39] Shortly afterward, the sheikhs were rewarded with new ranks and civil service positions. It was further decided that the cost of all the meals of the Sheikhs' tekkes would be met by the government, and a monthly cash stipend would be given to them. Sheikh Mehmed Efendi's son, Selim Efendi, took a higher ranking *müderris* title in the government hierarchy and a wage monthly was given to him in appreciation.[40]

To sum up, these examples of revolts indicate that using ulema as mediators in the rebellions was not always the first choice of the government. Some government elites shared an agreement on using military force to suppress the rebels. Under normal circumstances, the government wanted to solve problems through the use of military power rather than resorting to the mediation or sermons of the ulema. However, the infrastructural capacities of the government, the military, and available resources to put toward increasing internal problems were limited, and the ulema filled this deficiency. When the government failed to discourage rebel attacks with military force, they sent ulema to mediate between the rebels and the central government. In this framework, the ulema was preferred by the central government as a keeper of order and a security tool in Ottoman provincial territories, filling gaps in political and military power. The position of the ulema as a political elite in the government, their mediator role between the rulers and the people, their strong moral authority, and their social influence paved the way for their respected position in the government administration. Rather than direct intervention by the central government in provincial areas, the ruling elite preferred to use provincial ulema as mediators and even as advisors to the government. This also forced the government to negotiate and interact with the ulema before implementing reform policies in the territories. This mediation on the part of the ulema needs further elaboration.

Also, the rebellions clearly showed the need for the government to develop infrastructural power, to improve relations with provincial powers, and to increase its administrative capacity vis-à-vis increasing internal threats. In this respect, the utility of the ulema as mediators in dispute resolution determined the capacity of the government at the provincial level and symbolized relations between the central government and its provincial districts. The ulema fulfilled the social and political functions of the government by acting as a mediator in these uprisings. At the same time, the mediation role of the ulema demonstrates that various areas were inaccessible to the center and that government resources were inadequate to supervise those areas. And this resulted in the increase of the ulema's power in these regions.

Conclusion

The Ottoman ulema's strongly rooted role in government practices provided the government's relations with society. They were a superior source of sovereignty that gave legitimacy to government politics in the eyes of the people. Their public statements and sermons were considered due to their strong effect over subjects, especially in the provincial territories of the empire, and central authorities resorted to them immediately. Therefore, the government reached out to the ulema in conditions and regions where the government was not effective on its own.

The process of resolving conflicts between tribes and individuals provided ulema with larger roles in emergency situations given their powerful position in society. Especially during times of crisis, the Ottoman ulema attempted to minimize the scope of the crises and helped maintain government control over subjects. This attitude of ulema contributed to increasing both their religious and authoritative prestige in the eyes of the public, which was desired by the government. The ulema transformed into the most influential figure for implanting religious order and solidarity and for keeping subjects together. As a result of these social and political duties, the ulema were empowered and gained status as useful, influential allies for the rulers of the Ottoman Empire. These positions helped the government maintain order and security in Ottoman territories. Also, the Ottoman ulema gained valuable allies in society through the task of creating Muslim subjects who were loyal and obedient to the government and thereby stabilizing and prolonging the life of the government. The Ottoman Empire's strategy concerning religion and the ulema remained essentially unchanged until the end of the Empire.

A little-known aspect of the Ottoman ulema's leadership role as a community organizer in the Muslim community shows how the ulema accessed community members and served as an informer to the center about the opinions of provincial rulers and the public via prepared reports. The central authorities benefited from such reports of the *ulema* on important subjects such as the opinions of provincial administrators about the central government, provincial revolts, and the effects of implementing new policies and administrative regulations in the districts. These reports and letters of the ulema showed that the ability of the government to govern in provincial regions had effectively increased and that the control mechanisms of the government over provincial administrations had strengthened.

To sum up, I deal with how the ulema contributed to the continuity and sustainability of the government through their unofficial mission of mediation with examples from various Anatolian regions. Taking government interests in the nineteenth century under consideration, such as its centralization programs, the ulema stood in the favor of the government, helped the government mobilize the population, and helped communities adapt to increased government authority over the provincial. The ulema provided the central government with support and encouragement in maintaining order and stability in the empire by way of acting as a mediator.

Conclusion

The purpose of this book was to embark on a comprehensive study of the social and political aspects of the Ottoman ulema in the nineteenth century. The study focused on crucial aspects of the nineteenth century Ottoman ulema, such as their educational and professional careers from the beginning of their education in a primary school until the end of their professional lives. The transformation of the professional identity of ulema in this century was explored with reference to the Şeyhülislam Office's institutional infrastructure, and the educational and professional conditions of provincial ulema. This study also systematically examined and interpreted the social origins, educational, professional, and social backgrounds, and administrative networks and relations of Ottoman ulema who lived in the late nineteenth century in the Anatolian provinces. In this regard, this book dealt with the ulema and the Ilmiye as part of a transformation process in a changing Ottoman Empire. It focused on the growing role of the ulema in society as active and skilled, educated officials of the central government in the late nineteenth century.

The central government invested a great amount of energy in the professional transformation of the Şeyhülislam Office in regard to acquiring qualified members for the newly established bureaucratic government structure as part of its centralization and institutionalization policy. In this regard, the nineteenth century saw a transformation of the professional identity of the Ilmiye members and their integration into the bureaucratic administration. The regulations introduced by the central government established a regular, comprehensive policy for all officials, including members of the Ilmiye. This policy was fully implemented through promotion and retirement laws, the remuneration system, institutional expansion, full-time paid and hierarchically organized professional officials, and formalized record keeping within the Ottoman Ilmiye hierarchy in the nineteenth century.

Ulema of Anatolian origin were on an equal professional footing with Istanbul ulema if they were educated in Istanbul madrasas. Ulema candidates who lived on the periphery of the Ottoman Empire had the same opportunities to study in a madrasa in Istanbul. After studying in their hometowns, they could continue their careers by pursuing education at high-ranking madrasas in Istanbul like Süleymaniye Madrasa. Madrasa graduates who studied in Istanbul easily obtained high-level positions in the hierarchy of the Ilmiye. There were many examples of Anatolian origin ulema who were educated in the Istanbul madrasas and rose to key positions in the Ilmiye hierarchy. Among them were such high-level posts as Süleymaniye müderris, Anatolian and Rumelia kazaskership, and even Şeyhülislam. The attainment of high-ranking posts was closely related to their level of education, skills, and proficiency throughout their careers. In this sense, the first, and one of the most important conclusions, of this study is that the educational backgrounds, not the social origins, of the ulema, determined their position in the Ilmiye hierarchy. Moreover, well-educated men were needed at a time when new, modern institutions were being established. This need for qualified people increased the importance of the ulema, who were the only educated group of the time. Therefore, other important administrative posts were also open to them, such as teacher, provincial council member, and inspector.

Furthermore, the standing of the ulema did not fall following the reorganization of madrasa education and the establishment of new modern schools to meet the growing need for trained administrative, judicial, educational, and religious personnel. On the contrary, the new models of training were accomplished upon the initiative of the ulema. Given that the ulema were embedded in the new schools and institutions, they continued to obtain advantageous positions and improved their conditions and status. In this regard, the ulema expanded its position and role in the newly created institutions and became a significant group within the new modern bureaucratic state apparatus in the nineteenth century, given the quality of their education, which lasted about twenty-five years, and the trajectories of their ensuing professional lives.

The introduction of modern schools did not prevent students from attending madrasas and did not result in the decline of the importance of madrasa education. The government could not create modern schools altogether distinct from madrasa education. Madrasa education continued to develop and expand in higher education in the nineteenth century, and the central government encouraged education in the madrasas. They retained their status as the empire's most prestigious educational institutions, continued to produce many graduates, and opened up employment opportunities for their graduates until the end of the empire.

Through a quantitative analysis of the biographies of ulema in the group found in the Meşihat Archive and Prime Ministry Ottoman Archive, this study demonstrates that the ilmiye class underwent important changes and progressed its position and role in newly created institutions toward the nineteenth century. During this period, the institutionalization of the şeyhülislam office and the employment of Ilmiye members went hand in hand. A new phase of state-building, institutionalization, and centralization—known as the Tanzimat reforms—provided many job opportunities for ulema candidates in almost every field of state bureaucracy in the nineteenth century. The ulema gradually turned into professional officials by obtaining new governmental positions and status in the organization of new judicial and educational systems. To be appointed to these bureaucratic duties, a quality madrasa education, personal merit, and the actual knowledge and abilities of the ulama were prerequisites.

After ulema candidates graduated from a madrasa, they had two options; they could be appointed to various ranked positions such as müderris, kadı, mufti, and naib or they could take on administrative posts such as being teachers in modern schools, council members, and inspectors. However, it was seen that ulema attended one of the new style schools of the late nineteenth century to obtain more prestigious and recognized career paths in the state bureaucracy. In our sample group, a significant number of ulema were encountered in the newly established schools such as *Darülfünün*, *Mekteb-i Hukuk*, *Darülmuallimin*, and *Mekteb-i Nüvvab*. After graduating from these Western-style schools, the ulema's career could expand considerably, and they could hold many positions in the modern state bureaucracy as judges and scholars.

The ulema mostly filled administrative positions due to the government's need for qualified, competent employees. Graduates could easily find jobs, especially in the fields of administration and education. In our case studies, no one indicated that they were unemployed after graduating. Most found a job within one year of graduating from a madrasa.

Madrasa education in Anatolian towns was similar in terms of stages and curricula. Books and texts studied in Istanbul and the provinces were similar. However, each madrasa had its own character and strengths, and the scientific atmosphere of Istanbul madrasas continued to attract students in the nineteenth century from throughout the empire. Therefore, there was considerable student migration to Istanbul from surrounding cities and even far away provinces such as Erzurum, Bitlis, and Van. Education at Istanbul madrasas was always an advantage in terms of launching a successful career in the Ilmiye hierarchy. However, this does not mean that Istanbul madrasas held a monopoly on winning good posts and advancement; there were many respectable, recognized madrasa centers in the provinces, such as in Sivas, Konya, and Erzurum.

Despite criticisms in the mainstream historiography that madrasas were old-fashioned and failed to integrate into the new intellectual policy of the Ottoman Empire, the curricula of Ottoman madrasas did change after the beginning of the Tanzimat in order to adapt to the new system. The personnel records of the late Ottoman ulema illustrated that the ulema succeeded in adapting to the newly established modern schools. Assumptions about the decrease in the paramount importance of madrasas and ulema in most of the current literature are linked to a decline paradigm that tends to obscure the transformation of institutions and the coexistence of old and new types and situations.

One of the most important criteria affecting the career of an *alim* was the quality of his education and intellectual merit rather than his personal relations. In practice, the ulema rose up in the Ilmiye hierarchy if they received a good education in Istanbul madrasas, regardless of whether they were of central or provincial origin. The Şeyhülislam Office generally expected ulema to complete the following four steps before receiving appointments: To graduate from a madrasa and possess a graduation certificate of service, to pass the *rüus* exam, to serve as a *mülazım* for several years (which later became a short waiting period due to the government's growing need for better- qualified personnel) in one of the bureaus of the Şeyhülislam Office, and to pass the professional exam. These recruitment standards established by the Şeyhülislam Office were required of any candidate who wished to pursue a career in the Ilmiye post. If a candidate did not meet these recruitment standards required by the Şeyhülislam, he was not appointed to the Ilmiye position. The Ilmiye members' appointment was thereby made according to their proficiency and knowledge. Examination results became the only criteria to hold a rank in the Ilmiye as part of the institutionalized government of the nineteenth century.

The professional careers of the ulema after their graduation from a madrasa were studied with reference to important professional milestones. In tracing the social history of the ulema since the 1880s, this study shed light on the development of new professional careers of the Ilmiye members. In following the professional lives of ulema, this study focused on their appointment process, their salaries and promotions, their social security and retirement benefits, their rewards, and disciplinary measures. While answering the question of what kind of professional activities the ulema performed in the nineteenth century, this study proposed that the story of the collapse of the nineteenth-century ulema is a fairy tale - they continued to be deeply involved in the political and social life of the Ottoman Empire.

This statistical analysis of the ulema made new interpretations of the entire lives of the ulema by uncovering broader patterns of their careers during this critical period in their history. The analysis of ulema from various Anatolian provinces indicates that ulema positions were open to anyone and that there was no restriction to becoming an *alim* if candidates fulfilled the basic criteria for office. The government wanted candidates to prove their capabilities and competence before being appointed, so the recruitment of ulema to the Ilmiye positions was made according to the educational quality of the candidates. Unqualified and improper candidates were eliminated from the recruitment processes. The career success of officials was directly related to their educational backgrounds.

Ulema helped to extend the central government's authority in distant regions of the empire, where its management capacity had been weak. The central government attempted to improve its control over these regions with the help of the ulema by granting them titles and giving them gifts. The ulema had deep networks in provincial communities and a profound influence on Muslim subjects. They thereby played a leading role in maintaining public order in the provinces and they became intermediaries between the state and society. They used their influence to achieve compromises, integrate different elements of society, and prevent riots, turmoil, anarchy, and conflict, thereby allowing the government to peacefully manage many conflicts within society. In this regard, the relationship between the central government and the ulema was based on mutual interest. Where the capacity of state control over rural areas is limited due to the lack of qualified bureaucrats and financial resources, the ulema played a key role in the loyalty of Muslims to the state and the maintenance of state order in provincial areas. At this point, the central government needed the ulema's support to maintain the government's existence and consolidate social order and security, so the state strategically appealed to the help of the ulema and tried to regulate society with their mediatory service. One essential function of the ulema was to help the ruling class to preserve order and security through the ulema's mediatory role in provincial places. In order to utilize the ulema's great effect on society as the religious leaders, the Ottoman ruling elite showed an inclination to cooperate with the ulema. Similarly, the ulema needed the state's protection to preserve their social status, prestige, and privileges. Therefore, a large number of ulema formed an alliance with the central state and local authorities. Under this partnership, the ruling elite obtained legitimacy and the ulema maintained their dignity and prestige in the political and social fields so long as they continued this mediatory role.

A similar situation appears to have been true for other administrative ranks. The new, developing bureaucratic procedures in the nineteenth century had wide-ranging influence over other government officials in such areas as professionalization, punishment and reward systems, and performance evaluations, examinations for graduation, appointments, and promotions. In this regard, the central government by increasing its direct control over the Ilmiye members incorporated them into the centralized state system and they became more and more intertwined with state service. During this period, the ulema continued indeed to be an important part of Ottoman society and government and they adapted to the new rules of the current bureaucratized system of the centralized state as having new career opportunities. While this newly centralized state system limited the authority and dominance of the ulema, on the other hand, it opened up new areas for the ulema with their official identities in the education, judicial and religious affairs of the state bureaucracy.

Appendices

Appendix A The Personnel Record of Mufti Nadir Cemil Efendi

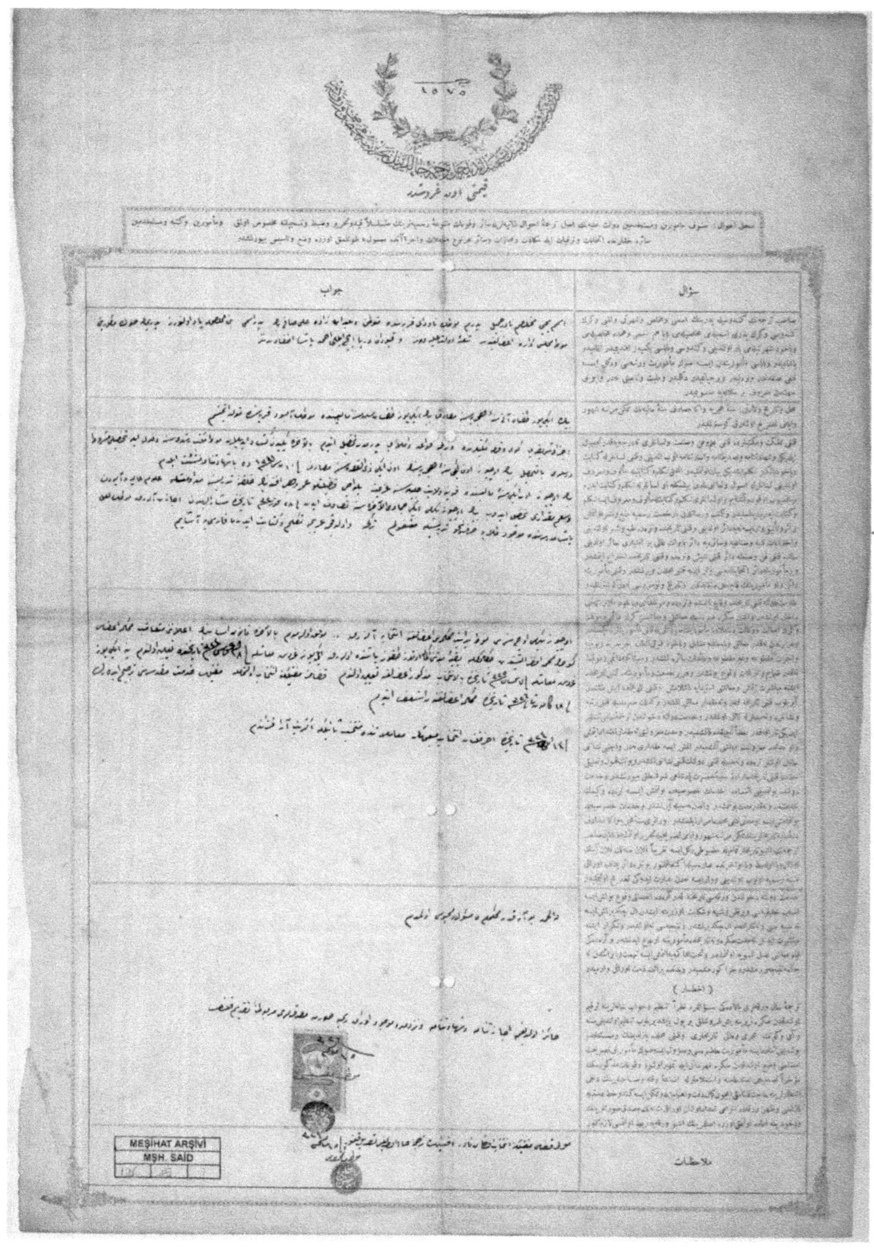

سؤال	جواب
ملاحظات	

Appendix B Transcription of the Personnel Record of Mufti Nadir Cemil Efendi

Memurin ve ketebe ve müstahdemin tescil edilecek tercüme hallerinin tahririne mahsus varakadır. Kıymeti on kuruştur.

Sicill-i ahval Sunuf-ı memurin ve müstahdemin Devlet-i aliyyenin asıl tercüme-i ahvâl zâtileriyle sair vukuât mütevvia-i resmiyelerinin mütesilsilen kayd u tahrir ve zabt ve tesciline mahsus olmak ve memurin ve ketebe ve müstahdemin-i saire haklarında intihabat ve terakkiyât ile mükâfât ve mücâzât ve sair her nev muamelât ve icraâtta ma'mul bih tutulmak üzere vaz u te'sis buyurulmuştur.

Sual Sahibi tercümenin kendisiyle pederinin ismi ve mahlası ve şöhreti ve lakabı ve gerek kendisi ve gerek pederi isimle mi mahlasla mı veya hem isim hem de mahlasla mı veyahut şöhretiyle mi yad olunduğu ve kendisi ve babası beğ midir efendi midir ağa mıdır paşa mıdır ve babası memurinden ise son memuriyet ve rütbesi ve değil ise hangi sınıftandır ve nerelidir ve ber hayat mıdır değil midir ve millet-i tâb'iyeti nedir ve ebeveyni cihetinden ma'ruf bir sülaleye mensub mudur.

Cevab İsmim Yahya mahlasım Nadir Cemil pederim Mut'un Navdalı Karyesinde mutavattın ve Abdullahzade Ali Safi Bey peder ismi ben mahlasımla yad olunuruz. Pederimin son memuriyeti Mut Meclis İdaresi azalığıdır. Tebayı devleti aliyyedeniz. Ve kapudan-ı derya İçelili Ahmed Paşa ahfadındanız.

Sual Mahal ve tarih-i velàdeti: Sene-yi Hicriyye ve ona müsâdif sene-yi maliyenin mümkün mertebe şuhur ve eyyamı tasrih olunarak gösterilmelidir.

Cevab 1296 sene-i hicriyesine müsadif 1295 senesi maliyesinde Mut'un Albor? Karyesinde tevellüt etmişim.

Sual Hangi memleket ve mekteplerde hangi ilim ve fen ve sanat ve lisanları ne dereceye kadar tahsil eylediği şehadetname ve tasdikname ve icazetname alıp almadığı ve hangi lisanlarla kitabet veyahut yalnız tekellüm ettiği beyan olunmalıdır. Ancak tekellüm ve kitabetiyle meluf ve mar'uf olmadığı lisanların usul ve lügatını adı bilmekle o lisanlarla tekellüm ve kitabet ederim denilmeyip okudum aşinayım ve o lisanları tekellüm ve kitabetle meluf ve ma'ruf ise tekellüm ve kitabet ederim denilmelidir. Ve kütüb ve resailden ba ruhsat-ı resmiye tab ve neşr olunmuş bir eser ve telifi var ise neye dair olduğu ve hangi tarihde ve nerede tab ve neşr olunduğu ve ihtiraat-I fenniye ve sanaiye ve saireye dair ba berat-I ali bir imtiyazı haiz olduğu halde hangi fen ve sanata dair hangi şeyi ve nerede ve hangi tarihde ihtira etmiştir ve bir memuriyete dair intihabnamesi var ise hangi mahalden verilmiştir ve hangi memuriyete dair ve o memuriyetin kaçıncı sınıfındandır ve tarih ve numerous nedir gösterilmelidir.

Cevab Ecza-yı şerifeyi köy ve kasaba mekteplerinde ve Türkçe kavaid ve imlayı pederimden tahsil ettim. Bilahare yeniden küşad edilen Mut mektebi rüşdiyesine duhul ile tahsili meşrut dersleri bittahsil 1312 sene-i hicriyesinin 12 Zilkadesine müsadif 10 Mayıs 1311 de ba şehadetname neşet eyledim. 1312 sene-i maliyesinde Konya vilayeti celilesine azimet Yalvacı Faziletlü Ömer Vehbi Efendinin halka-i tedrisine müdavemetle ulum-u aliye miktarı tahsil edip 1322 cemaziyelahiresine tesadüf eden 28 Temmuz 320 tarihinde müşarunileyhden icazet alarak Mut'un Laal Paşa madrasasinde mevcud talebe sarf ve nahv tedrisiyesiyle meşgulüm Türkçe ve oldukça Arapça tekellüm ve kitabet ederim. Farisiye aşinayım.

Sual Hizmet-i devlete hangi tarihte ve kaç yaşında ve nerede ve muvazzafan mı veyahut mülazemetle mi dahil olmuştur ve ondan sonra sırasıyla maaşlı ve maaşsız gerek daimi ve muvakkat ve gerek asalet ve vekalet veya ilave-i memuriyet suretleriyle hangi memuriyetlere geçmiştir ve her birinden ne kadar maaş veya maaşa mukabil veyahut fevkalade harcırah ve yevmiye ve ücret-i maktua ve gayr-i maktua ve aidat-ı saire almıştır muayyen netice daimi ve muvakkat ne kadar zamayim ve tenzilat vuku bulmuştur ve her bir hizmet-i memuriyette hangitarihte işine mübaşeret etmiş ve maaşını istifaya başlamış ve hangi tarihte iş başından ayrılıp ve hangi tarihe kadar ve ne mikdar maaş almıştır ve kezalik sırasıyla hangi rütbe ve nişanlara ve ne sebeplerle nail olmuştur ve hizmet-i devlete duhulünden tercüme-i hâlini tanzim eylediği tarihe kadar bazen açıkta kalmış mıdır ve müddet-i ma'zuliyeti ne mikdar imtidâd etmiş ve o müddette ma'zuliyet maaşı almış mıdır almış ise mikdarı nedir ve ecnebi nişânını hamil olanlar nerede ve ne sebeple devletin ve hangi nişanını almıştır ve bunun kabul ve taliki hakkında hangi tarihte irâde-i seniyye—i hazret-i padişâhı şeref müteallik buyurulmuştur ve hizmet-i devlette bulunmadığı esnada hidemat-ı hususiyede bulunmuş ise nerede ve kimin hizmetinde ve ne kadar hizmette bulunmuştur ve ondan ne sebeple ayrılmıştır ve hidemat-ı hususiyede bulunmamış ise o müddeti hangi mahalde imrar eylemiştir Buraları sene-yi hicriye ve ona müsadif sene-i maliye tarihlerinin mümkün mertebe şuhur ve eyyamı tasrihiyle tahrir olunmalıdır şayet sahib-i tercümenin işbu tarihler tamamıyla mazbutu değil ise takriben falan senenin falan ayının evail veya evasıt veya avahirinde ibaresiyle iktifa kılınır Bunlara dair yedinde evrak—ı müsbite-i resmiye olup olmadığı ve var ise neden ibaret idüği tasrih olunmalıdır.

Cevab 1323 senesi Mut’un bidayet mahkemesi azalığına intihaba alınarak muvaffak oldum. Bilahare Kanunu esasinin ilanını müteakip mahkeme azası Küçük Mehmet Efendi işinden çekilmekle bakiye-i müddetini ikmal ve 39 yaşında olarak 200 kuruş maaşla 8 Ağustos 322 tarihinde tayin olundum. Yine 200 Kuruş maaşla 7 Nisan 325 tarihinde bil-intihab mezkur azalığa tayin olundum. Kazamız müftülüğüne intihab olunmamla müftülük hizmet-i mukaddesesini tercih ederek 18 Kânunusani 326 tarihinde mahkeme azalığından istifa ettim.

14 Eylül 324 tarihinde icra kılınan inthab-ı mebusan muamelatında müntehib-i saniliğe ekseriyet ara kazandım.

Sual Hizmet-i devlete duhulünden varakası tarihine kadar arada infisali vuk’u bulmuş ise esbab-ı hakikiyesi ve bir zan ve şüphe ve şikayet üzerine işten el çektirilmiş ise ne sebebe mebni ve ne tarihte el çektirilmiştir ve neticesi ne olmuştur ve tekrar işine mübaşeret edenler ne müddet sonra ve ne tarihte memuriyetine irca’ edilmiştir ve aradaki eyyam maaşı nasıl tesviye olunmuştur ve taht-ı muhakemeye alınmış ise töhmet veya beraâtten ne hükme netice verilmiştir ve ceza görmüş müdür ve yedinde beraât-ı zimmet-i evrakı var mıdır.

(İhtar)

Tercüme-i hal varakaları baladaki suallere nazaran tanzim ve cevap hanelerine terkim olunduktan sonra ve zirine beş kuruşluk bir pul yapıştırılıp tanzim olunduğu sene ve ay ve günün hicri ve mali tarihleri ve hangi mahalde yazdırıldığının ve müstahdem bulunduğu esnada ise memuriyet-i hazırası ve ma’zul ise son memuriyeti tasrihiyle imzası vaz olunduktan sonra mühr-i zati ile temhir olunur vukuât-ı mezkurenin muahharen tashihi istidasına ve isti’lamlarla izaa-i vakte ve sahiplerinin dahi intizarlarına hacet kalmamak için kemal-i dikkat ve ihtimam ile ve mümkün ise kendi hatt-ı destiyle yazılması ve varakada envai tadad olunan evrak-ı müsbitenin musaddak suretlerinin veyahut yine iade olunmak üzere asıllarının işbu varakaya rabt olunması lazım gelir.

Cevab Lehülhamd, bu ana kadar mahkum ve mesul ve mahbus olmadım.

Mülahazat Mut Kazası Müftülüğüne intihab olunan Nadir Efendinin Tercüme-i Hal olduğu tasdik kılınır. Mut Kaymakamı Hüseyin Hilmi

Haiz olduğum icazetname ve şehadetname mevcud evrak-ı resmiye suret-i musaddakaları merbutan takdim kılındı

15 Mayıs 326
Mut Müftüsü Nadir Cemil

SOURCE MA. USAD. No: 1575. Nadir Cemil Efendi of Mut. 14 Eylül 1323/ 27 September 1907.

Appendix C Ali Avni Efendi's Certificate of Graduation from the Madrasa

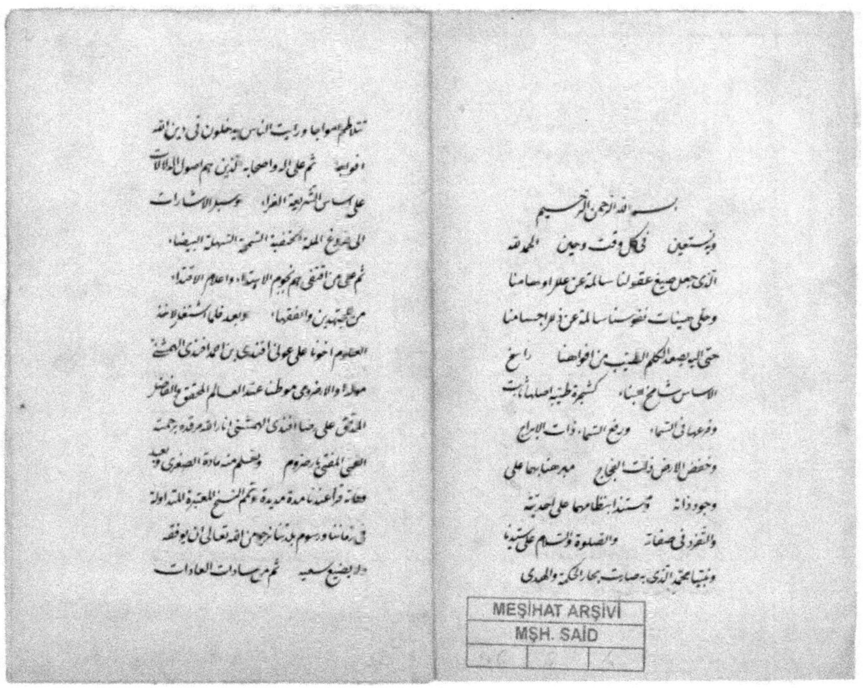

بسم الله الرحمن الرحيم
وبه نستعين في كل وقت وحين الحمد لله
الذي جعل صحيح عقولنا سالمة عن علل اوهامنا
وحلى جنبات نفوسنا سالمة عن ذرائع اجسامنا
حتى اليه يصعد الكلم الطيب من افواهنا راسخ
الاساس شامخ البناء كشجرة طيبة اصلها ثابت
وفرعها في السماء ورفع السماء ذات الابراج
وخفض الارض ذات الفجاج مبرهنا بهما على
وجود ذاته ومستدلا بنظامهما على احديته
والتفرد في صفاته والصلوة والسلام على سيدنا
ونبينا محمد الذي به صارت بحار الحكمة والهدى

متلاطمة امواجا ورايت الناس يدخلون في دين الله
افواجا ثم على آله واصحابه الذين هم اصول الدلالات
على اساس الشريعة الغراء وسبل الاشارات
الى فروع الملة الحنيفية السمحة السهلة البيضاء
ثم على من اقتفى بهم نجوم الاهتداء واعلام الاقتداء
من المجتهدين والفقهاء وبعد فلما اشتغل لاخذ
العلوم اخونا علي عوني افندي بن احمد افندي الهمشيني
مولدا والارضرومي موطنا عند العالم المحقق والفاضل
المدقق علي رضا افندي الهمشيني انار الله مرقده برحمته
العلي المفتي بارضروم وتعلم منه مادة الصغرى وبعد
معاناة قراءته مدة مديدة وتمم النسخ المعتبرة المتداولة
في زماننا ورسوم بلدنا نرجو من الله تعالى ان يوفقه
[illegible] بتضييع سعيه ثم من سادات العادات

الحاج علي عن شيخ الحرمين شيخ جميع بلاد المسلمين
وخاتم حفاظ المحدثين الشيخ عبد الله بن سالم البصري
ثم المكي اسكنه الله تعالى فراديس جنانه ورزقه
حلل غفرانه ثم ان ذلك المولى المغفور له اخذه بوسائط
عن الحسين النخلي وهو قد اخذها عن جمال الدين
محمود وهو عن جلال الدواني وهو عن السيد
الشريف الجرجاني عليه رحمة واهب الاماني وهو
عن الابهري وعن مبارك شاه وهو عن قطب الدين
الرازي وهو عن العلامة الشيرازي وهو
عن الكاتب القزويني وهو عن الامام فخر الدين الرازي
وهو عن الامام ابي حامد محمد الغزالي وهو عن امام
الحرمين وهو عن ابي الطيب بن محمد بن سليمان
الصعلوكي وهو عن ابراهيم المروزي وهو عن ابي

العباس احمد وهو عن ابي القاسم عثمان وهو
عن ابي ابراهيم بن اسمعيل وهو عن ابي عبد الله محمد بن
ادريس الشافعي وهو عن محمد بن حسن الشيباني
وهو عن امام الائمة سراج الملة والامة ابي حنيفة
وهو عن حماد وهو عن ابراهيم النخعي وهو عن
علقمة وهو عن ابي عبد الرحمن بن الاسود بن يزيد
وابي عبد الرحمن عبد الله ابن حبيب والاولان
عن عبد الله بن مسعود رضي الله تعالى عنه
والثالث عن علي بن ابي طالب رضي الله تعالى
عنه وهم عن خاتم النبيين ورسول رب
العالمين صلى الله تعالى عليه وسلم
مع اله وصحبه وتابعيه اجمعين ثم اني اوصي
اولا نفسي وثانيا اياك مع جميع تلامذتي

واحبتي بما يدور عليه الفوز بسعادة الدارين ومجمع
كل خير الاولين والآخرين وامر به الله الانبياء
والمرسلين وجميع اممهم من الخواص وكافة المسلمين
وهو التقوى لا سيما غايتها لقوله تعالى يا ايها الذين
امنوا اتقوا الله حق تقاته ولا تموتن الا وانتم مسلمون
وقوله تعالى ان اكرمكم عند الله اتقيكم وقوله تعالى
ان الله مع الذين اتقوا والذين هم محسنون وذلك
انما يحصل بالتخلية والتحلية فالتخلية تطهير القلب
عن جميع الاخلاق الذميمة والخصال الردية
من الكبر والعجب والحقد والحسد والبخل وغيرها
وذلك انما يتيسر بترك شيء حبه رأس كل الخطيات
واعراضه مفتاح كل السعادات واما التحلية فاتصاف
القلب بالصفات المرضية والاخلاق الحميدة

مثل العفة والاستقامة والزهد والخشية والتواضع والجود
فغايتها تطهير القلب عما سوى الله تعالى وتحليته وتنويره
باستغراق ذكره الموصل الى وصله تعالى في الدارين
والجمع مناط هذا الشأن هو التبعية الكاملة لافضل خلق الله
عليه السلام لسانا وجنانا واركانا في الديانات والعبادات
والمعاملات فعليك الاعتصام بعزايم الكتاب والسنة
والاشتغال بالوظائف العلمية نشرا وعملا واصرف
ريعان عمرك على اكمال نفسك على العمر بقوله تعالى
عليكم انفسكم وحاسب نفسك كل يوم صباحا ومساء
وتذكر ما جاء في الاثر من استوى يوماه فهو مغبون
وتذكر ايضا ما قيل من جاوز الاربعين فلم يغلب خيره شره
فليتجهز الى النار ولكن بضاعة مال دنياك العمر
بالحديث القدسي يا دنيا اخدمي من خدمني واتعبي

SOURCE MA. USAD. no: 303. Ali Avni Efendi of Trabzon 20 Mayıs 1309/ 1 June 1893.

Appendix D Questions from Mehmet Şaban Efendi's Examination for the Position of Müderris

بسم الله الرحمن الرحيم

SOURCE MA, USAD no: 541. Hacı Mehmed Şaban Efendi of Trabzon. 2 Şaban 1332/ 26 June 1914.

Appendix E Answers Given by Mehmet Şaban Efendi During his Examination for the Position of Müderris

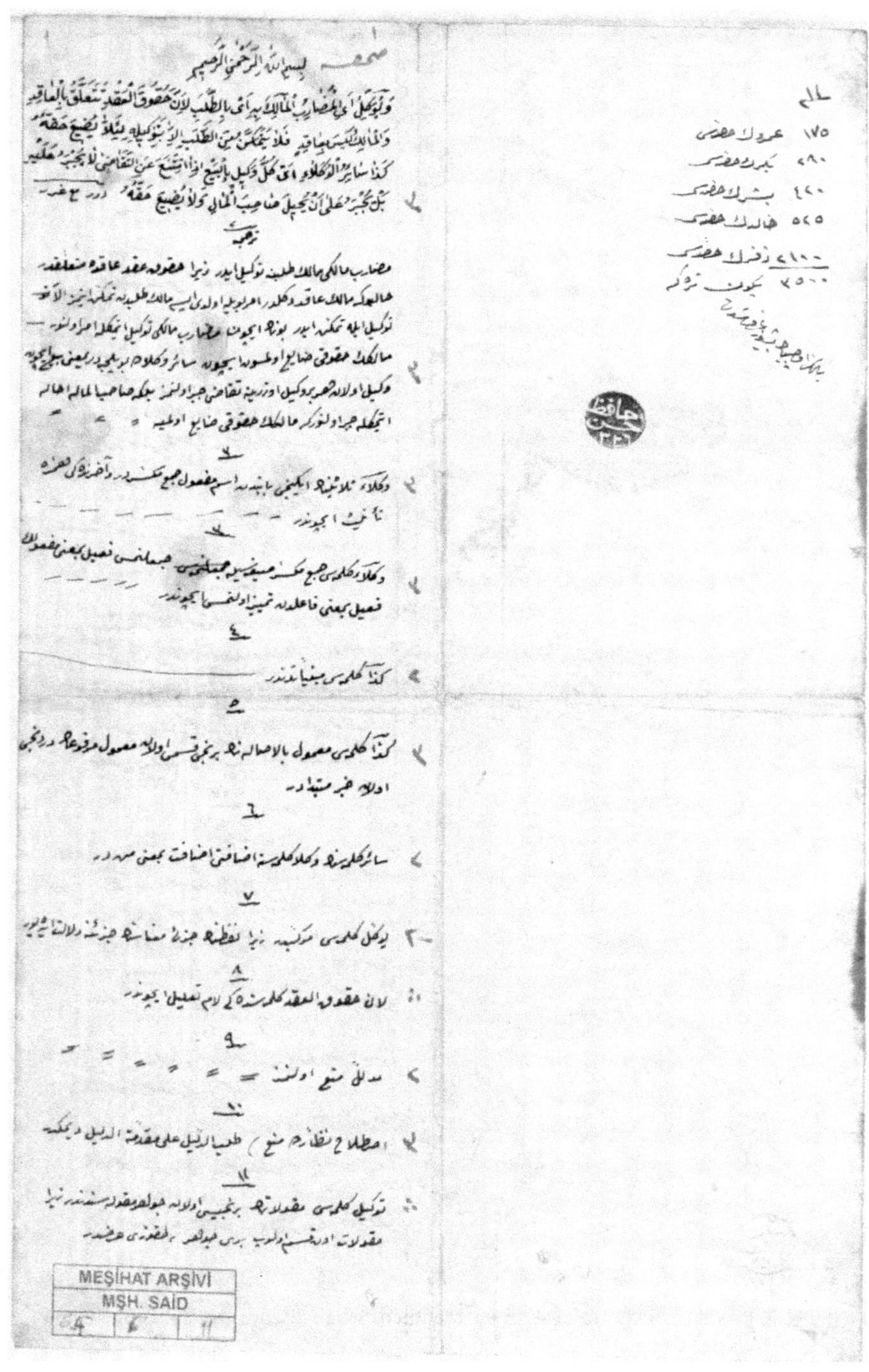

بسم الله الرحمن الرحيم

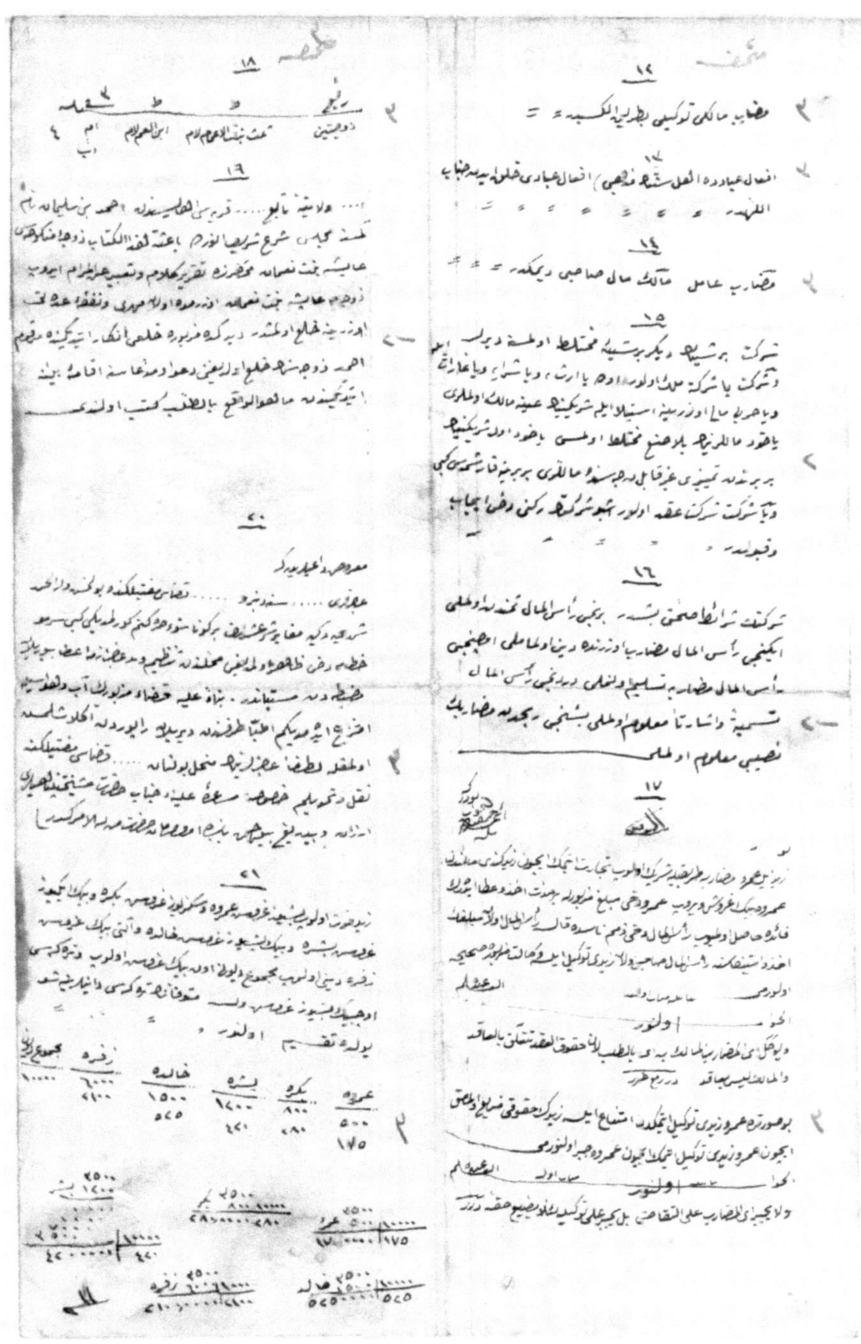

SOURCE MA, USAD no: 541. Hacı Mehmed Şaban Efendi of Trabzon. 2 Şaban 1332/ 26 June 1914.

Appendix F Naib Abdullah Efendi's Identity Card and Certificate of Graduation from the Madrasa

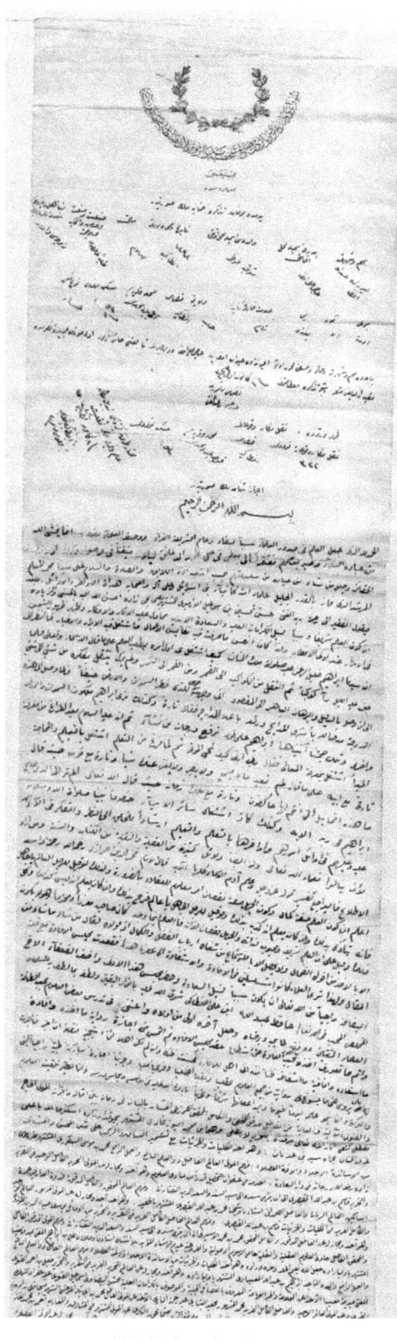

SOURCE MA. USAD. no: 939. Abdullah Efendi of Konya. 21 Temmuz 1326/ 3 August 1910.

Appendix G Questions from the Tabur İmameti Examination of Abdullah Efendi

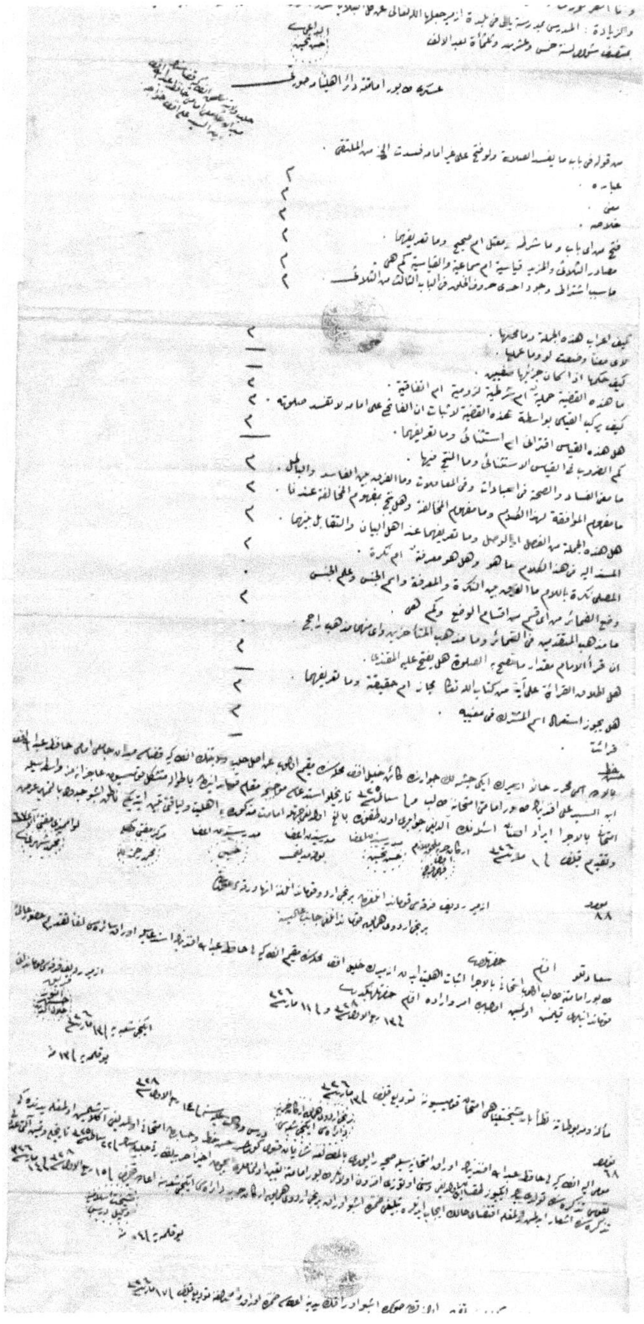

SOURCE MA. USAD. no: 939. Abdullah Efendi of Konya. 21 Temmuz 1326/ 3 August 1910.

Appendix H Abdullah Efendi's Certificate of Graduation from Taşra Mekatib-i İbtidaiye Muallimi

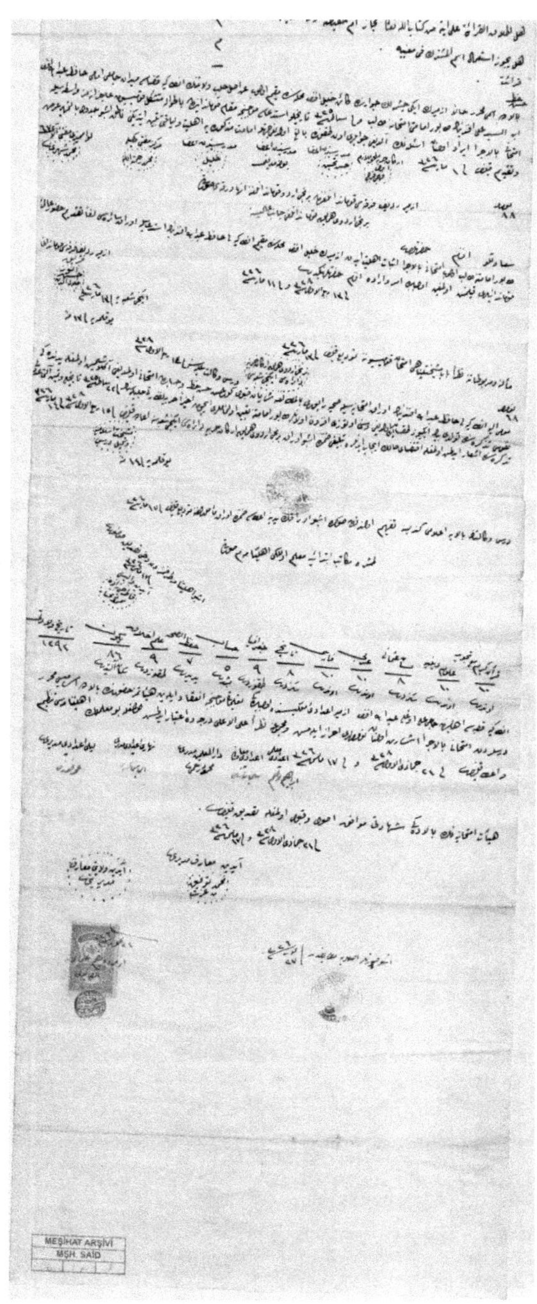

SOURCE MA. USAD. no: 939. Abdullah Efendi of Konya. 21 Temmuz 1326/ 3 August 1910.

Appendix I Recommendation Letter for Terzizade Mustafa Hulusi Efendi's Appointment as Mufti of İzmir

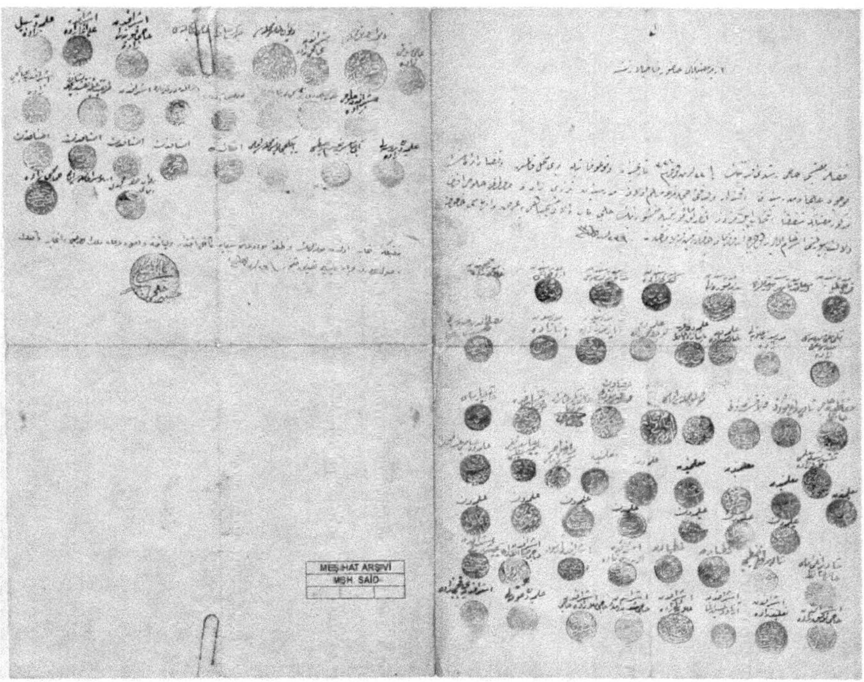
MEŞİHAT ARŞİVİ
MŞH. SAİD

SOURCE MA. USAD. no: 1207, Mustafa Hulusi Efendi of Aydın. 31 Kanunusani 1307/ 31 January 1921.

Appendix J Documentation of the Specialized Madrasa Degrees of Mehmed Tevfik Efendi

SOURCE MA. USAD. no: 169. Mehmed Tevfik Efendi of Ankara. 15 Safer 1310/ 8 September 1892.

Appendix K Table of the Salaries of the Ilmiye Members in the District of Gediz

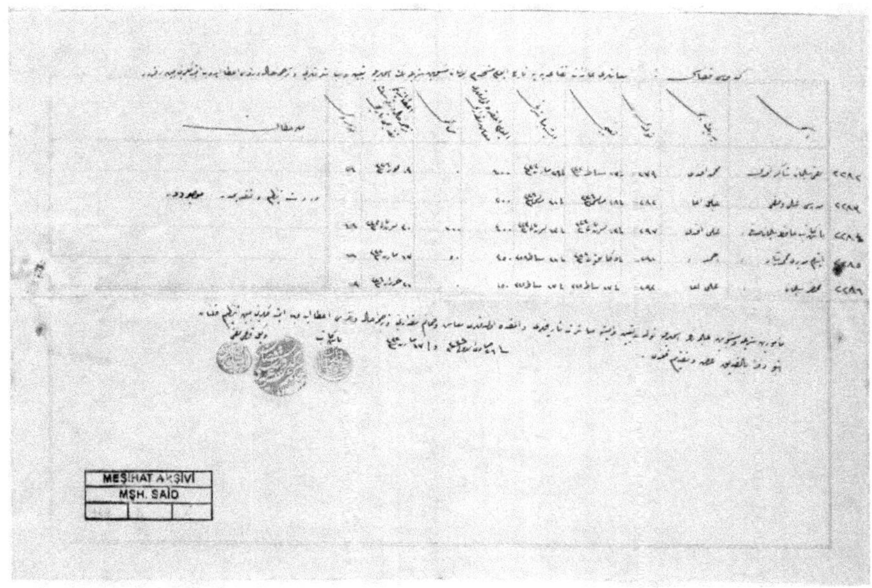

MEŞİHAT ARŞİVİ
MŞH. SAİD

SOURCE MA. USAD. no: 2282. Süleyman Şakir Efendi of Hüdavendigar. 17 Temmuz 1326/ 30 July 1910.

Appendix L Mahmud Esad Efendi's Examination for the Position of Naibship

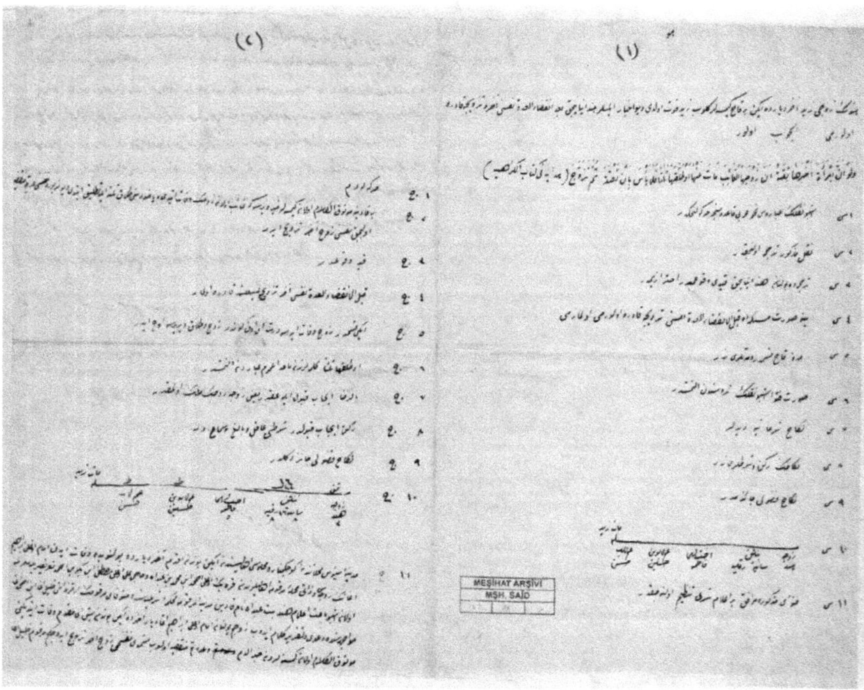
MEŞİHAT ARŞİVİ
MŞH. SAİD

SOURCE MA. USAD. No: 2385 Mahmud Efendi of Sivas 1 Mart 1327/ 14 March 1911

Appendix M Mahmud Esad Efendi's Examination for the Position of Naibship

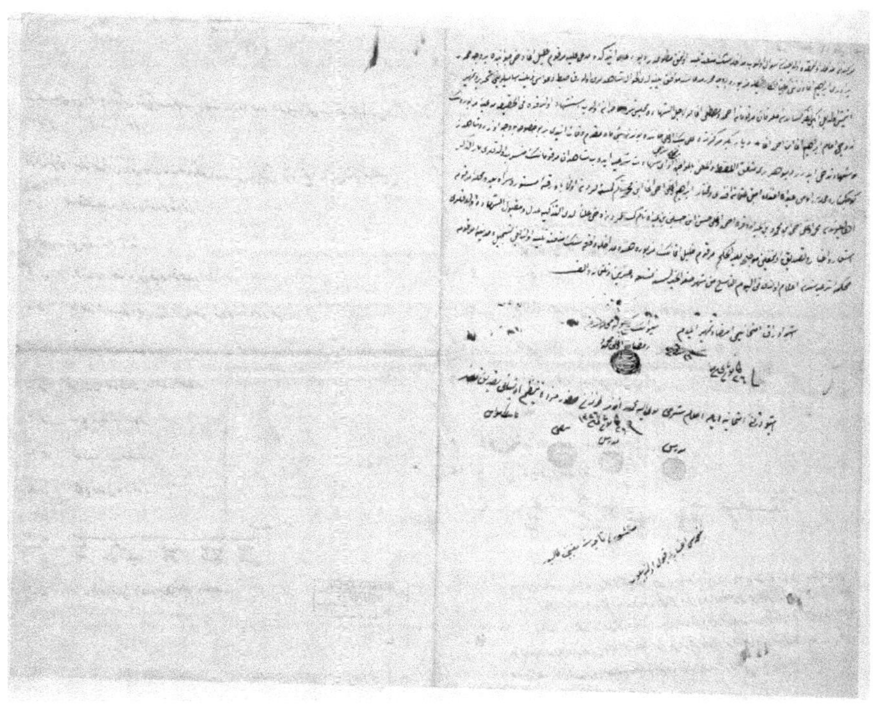

SOURCE MA. USAD. No: 2385 Mahmud Efendi of Sivas 1 Mart 1327/ 14 March 1911

Appendix N Score of Mehmed Efendi's Examination for Appointment as Imam of Hacı Ali Mosque

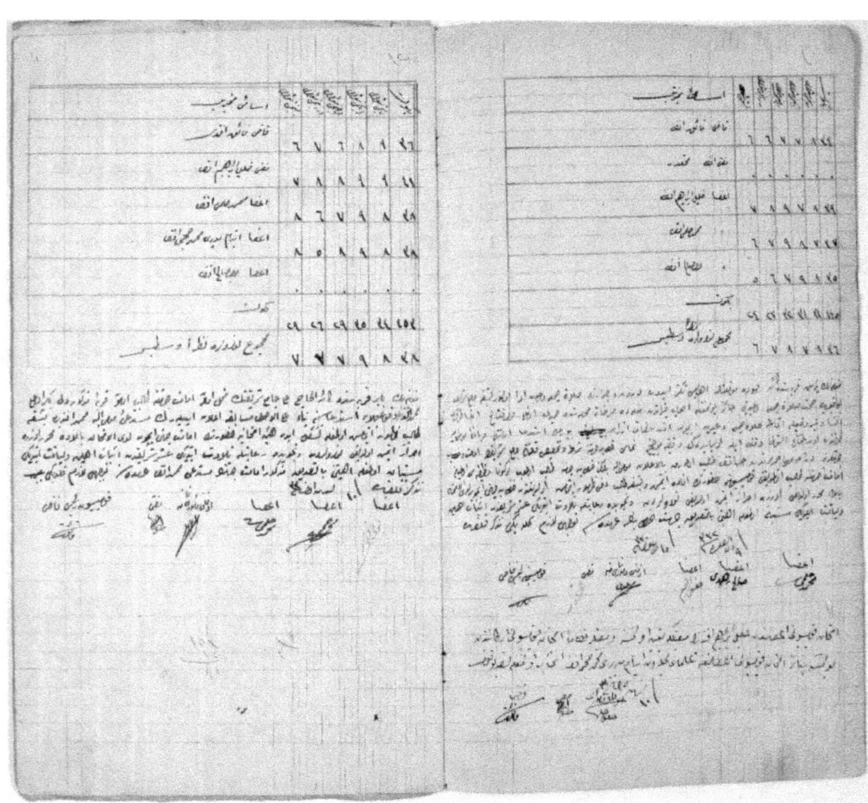

SOURCE BOA. EV. d. 39419/ 5. 29 Mayıs 1333/ 29 May 1917.

Appendix O Müderris and Madrasa Student

SOURCE BOA. FTG 1212/1

Appendix P Müderris and Madrasa Student

SOURCE BOA. FTG 1985/1

Notes

1 Introduction: The Decline Paradigm of the Ulema Reconsidered

1 For the definition of the term "ulema," see Mehmet İpşirli, "İlmiye," in *TDV İslam Ansiklopedisi* 22 (Istanbul: Türkiye Diyanet Vakfı Yayınları, 2000), 141–145. Ulema, the Turkish spelling of the Arabic term "ulama," is the plural form of *alim* (scholar) deriving from the Arabic root *ilm* (scientific knowledge) and means "to know or to be aware of." The term generally refers to a scholar of the religious sciences such as Islamic law, hadiths, and Qur'anic verses. The ulema include those who studied in madrasas and received graduation certificates after proving their ability as well as those who were appointed as kadıs, mosque functionaries, *müderrises*, judges, and jurisconsults in the cadres of the Ottoman state.

2 Amit Bein, *Ottoman Ulema, Turkish Republic: Agents of Change and Guardians of Tradition* (California: Stanford University Press, 2011), 1.

3 Mehmet İpşirli, "Osmanlı'da İlmiyeye Dair Çalışmalar Üzerine Gözlemler," in *Dünden Bugüne Osmanlı Araştırmaları: Tesbitler, Problemler, Teklifler*, eds. Ali Akyıldız, Ş. Tufan Buzpınar, and Mustafa Sinanoğlu, (Istanbul: İsam Yayınları, 2007), 270; Fahri Unan, "Osmanlı Resmi Düşüncesinin İlmiye Tariki İçindeki Etkileri: Patronaj İlişkileri," *Türk Yurdu* 45, XI (1991): 7.

4 Roderic H. Davison, *Reform in the Ottoman Empire, 1856-1876* (Princeton: Princeton University Press, 1963), 67–69; Avigdor Levy, "The Ottoman Ulema and the Military Reforms of Sultan Mahmud II," *Asian and African Studies* 7, (1971): 13–39.

5 For a further elaboration of the decline paradigm of Ottoman ulema in the literature, see, for example, Stanford J. Shaw and Ezel Kural Shaw, *History of the Ottoman Empire and Modern Turkey* (Cambridge: Cambridge University Press, 1976); Bernard Lewis, *The Emergence of Modern Turkey* (London: Oxford University Press, 1968); Carter V. Findley, *Bureaucratic Reform in the Ottoman Empire: The Sublime Porte, 1789-1922* (Princeton: Princeton University Press, 1980); Niyazi Berkes, *The Development of Secularism in Turkey* (Montreal: McGill University Press, 1964); Feroz Ahmad, *The Making of Modern Turkey* (London: Routledge, 1993); Eric J. Zürcher, *Turkey: A Modern History* (London: I. B. Tauris, 1993); Roderic H. Davison, *Reform in the Ottoman Empire, 1856-1876* (New Jersey: Princeton University Press, 1963) İsmail Hakkı Uzunçarşılı and Enver Ziya Karal, *Osmanlı Tarihi*, 8 vols.

(Ankara: Türk Tarih Kurumu Yayınları, 1972). For criticism of the decline theory, see Cemal Kafadar, "The Question of Ottoman Decline," *Harvard Middle Eastern and Islamic Review* 4, 1–2 (1997–98): 30–75.

6 For an example of a proponent of external dynamics, see Bernard Lewis, *Emergence of Modern Turkey*, 125. "The reforms were basically the forcible imposition, on a Muslim country, of practices and procedures derived from Europe. . ."

7 İlber Ortaylı, *İmparatorluğun En Uzun Yüzyılı* (Istanbul: İletişim Yayınları, 2003).

8 For the theoritical framework of bureaucracy in Weberian terms see Max Weber, *Economy and Society: An Outline of Interpretive Sociology*, ed. Guenther Roth and Claus Wittich, 2 vols., New York: Bedminster Press, 1968. Bureaucracy definition: *"Bureaucracy is an organizational structure that is characterized by many rules, standardized processes, procedures and requirements, number of desks, meticulous division of labor and responsibility, clear hierarchies and professional, almost impersonal interactions between employees."*

9 For the concept of professionalization, see the characteristics of an ideal bureaucracy in Weber's view. *"The professionalization is a social process that handled with an ideal bureaucracy based on division of work, hierarchy, written documents or records, impersonality, rationality, neutrality, and a career system."* Weber, *Economy and Society: An Outline of Interpretive Sociology.*

10 Uriel Heyd "The Ottoman Ulema and Modernization in time of Selim III and Mahmud II," in *The Modern Middle East*, eds. Albert Hourani, Philip Khoury, and Mary Wilson (London: I. B. Tauris, 2014): 39–53.

11 Ibid., 68.

12 Ibid., 33–36.

13 Arnold H. Green, *The Tunisian Ulama 1873-1915: Social Structure and Response to Ideological Currents* (Leiden: Brill, 1978), 12–13.

14 Moshe Maoz, "The Ulama and the Process of Modernization in Syria during the mid-Nineteenth Century," in *The Ulama in Modern History. Studies in Memory of Professor Uriel Heyd*, ed. Gabriel Baer (Jerusalem: Israel Oriental Society, 1971), 83–84.

15 Levy, "The Ottoman Ulema and the Military Reforms of Sultan Mahmud II,": 13.

16 Ibid., 13.

17 Lewis, *The Emergence of Modern Turkey*, 122-125. Bernard Lewis begins the book with the sentence: "The theme of this book is the emergence of a new Turkey from the decay of the old." This sentence is a summary of the author's approach throughout the book visibly the Ottoman Empire in the nineteenth century.

18 Berkes, *The Development of Secularism in Turkey*, 169.

19 Ibid., 169.

20 Ibid., 236.

21 Ibid., 16.

22 Richard L. Chambers, "The Ottoman Ulama and the Tanzimat," in *Scholars Saints and Sufis: Muslim Religious Institutions Since 1500*, ed. Nikki R. Keddie (Berkeley: University of California Press, 1978), 33–46.

23 Ibid., 33–46.

24 Nikki Keddie, "The Roots of the Ulama's Power in Modern Iran," in *Scholars Saints and Sufis: Muslim Religious Institutions Since 1500*, ed. Nikki R. Keddie (Berkeley: University of California Press, 1978), 229.

25 Shaw and Shaw, *History of the Ottoman Empire and Modern Turkey*, 282.

26 Findley, *Bureaucratic Reform in the Ottoman Empire: The Sublime Porte, 1789-1922*, 55.

27 Ibid., 54.

28 Ibid.

29 Mehmet İpşirli, "II. Mahmud Döneminde Vakıfların İdaresi," in *Sultan II. Mahmut ve Reformları Semineri* (Istanbul: İstanbul Üniversitesi Edebiyat Fakültesi, 1990): 49–57.

30 Ahmet Cihan, *Reform Çağında Osmanlı İlmiye Sınıfı* (Istanbul: Birey Yayınları, 2004), 13–15.

31 Ibid., 14.

32 Ibid., 25.

33 Bein, *Ottoman Ulema, Turkish Republic: Agents of Change and Guardians of Tradition.*

34 Susan Gunasti, *The Qur'an Between the Ottoman Empire and the Turkish Republic : An Exegetical Tradition* (Routledge: Routledge Studies), 2019.

35 M. Alper Yalçınkaya, *Learned Patriots : Debating Science, State, and Society in the Nineteenth- Century Ottoman Empire*, (Chicago: The University of Chicago Press, 2015).

36 Karon D. Salch, Şeyhülislam *and the Tanzimat*, PhD diss., (Montreal: McGill University, August 1980), viii; Ümit Cizre Sakallıoğlu, "Parameters and Strategies of Islam-State Interaction in Republican Turkey," *International Journal of Middle East Studies* 28, no. 2 (May 1996): 232.

37 Keddie, "The Roots of the Ulama's Power in Modern Iran," 171.

38 See Abdurrahman Atçıl, *Scholars and Sultans in the Early Modern Ottoman Empire* (Cambridge: Cambridge University Press, 2017).

39 See Meir Hatina, *"Ulama", Politics, and the Public Sphere: An Egyptian Perspective* (Salt Lake City: The University of Utah Press, 2010).

40 Ortaylı, *İmparatorluğun En Uzun Yüzyılı*, 119; Ercüment Kuran and Mümtazer Türköne, *Türkiye'nin Batılılaşması ve Milli Meseleler* (Ankara: Türkiye Diyanet Vakfı Yayınları, 2007), 3.

41 Ortaylı, *İmpratorluğun En Uzun Yüzyılı*, 119.

42 David Kushner, "The Place of the Ulema in the Ottoman Empire During the Age of Reform (1839-1918)," *Turcica* 19 (1987): 70.

43 Ibid., 72–73.

44 Halil İbrahim Erbay, *Teaching and Learning in the* Madrasas *of Istanbul During the Late Ottoman Period*, PhD diss., (London: University of London School of Oriental and African Studies, 2009).

45 Jun Akiba, "From Kadi to Naib: Reorganization of the Ottoman Sharia Judiciary in the Tanzimat Period," in *Frontiers of Ottoman Studies: State, Province, and the West*, eds. Colin Imber and Keiko Kiyotaki (London: I. B. Tauris, 2005); Jun Akiba, "A New School for Qadis: Education of the Sharia Judges in the Late Ottoman Empire," *Turcica* 35 (2003).

46 Kushner, "The Place of the Ulema in the Ottoman Empire During the Age of Reform (1839-1918)," 55; Levy, "The Ottoman Ulema and the Military Reforms of Sultan Mahmud II," 13–39.

47 For an example of the degeneration of the ulema and the madrasas, see Sir Hamilton Gibb and Harold Bowen, *Islamic Society and the West: A Study of the Impact of Western Civilization on Moslem Culture in the Near East* (London: Oxford University Press, 1950), 105–13.

48 See Esad Efendi, *Vak'a-nüvis Es'ad Efendi Tarihi, 1237-1241/1821-1826/ Sahhaflar Şeyhi-Zade Seyyid Mehmed Es'ad Efendi; Bahir Efendi'nin zeyl ve ilaveleriyle*, Ziya Yılmazer, ed., (Istanbul: Osmanlı Araştırmaları Vakfı, 2000); Mehmed Esad Efendi, *Üss-i Zafer: Yeniçeriliğin Kaldırılmasına Dair*, ed. Mehmet Arslan (Istanbul: Kitabevi, 2005).

2 The Re-organization of the Şeyhülislam Office *(*1826–1914*)*

1 The administrative system of the Ottoman Empire in the classical period consisted of three categories: the Ilmiye, seyfiye, and kalemiye. The Ilmiye was an important group constituting the Ottoman bureaucratic system together with the military group known as the seyfiye and the bureaucrat group, the kalemiye. The Ilmiye class, consisting of the madrasa-trained ulema, held special positions within the society such as the şeyhülislam, sharia court judges (kadı, naib), jurisconsults (mufti), chief of the prophet's descendants (nakibuleşraf), chief justice (kazasker), and madrasa teacher (müderris).

2 Özkul, *Gelenek ve Modernite Arasında Osmanlı Uleması*, 22–23.

3 Cengiz Kırlı, "Kahvehaneler ve Hafiyeler: 19. Yüzyıl Ortalarında Osmanlı'da Sosyal Kontrol," in *Tanzimat Değişim Sürecinde Osmanlı İmparatorluğu*, eds. Halil İnalcık and Mehmet Seyitdanlıoğlu (Ankara: Phoenix Yayınevi, 2006), 426.

4 BOA. İ. DH. 1267/ 99649. 13 Şubat 1307/ 25 February 1892.

5 *Düstur*, Tertib-i Sani, VII, 541–546.

6 BOA. Y. PRK. DH. 10/ 98. 14 Zilhicce 1316/ 25 April 1899; BOA. BEO. 2563/192165. 13 Nisan 1321/ 26 April 1905.
7 BOA. İ. DH. 1267/ 99649. 13 Şubat 1307/ 25 February 1892.
8 BOA. Y. PRK. DH. 10/ 98. 14 Zilhicce 1316/ 25 April 1899.
9 BOA. C. ADL. 13/ 847. 29 Cemaziyelevvel 1268/ 21 March 1852.
10 BOA. A. MKT. MVL. 20/ 58. 30 Zilkade 1265/ 17 October 1849.
11 BOA. İ. DH. 285/ 17944. 24 Rabiyülevvel 1270/ 25 December 1853.
12 BOA. İ. MVL. 293/ 11821. 3 Rabiyülahir 1270/ 3 January 1854.
13 BOA. MF. MKT. 449/ 36. 11 Muharrem 1317/ 22 May 1899.
14 François Georgeon, *Sultan Abdülhamid*, (trans.) Ali Berktay, (Istanbul: İletişim Yayınları, 2012), 274; Süleyman Tevfik Özzorluoğlu, *Abdülhamid'in Cinci Hocası Şeyh Ebü'l-Hüda* (Istanbul: Yeditepe Yayınları, 2011), 53.
15 BOA. BEO. 612/ 45881. 6 Zilkade 1312/ 1 May 1895.
16 All ordinary Muslims attended the Friday prayer in their neighbor mosques. The khatib gave the weekly sermon under the leadership of the imam who was the principal religious officer of the mosque.
17 BOA. DH. SYS. 52/ 4. 7 Rabiyülahir 1330/ 26 March 1912.
18 Uzunçarşılı, *Osmanlı İlmiye Merkez Teşkilatı'nda Reform*, 186. To preach to the people in places like the mosque and prayer rooms, to show them the right way to live, to warn them by informing them about religious and worldly matters, and to inform them of the orders and prohibitions of Allah is known as the homily (sermon), and the person fulfilling this service is called the preacher *(vaiz)*.
19 BOA. İ. DUİT. 20/ 53. 24 Cemaziyelevvel 1337/ 25 February 1919.
20 BOA. İ. MMS. 183/ 7. 13 Cemaziyelevvel 1332/ 9 April 1914.
21 BOA. Y. EE. 5/ 19. 18 Şevval 1307/ 7 June 1890.
22 BOA. DH. SYS. 52/ 4. 7 Rabiyülahir 1330/ 26 March 1912; BOA. Y. PRK. UM 10/28. 1 Zilhicce 1304/ 21 August 1887
23 BOA. DH. SYS. 52/ 4, 18. 7 Rabiyyülahir 1330/ 26 March 1912.
24 Fatwas were issued by the ulema in response to the questions of private individuals or official institutions to resolve their day-to-day problems and important issues of the moment.
25 Donald Eugene Smith, *Religion and Political Modernization* (New Haven: Yale University Press, 1974), 70.
26 BOA. A.} MKT. NZD 142/ 74. 20 Receb 1271/ 8 April 1855; BOA. MV. 234/ 97. 12 Cemaziyelevvel 1332/ 8 April 1914; BOA. DH. SYS. 52/ 4. 7 Rabiyyülahir 1330/ 26 March 1912.
27 BOA. DH. SYS. 52/ 4. 7 Rabiyyülahir 1330/ 26 March 1912.
28 BOA. DH.SYS 52/ 4, 15. 7 Rabiyyülahir 1330/ 26 March 1912
29 Yurdakul, *Osmanlı İlmiye Merkez Teşkilatı'nda Reform*, 29.

30 *Fetvahane* is the fatwa department of legal consultation for private applications. And *Fetva Emini* is the title of the director of the *Fetva Kalemi* in the Şeyhülislam Office and was responsible for controlling the correspondence in the *fetva* room.

31 Yurdakul, *Osmanlı İlmiye Merkez Teşkilatı'nda Reform*, 32.

32 Uriel Heyd, "Some Aspects of the Ottoman Fetva," *School of Oriental and African Studies, University of London Bulletin* 32, 1 (1969): 46.

33 BOA. İ. DUİT. 90/ 64. 10 Cemaziyelahir 1335/ 3 April 1917.

34 Yakut, *Şeyhülislamlık: Yenileşme Döneminde Devlet ve Din*, 113.

35 For the term "kazasker," see Mehmet İpşirli, "Kazasker," in *TDV İslam Ansiklopedisi* 25 (Istanbul: Türkiye Diyanet Vakfı Yayınları, 2000), 141. The duty of the kazasker is the second highest position in the Ilmiye hierarchy after the position of şeyhülislam. The first traces of the kazasker institution in the Ottoman Empire which are thought to have been taken from the Anatolian Seljuks are found during the time of Murad I (1359–89). Murad I appointed the first kazasker and made him the most important ulema. At the time of Mehmed II (1451–81), the second kazasker was appointed and divided the responsibilities between the two as Anatolia and Rumelia, giving a slight superiority to the kazasker of Rumelia.

36 Musa Çadırcı, "Tanzimat'ın İlanı Sıralarında Osmanlı İmparatorluğu'nda Kadılık Kurumu ve 1838 Tarihli Tarik-i İlmiyeye Dair Ceza Kanunnamesi," *Ankara Üniversitesi TDCF Tarih Araştırmaları Dergisi* XIV, 25 (1982): 139–161.

37 For more on the "bribery," see Cengiz Kırlı, "Yolsuzluğun İcadı: 1840 Ceza Kanunu, İktidar ve Bürokrasi," *Tarih ve Toplum* 4 (2006): 45–119.

38 Çadırcı, "Tanzimat'ın İlanı Sıralarında Osmanlı İmparatorluğu'nda Kadılık Kurumu ve 1838 Tarihli Tarik-i İlmiyeye Dair Ceza Kanunnamesi," 144.

39 Yurdakul, *Osmanlı İlmiye Merkez Teşkilatı'nda Reform*, 216.

40 Ibid., 215.

41 Mustafa Ergün, "II. Meşrutiyet Devrinde Medreselerin Durumu ve Islah Çalışmaları," *Ankara Üniversitesi Dil ve Tarih-Coğrafya Fakültesi Dergisi* 1–2 (1982): 59–89.

42 Akiba, "From Kadi to Naib: Reorganization of the Ottoman Sharia Judiciary in the Tanzimat Period," 140; Akiba, "A New Scholl for Qadis: Education of the Sharia Judges in the Late Ottoman Empire," 49.

43 Yasemin Bayezit, "Tanzimat Devri *Şeyhülislam*larından Meşrepzade Arif Efendi ve Kadılık Kurumundaki İstihdam Sorunu," *Bilig Türk Dünyası Sosyal Bilimler Dergisi* 54, (Summer 2010): 62.

44 Akiba, "A New Scholl for Qadis: Education of the Sharia Judges in the Late Ottoman Empire," 149.

45 Ibid., 149.

46 Ibid., 153.

47 Akiba, "From Kadi to Naib: Reorganization of the Ottoman Sharia Judiciary in the Tanzimat Period," 48.

48 Ibid., 48.

49 Mevleviyet is the highest-level post of judiciary office in the first grade regions.

50 According to the *mülazemet* system introduced at the end of the sixteenth century as a result of an increase in the number of students graduating from the madrasas and the excessive number of ulema wanting to work in The Ilmiye positions, newly graduated ulema waited for one to seven years. It was expected to reach professional maturity and the qualifications required to be appointed for a position in The Ilmiye hierarchy during the *mülazemet* period.

51 Yakut, *Şeyhülislamlık: Yenileşme Döneminde Devlet ve Din*, 61.

52 Akiba, "From Kadi to Naib: Reorganization of the Ottoman Sharia Judiciary in the Tanzimat Period," 43–60.

53 The book explaining the principles of Islamic belief.

54 Yakut, *Şeyhülislamlık: Yenileşme Döneminde Devlet ve Din*, 61.

55 Akiba, "A New School for Qadis: Education of the Sharia Judges in the Late Ottoman Empire," 136.

56 İrfan Gündüz, *Osmanlılarda Devlet-Tekke Münasebetleri* (Ankara: Seha Neşriyat, 1989), 205; Mustafa Kara, *Din, Hayat ve Sanat Açısından Tekkeler ve Zaviyeler* (Istanbul: Dergah Yayınları, 1980), 301–18.

57 For the term of "tekke," see Mehmet Zeki Pakalın, "Tekke," *Osmanlı Tarih Deyimleri ve Terimleri Sözlüğü* 2 (Istanbul: Milli Eğitim Basımevi, 1993). One of the institutions with an important place in the history of Islamic culture is the *tekke*. *Tekke* is also known as *zaviye*, *asitane*, *hankah*, and *dergah*. The heads of dervishes sitting in dervish lodges or *tekkes* are called "tekke şeyhi," "zaviyedar," or "postnişin." They directed and administered the *tekkes*.

58 Bilgin Aydın, "Osmanlı Devleti'nde Tekkeler Reformu ve Meclis-i Meşayihin Şeyhülislamlık'a Bağlı Olarak Kuruluşu, Faaliyetleri ve Arşivi," *İstanbul Araştırmaları* 7 (Fall 1998): 98.

59 Muharrem Varol, "Osmanlı Devleti'nin Tarikatları Denetleme Siyaseti ve Meclis'i Meşayihin Bilinen; Ancak Bulunamayan İki Nizamnamesi," *Türk Kültürü İncelemeleri Dergisi* 23 (2010): 41.

60 BOA. ŞD. 2569/ 21. 11 Şaban 1308/ 22 March 1891. Article 17

61 Ibid., Article 5.

62 Muharrem Varol, "Osmanlı Devleti'nin Tarikatları Denetleme Siyaseti ve Meclis'i Meşayihin Bilinen; Ancak Bulunamayan İki Nizamnamesi." *Türk Kültürü İncelemeleri Dergisi* 23 (2010): 55; BOA, ŞD. 2569/21. 11 Şaban 1308/ 22 March 1891.

63 Yakut, *Şeyhülislamlık: Yenileşme Döneminde Devlet ve Din*, 67.

64 Ibid., 67.

65 Ferhat Koca, "Fetvahane." in *TDV İslam Ansiklopedisi* 12 (Istanbul: Türkiye Diyanet Vakfı Yayınları, 1995), 498–499
66 Yakut, *Şeyhülislamlık: Yenileşme Döneminde Devlet ve Din*, 68.
67 *Düstur*, Tertib-i Sani, VII, 127–133.
68 BOA. İ.DH. 1267/ 99649. 13 Şubat 1307/ 25 February 1892.
69 Yakut, *Şeyhülislamlık: Yenileşme Döneminde Devlet ve Din*, 68.
70 BOA. A.} AMD. 31/ 20. 20 Ramazan 1267/ 18 July 1851; BOA. MF. MKT 269/ 57 24 Zilhicce 1312/ 18 June 1895; BOA. MF. MKT 280/ 28. 13 Rabiyülevvel 1313/ 3 September 1895. See also, Ayşe Polat, "Osmanlı'da Matbu İslam'ın Onay ve Denetimi: Tedkik-i Mesahif ve Müellefat-i Şer'iyye Meclisi," *FSM İlmi Araştırmalar İnsan ve Toplum Bilimleri Dergisi*, 11 (2018): 87–120.
71 Atilla Çetin, "Sicill-i Ahval Defterleri ve Dosyaları Hakkında Bir Araştırma," *Vakıflar Dergisi* 29 (2005): 90–92.
72 Yakut, *Şeyhülislamlık: Yenileşme Döneminde Devlet ve Din*, 79.
73 BOA. BEO 3542/ 265639. 14 Rabiyülevvel 1327/ 5 April 1909.
74 MA, USAD no: 529. Hacı Ahmet Necati Efendi of Erzurum. 22 Kanunuevvel 1329/ 4 January 1910.
75 Jun Akiba, "A New School for Qadis: Education of the Sharia Judges in the Late Ottoman Empire," 154.
76 BOA. İ. DUİT. 90/ 64. 10 Cemaziyelahir 1335/ 3 April 1917.
77 MA, USAD no: 416. İbrahim Muhyiddin Efendi of Sivas. 5 Nisan 1327/ 18 April 1911.
78 Among the officers in larger mosques, the *müezzin* gives the call to prayer from the minaret. They can be thought of as deputy imams, and especially in cases when there was no imam, the müezzin acted as imam and became the prayer leader.
79 Mübahat Kütükoğlu, "Darü'l-Hilafeti'l-Aliyye Medresesi ve Kuruluşu Arefesinde İstanbul Medreseleri," *İslam Tetkikleri Enstitüsü Dergisi* 7, 1–2 (1978): 212.

3 Ulema's Educational Career

1 BOA. Y. EE. 112/ 6. *Maarif-i Umumiye Nizamnamesi*, 24 Cemaziyelevvel 1286/ 1 October 1869; see, for instance MA. USAD. no: 568. Mehmed Kazım Efendi of Konya 21 Muharrem 1310/ 15 August 1892. Mehmed Kazım Efendi studied four years at a *sibyan mekteb*.
2 For instance, MA. USAD. no: 900. Salih Efendi of Kütahya. 22 Mart 1332/4 April 1916. Salih Efendi started his *sibyan* education at the age of six; MA. USAD. no: 1465. Ömer Faruk Efendi of Uşak. 30 Kanunusani 1331/ 12 February 1916. Ömer Faruk Efendi started his education at the age of nine.

3 For the "sibyan muallim," see Cahit Baltacı, "Osmanlı Devleti'nde Eğitim ve Öğretim," *Türkler* XI (2002) 446.; Teachers in *sibyan mektebs* were called *sibyan muallim*. The *talebes* at the *sibyan mektebs* were taught by *muallims* who had graduated from madrasas and by *muallims* who received a special education although not a madrasa education. It was expected that these *muallims* would teach basic mathematics and literacy as well as basic religious education to *talebes*. Initially, the ulema like the imam *and* müezzin of a given district were given the authority to become *sibyan muallimi*, but this situation was changed in the Tanzimat period. In 1868, the *Dar'ül-Muallimin-i Sibyan* was established to educate *sibyan muallims* and only graduates of this school were to be appointed as *sibyan muallims*. However, this was not valid in practice, and the region's ulema continued to be appointed as *sibyan muallims* after the establishment of this school. For instance, see BOA. MF. MKT. 9/ 95. 11 Muharrem 1290/ 12 March 1873. Upon the death of the *sibyan muallimi* Şükrü Efendi of the Ergani Madeni Sibyan Mekteb in 1873, the district's famous *alim*, Osman Tevfik Efendi, was appointed as *sibyan muallim*.

4 Mustafa Öcal, "Amin Alayı," in *TDV İslam Ansiklopedisi* 3 (Istanbul: Türkiye Diyanet Vakfı Yayınları, 1991), 63.

5 For instance, MA. USAD. no: 3911. Mehmed Kamil Efendi of Konya, 25 Teşrinievvel 1331/ 7 November 1915. Mehmed Kamil received his first *sibyan* education at the Antakiye Habib Altı Madrasa.

6 For instance, MA. USAD. no: 303. Ali Avni Efendi of Trabzon 20 Mayıs 1309/ 1 June 1893. Ali Avni Efendi first studied with the neighborhood imam.

7 MA. USAD. no: 199. Ahmed Hulusi Efendi of Ankara. 21 Teşrinievvel 1308/ 2 October 1892.

8 MA. USAD. no: 2712. Hüseyin Efendi of Konya. 4 Ağustos 1308/ 16 August 1892.

9 Bereketzade İsmail Hakkı, *Yad-ı Mazi* (Istanbul: Nehir Yayınları, 1997), 23; see also MA. USAD. no: 2329. Mehmed Necib Efendi of Sivas, 28 Temmuz 1308/ 9 August 1892; MA. USAD. no: 568. Mehmed Kazım Efendi of Konya 21 Muharrem 1310/ 15 August 1892.

10 For instance, MA. USAD. no: 175. Ahmed Hilmi Efendi of Trabzon 12 Eylül 1308/ 24 September 1892. Ahmed Hilmi became a hafiz at the *sibyan mekteb* in 1848 at the age of seven.

11 For instance, MA. USAD. no: 1015. Haci Hasan Rüşdü Efendi of Mamuratülaziz 10 Kanunuevvel 1308/ 22 December 1892. Haci Hasan Rüşdi Efendi learned *sarf* and *nahv* (Arabic grammar) at the *sibyan mekteb*; MA. USAD. no: 1420 Abdülkadir Efendi of Trabzon 21 Temmuz 1326/ 3 August 1910, Abdülkadir Efendi studied *sarf*, *emsile* and *bina* (Arabic grammar classes) at the *sibyan mekteb*.

12 For the "rüşdiye," see Cemil Öztürk, "Rüşdiye," in *TDV İslam Ansiklopedisi* 35 (Istanbul: Türkiye Diyanet Vakfı Yayınları, 2008), 300–303. Education in *rüşdiye*

schools was a modern concept. Although there were no strict rules to attend a *rüşdiye* school as secondary education, some ulema candidates attended to these modern schools before starting their madrasa education. The training period for *rüşdiye mektebs* was generally set at four years, and Turkish, Arabic, and Persian grammar, religion, arithmetic, geometry, general and Ottoman history, geography, and physical education were taught in the *rüşdiyes*. The central curriculum was based on the religious sciences, but the students also acquired a modern education such as the learning of foreign languages (German and French). For instance, MA. USAD. no: 871 Ahmed Cemil Efendi of Diyarbakır. 9 Mayıs 1326/ 22 May 1910. Ahmed Cemil Efendi learned French and Persian in a rüşdiye mekteb.

13 J. E. Gilbert. "Institutionalization of Muslim Scholarship and Professionalization of the Ulama in Medieval Damascus," *Studia Islamica* 52 (1980): 122.

14 Baltacı, "Osmanlılarda Mektep," 6–7.

15 *Düstur*, Tertib-i Sani, II, 127–136. *Medaris-i Suret-i İdaresi.*

16 BOA. İ. DUİT. 20/ 53, 24 Cemaziyelevvel 1337/ 25 February 1919.

17 *Düstur*, Tertib-i Sani, II, 127. *Medaris-i Suret-i İdaresi*, article 14.

18 *Düstur*, Tertib-i Sani, II, 128. *Medaris-i Suret-i İdaresi*, article 16.

19 Halil İnalcık, *The Ottoman Empire: The Classical Age, 1300-1600* (London: Phoenix Press, 1997), 168–169.

20 The Istanbul madrasas like Süleymaniye were the most important building blocks of the Ottoman madrasa education system. The *Dar'ül-Hadis* madrasas were the final step in the madrasa system. The system of this madrasa became the foremost madrasa system of the empire, and it continued to be among the highest-ranking madrasas until the end of the Ottoman Empire.

21 *Düstur*, Tertib-i Sani, IX, 598–601.

22 *Düstur*, Tertib-i Sani, VI, 1325–1330, Islah-ı Medaris Nizamnamesi, 10 Zilkade 1332/ 29 Eylül 1914.

23 *Düstur*, Tertib-i Sani, IX, 598–601.

24 Kütükoğlu, "Darü'l-Hilafeti'l-Aliyye Medresesi ve Kuruluşu Arefesinde İstanbul Medreseleri," 3–12.

25 For instance, MA. USAD. no: 169. Mehmed Tevfik Efendi of Ankara. 15 Safer 1310/ 8 September 1892. Mehmed Tevfik of Ankara became the ministry of *meclis-i meşayih*, a high- ranking position in the Ilmiye system, after he studied in the *musila-i Süleymaniye* madrasa and had the *paye* of *Rumelia.*

26 Rainer A. Müller, "Student Education, Student Life," in *A History of the University in Europe* II, (ed.) Hilde De Ridder-Symoens (Cambridge: Cambridge University Press, 1996), 345.

27 George Makdisi, *The Rise of Colleges: Institutions of Learning in Islam and the West* (Edinburgh: Edinburgh University Press, 1981), 94.

28 For instance, MA. USAD. no: 939. Abdullah Efendi of Konya. 21 Temmuz 1326/ 3 August 1910. Hafiz Abdullah Efendi studied at Koyalı Mosque at Konya; MA. USAD. no: 594. Mehmed Rüşdü Efendi of Konya, 29 Mart 1312/ 10 April 1896. Mehmed Rüşdü Efendi studied in İbradi Mosque in the İbradi district of Konya before attending the madrasa in Konya.

29 BOA. BEO. 3531/ 264809. 17 Rabiyülevvel 1327/ 8 April 1909; BOA. C. MF. 171/ 8510. 29 Zilkade 1272/ 1 August 1856; BOA. C. MF. 61/ 3009. 21 Zilkade 1260/ 2 December 1844.

30 BOA. C.MF. 162/8061. 17 Şaban 1280/ 27 January 1864; BOA. İ. DH 519/35335. 3 Zilhicce 1280/ 10 May 1864.

31 BOA. TS. MA. e 627/ 17. 27 Cemaziyelevvel 1310/ 17 December 1892.

32 BOA. Y. MTV. 100/ 69. 13 Temmuz 1310/ 25 July 1894; BOA. TS. MA. e 627/ 17. 27 Cemaziyelevvel 1310/ 17 December 1892.

33 BOA. BEO. 4049/ 3036, 36. 23 Cemaziyelevvel 1330/ 10 May 1912.

34 For instance, MA. USAD. no: 165. Abdülgaffar Efendi of Konya. 15 Zilkade 1310/ 31 May 1893. Although Abdülgaffar of Konya was registered at the Ibrahim Pasha Madrasa in 1858, he studied the *Mantık* (the book of logic), *Akaid* (the book of the basic principles of faith and Islamic belief), and *Celal* (the book of Arabic grammar) with Muhyiddin Efendi who worked at Sultan Mehmet Mosque. He took the *icazet* both from his müderris at İbrahim Pasha Mosque and Sultan Mehmet Mosque; MA. USAD. no: 2553. Abdullah Efendi of Konya. 8 Temmuz 1330/ 21 July 1914. Abdullah Efendi of Konya studied *Sarf* and *Nahv* (Arabic grammar book) with Ali Rıza Efendi and also studied *Sarf*, *Nahv*, *Mantık*, *Meani* (advanced Arabic grammar), *Hadis* (Hadith/the sayings of Prophet Muhammad), and *Tefsir* (exegegesis on the Quran) with Gümüşhaneli Hacı Osman, Tokatlı Nuri, Haci Hafiz Osman Efendi at other madrasas; MA. USAD. no: 3323. Mustafa Mahfi Efendi of İzmit 22 Teşrinievvel 1308/ 3 November 1892. Mustafa Mahfi Efendi of İzmit took almost every course from a different müderris starting in his *ibtidai* school and throughout his educational life. For instance, he studied Quran and calligraphy with Mehmet Tahir Efendi at İzmit *İbtidai Mekteb* and learned the *Kıraat* (recitation of the Quran) at Dersaadet with Hafiz Niyazi Efendi. He learned *Sarf*, *Nahv*, *Mantık*, and *Fıqh* from Kurra Mehmed Tahir Efendi and also *Akaid* from Kangırılı İbrahim Efendi. Furthermore, he learned calligraphy, mathematics, and geography from Bedri Efendizade and the *Kavaidi Farisi* and *Gülistan* (Persian grammar books) from Musa Efendi. All of the sample madrasa students took more than one *icazet* from *müderrises* at different madrasas.

35 For instance, MA. USAD. no: 303. Ali Avni Efendi of Trabzon. 20 Mayıs 1309/ 1 June 1893. The *icazet* of Takvazade Ahmed Tevfik Efendi was approved by the governor and the mufti of Erzurum.

36 The classes were given regularly in large mosques through the *dersiams*, and these classes, called mosque classes, were open to anyone apart from the students. The children of craftsmen and apprentices could attend the mosque courses. The *dersiams* were required to teach the students, and they could give an *icazet* like *müderrises*; For instance, MA, USAD no:635. Mehmed Reşad Efendi of Kastamonu. 20 Haziran 1326/ 3 July 1910. Dersiam Şakir Efendi of Tokat gave an icazet to Mehmet Reşad Efendi; MA. USAD. no: 23. Hüseyin Avni Efendi of Ankara. 24 Receb 1316/ 8 December 1898, Hüseyin Avni Efendi took his *icazet* from Dersiam Abdürrahim Efendi; MA. USAD. no: 3400. Abdülhalim Efendi of Ankara. 18 Cemaziyelahir 1328/ 27 June 1910. Abdülhalim Efendi studied at Nuriosmaniye Mosque and took his *icazet* from Dersiam Necib Efendi; MA. USAD. no: 3475. Refi Efendi of Ankara. 5 Receb 1328/ 13 July 1910, Refi Efendi had an *icazet* from Ermenekli Süleyman Sırrı Efendi of Beyazit Dersiam.
37 Uzunçarşılı, *Osmanlı Devletinin İlmiye Teşkilatı*, 38.
38 BOA. ŞD. 655/ 55. 27 Rabiyülahir 1330/ 15 April 1912.
39 BOA. BEO. 3531/ 264809. 17 Rabiyülahir 1327/ 8 May 1909.
40 Makdisi, *The Rise of Colleges: Institutions of Learning in Islam and the West*, 94; Uzunçarşılı, *Osmanlı Devleti'nin İlmiye Teşkilatı*, 12,16,20,26.
41 Sami es-Sakkar, "Muid," 86–87.
42 Kemal Edib Kürkçüoğlu, *Süleymaniye Vakfiyesi* (Istanbul: Vakıflar Umum Müdürlüğü Neşriyat, 1962), 8–9.
43 For instance, some of the compulsory texts of Fatih madrasas were *Adut* and *Hidaye* for jurisprudence, *Telvih* for the fundamentals of fiqh, and *Keşşaf* for Quranic exegesis, Süheyl Ünver, *İstanbul Üniversitesi Tarihine Başlangıç: Fatih Külliyesi ve Zamanı İlim Hayatı* (Istanbul: İstanbul Üniversitesi Yayınları, 1946), 101.
44 *Takvim-i Vekayi*, No: 1570, 15 Safer 1290/14 April 1873.
45 BOA. A.} DVN. No: 35/ 67. 12 Cemaziyelahir 1246/ 16 April 1848.
46 *Düstur*, Tertib-i Sani, I, 127.
47 For instance, MA. USAD. no: 201. Halil Fehmi Efendi of Hüdavendigar. 14 Teşrinievvel 1308/ 26 October 1892. Halil Fehmi was taught by müderris Haci Ahmet Efendi at the Rüştempaşa Madrasa by staying day and night at the madrasa with whole day education; MA. USAD. no: 2289. Muhiddin Efendi of Diyarbakır. 12 Mart 1914/ 27 February 1329. *Molla* Muhyiddin Efendi learned from Haci İbrahim Efendi by day and night madrasa life.
48 *Düstur*, Tertib-i Sani, I, 322.
49 Bereketzade İsmail Hakkı, *Yad-ı Mazi*, 33.
50 BOA. DH. MKT. 1711/ 7. 4 Şaban 1307/ 26 March 1890.
51 For instance, MA. USAD. no: 120. Ahmed Esad Efendi of Kastamonu. 26 Eylül 1337/ 26 September 1921. Ahmed Esad Efendi of Kastamonu had to leave from Dar'ül-Hilafet'ül Aliyye Madrasa in the first years of his madrasa life due to health problems;

MA, USAD no: 1194. Mehmed Naim Efendi of Trabzon. 1 Haziran 1325/ 14 June 1909. In 1886, Mehmed Naim Efendi had to leave the madrasa that he had started in 1876 without receiving an *icazet* due to physical weakness that lasted for three years.

52 MA. USAD. no: 2827. Mustafa Efendi of Mamuratülaziz. 27 Ramazan 1330/ 9 September 1912. In 1886, Mustafa Efendi of Mamuratülaziz ended his madrasa education which he had started in 1869, as he was obliged to deal with his family.

53 Ekmeleddin İhsanoğlu, "Ottoman Educational and Scholarly-Scientific Institutions," in *History of the Ottoman State, Society and Civilization*, (ed.) Ekmeleddin İhsanoğlu (Istanbul: IRCICA, 2001): 385.

54 For instance, MA. USAD. no: 1021. Halil Fahri Efendi of Erzurum. 3 Teşrinisani 1308/ 15 November 1892. Halil Fahri Efendi learned literature, logic, and jurisprudence respectively.

55 MA. USAD. no: 3328. Mustafa Mahfi Efendi of İzmit 22 Teşrinievvel 1308/ 3 November 1892.

56 For instance, MA. USAD. no: 1420 Abdülkadir Efendi of Trabzon 21 Temmuz 1326/ 3 August 1910; MA. USAD. no: 3328. Mustafa Mahfi Efendi of İzmit 22 Teşrinievvel 1308/ 3 November 1892; Ekmeleddin İhsanoğlu, "Ottoman Educational and Scholarly-Scientific Institutions," 376.

57 BOA. İ. DUİT. 20/ 53, 24 Cemaziyelevvel 1337/ 25 February 1919; MA. USAD. no: 1249. Mehmed Tevfik Efendi of Ankara. 9 Muharrem 1310/ 3 August 1892.

58 *Düstur*, Tertib-i Sani, II, 127; MA. USAD. no: 2413. Mehmed Efendi of Ankara. 10 Mayıs 1332/ 23 May 1916.

59 *Takvim-i Vekayi*, No: 1570, 15 Safer 1290/14 Nisan 1873.

60 *Düstur*, Tertib-i Sani, II, 134–135. See also Adem Ölmez, "II. Meşrutiyet Devrinde Osmanlı Medreselerinde Reform Çabaları ve Merkezileşme," *Vakıflar Dergisi* 41 (June 2014): 27–40.

61 *Düstur*, Tertib-i Sani, II, 127.

62 *Düstur*, Tertib-i Sani, II, 127.

63 For instance, see the *icazetname* of Ali Avni Efendi, MA. USAD. no: 303. Ali Avni Efendi of Trabzon. 20 Mayıs 1309/ 1 June 1893; the *icazetname* of Hafiz Abdullah Efendi of Konya. MA. USAD. no: 939. Hafiz Abdullah Efendi of Konya. 21 Temmuz 1326/ 3 August 1910; the *icazetname* of Abdülgani Efendi of Trabzon; MA. USAD. no: 2121. Abdülgani Efendi of Trabzon. 22 Mayıs 1326/ 4 June 1910; the *icazetname* of Rüşdü Efendi of Mamuratülaziz. MA. USAD. no: 1015. Rüşdü Efendi of Mamuratülaziz. 10 Kanunuevvel 1308/ 22 December 1892.

64 Mehmet Zeki Pakalın, "Çömez," *Osmanlı Tarih Deyimleri ve Terimleri Sözlüğü* I, 381.

65 For instance, MA. USAD. no: 3420. Abdüllatif Lütfi Efendi of Mamuratülaziz. 24 Mayıs 1326/ 9 June 1910. Abdüllatif Efendi studied at an important madrasa in Istanbul, Şehzadebaşı Damat Cedid İbrahim Paşa Madrasa, and was taught by the famous Istanbul Müderris El Hac Ali Efendi even though he came from the small

district of Mamuratülaziz and far from Istanbul; MA. USAD. no: 901. Ahmed Cevdet Efendi of Aydın. 18 Cemaziyelahir 1326/ 18 June 1908. Ahmet Cevdet Efendi of Aydın first studied at Yusuf Efendi Madrasa in Aydın. After his müderris in this madrasa passed away, Ahmet Cevdet went to Denizli to continue his madrasa education. After completing the traditional madrasa education in those cities, he eventually came to Istanbul to attend the Dar'ül-Hadis Madrasa in 1890 and he was taught by the Ekmekçizade Mustafa Fehmi Efendi who was a famous Istanbul müderris; MA. USAD. no: 3595. Salih Nazım Efendi of Erzurum. 15 Mayıs 1326/ 28 May 1910. After Haci Salih Nazım Efendi of Erzurum studied *rüşdiye* at his hometown, he went to Istanbul for high-level education in madrasa. He was taught by the Huzur-u Hümayun scholar Ahmet Efendi.

66 MA. USAD. no: 3585. Hüseyin Hilmi Efendi of Konya. 10 Mart 1336/ 10 March 1910. Although Hüseyin Hilmi Efendi of Konya graduated from a Konya madrasa in the Akseki district, he attained the highest teaching position, the Fatih Dersiam*ship*.

67 For instance, MA. USAD. no: 2302. Mehmed Şakir Efendi of Mardin. 18 Temmuz 1327/ 31 July 1911. Mehmed Şakir was chosen as a *muid* with a salary of 75 piasters in 1909 in accordance with his exam results and the approval of the waqf commission while a student at the Kasımpaşa Madrasa.

68 For instance, MA. USAD. no: 169. Mehmed Tevfik Efendi of Ankara. 15 Safer 1310/ 8 September 1892. Mehmed Tevfik Efendi of Ankara reached one of the highest *the Ilmiye* positions and became the kazasker of Rumelia in 1890; MA. USAD. no: 1902. Şerif Mehmed Kamil Efendi of Hüdavendigar. 5 Ağustos 1309/ 17 August 1893. Şerif Mehmed Kamil Efendi of Hüdavendigar moved through the highest ranks in the *Ilmiye* hierarchy and received *mevleviyet* degrees after he completed his education with the highest degree of *Hamise-i Süleymaniye*; MA. USAD. no: 3469. Hafiz Emin Efendi of İzmit. 17 Haziran 1326/ 30 June 1910. Hafiz Emin Efendi of İzmit continued for 30 years from *İbtida-yi Hariç* to *Hamise-i Süleymaniye* rank.

69 An article in the *Düstur* stated that all their financial needs were met with revenues from the waqf of the madrasa, *Düstur*, Tertib-i Sani, I, 322. Article 2.

70 Yaşar Sarıkaya, *Merkez ile Taşra Arasında Bir Osmanlı Alimi Ebu Said El-Hadimi* (Istanbul: Kitap Yayınevi, 2008), 78–79.

71 Mehmet İpşirli, "Cer," in *TDV İslam Ansiklopedisi* 7 (Istanbul: Türkiye Diyanet Vakfı Yayınları, 1993), 388–389.

72 BOA. BEO. 984/ 73734. 26 Safer 1315/ 27 July 1897; BOA. DH. MKT. 2261/ 49. 20 Cemaziyelahir 1317/ 26 October 1899.

73 BOA. MVL. 48/ 512. 18 Cemaziyelahir 1283/ 28 October 1866; BOA. DH. MKT. 1427/ 92. 7 Şevval 1304/ 29 June 1887.

74 BOA. BEO, 319/ 23877. 19 Cemaziyelevvel 1311/ 28 November 1893; BOA. BEO. 322/ 24112. 26 Cemaziyelevvel 1311/ 5 December 1893.

75 Bereketzade İsmail Hakkı, *Yad-ı Mazi*, 25.

76 BOA. DH. MKT. 198/ 17. 14 Receb 1311/ 21 January 1894.

77 BOA. BEO. 473/ 35431. 25 Ağustos 1310/ 6 September 1894; BOA. BEO. 3462/259596. 3 Zilhicce 1326/ 27 December 1908.

78 BOA. DH. MKT. 1711/ 7. 4 Şaban 1307/ 26 March 1890.

79 BOA. DH. MKT. 1711/ 7. 4 Şaban 1307/ 26 March 1890; BOA. DH.MKT. 1711/21. 4 Şaban 1307/ 26 March 1890.

80 MA. USAD. no: 181. Ali Fahreddin Efendi of Bolu. 28 Mayıs 1326/ 22 May 1910.

81 MA. USAD. no: 648. Mustafa Nuri Efendi of Ankara. 29 Cemaziyelahir 1326/ 29 June 1908.

82 MA. USAD. no: 638. İsmail Efendi of Ankara. 15 Rabiyülevvel 1329/ 16 March 1911.

83 For instance, MA. USAD. no: 750. Ahmed Raşid Efendi of Aydın. 12 Temmuz 1326/ 25 July 1910.

84 Veysel Şimşek, "Ottoman Military Recruitment and the Recruit: 1826-1853," MA Thesis (Ankara: Bilkent University, 2005), 36.

85 BOA. MF. MKT. 787/ 37. 8 Rabiyülahir 1322/ 5 December 1904. For instance, MA. USAD. no: 3662. Mustafa Vasfi Efendi of Bolu. 21 Mayıs 1326/ 3 June 1910; MA, USAD no: 904. Abdülhadi Efendi of Bitlis. 18 Receb 1328/ 26 July 1910; MA. USAD. no: 945. Yusuf Ziya Efendi of Bitlis. 4 Kanunusani 1325/ 17 January 1910; MA. USAD. no: 120. Ahmed Esad Efendi of Kastamonu. 26 Eylül 1337/ 26 September 1921.

86 For instance, MA. USAD. no: 2777 Hasan Hüsnü Efendi of Hakkari. 14 Şubat 1326/ 27 February 1911. For instance, military officer Hafiz Mustafa Ali proved that Hasan Efendi was a madrasa student who attended the courses both at night and in the morning, and he informed the authorities with a written document.

87 MA. USAD. no: 638. İsmail Efendi of Ankara. 15 Rabiyülevvel 1329/ 16 March 1911.

88 MA. USAD. no: 2777. Hasan Hüsnü Efendi of Hakkari. 14 Şubat 1326/ 27 February 1911.

89 BOA. ŞD. 664/ 11. 14 Teşrinievvel 1331/ 27 October 1915.

90 BOA. MF. MKT. 213/ 36. 19 Muharrem 1312/ 23 July 1894; BOA. MF. MKT. 183/ 124. 28 Rabiyülevvel 1311/ 9 October 1893.

91 For the term "rüus," see, Pakalın "Rüus," *Osmanlı Tarih Deyimleri ve Terimleri Sözlüğü* III, 71. *Rüus* is an officially organized, regular exam within the Ilmiye system to appoint state positions. The graduates who have an *icazet* could enter this exam after a *mülazemet* period. If the madrasa graduates passed the examination, they were allowed to join the Ilmiye position. The certificate that they received after the exam was called a *rüus*. Also, when ulema were promoted to higher academic ranks, new *rüuses* were issued reflecting their changed rank.

92 *Takvim-i Vekayi*, No: 193, 16 Cemaziyelahir 1294/ 28 June 1877.

93 BOA. DH. MKT. 668/ 63. 19 Zilhicce 1320/ 19 March 1903.

94 BOA. İ. DUİT. 20/ 53. 24 Cemaziyelevvel 1337/ 25 February 1919. For instance, see, MA. USAD. no: 890. Mustafa Asım Efendi of Bitlis. 21 Haziran 1327/ 4 July 1911. Mustafa Asım Efendi of Bitlis was appointed to the madrasa in Bitlis where his father worked as müderris after his father passed away in 1911.

95 BOA. İ. DUİT. 20/ 53. 24 Cemaziyelevvel 1337/ 25 February 1919. *Tevcih-i Cihat Nizamnamesi.*

96 Ibid.

97 BOA. İ. DUİT. 20/ 53. 24 Cemaziyelevvel 1337/ 25 February 1919.

98 BOA. İ. DUİT. 20/ 53. 24 Cemaziyelevvel 1337/ 25 February 1919.

99 BOA. ŞD. 2927/ 32. 20 Muharrem 1309/ 26 August 1891.

100 Ibid.

101 Ibid.

102 BOA. MF. MKT 599/ 47. 11 Şevval 1319/ 21 January 1902.

103 A *berat* is a document which contained the signature of the sultan and indicated the duties and authority of those appointed to certain civil service positions. A *berat* is also called a "*menşur*", "*biti*", "*berat-ı şerif*", and "*nişan-ı şerif*".

104 BOA. İ. DH. 1291/101578. 5 Cemaziyelahir 1280/ 17 November 1863. The names of the civil servants to be assigned to the *Ilmiye* positions were presented to the sultan by the şeyhülislam, and their assignment was carried out via the sultan's *berat* in 1863. For instance, see, MA. USAD. no:2. Bekir Sıdkı Efendi of Ankara. 14 Kanunuevvel 1311/ 26 December 1895. Bekir Sıdkı Efendi of Ankara was appointed via a *berat* of the Sultan.

105 BOA. MF. MKT. 400/ 22. 24 Muharrem 1316/ 14 June 1898; BOA. MF. MKT. 443/ 9. 27 Zilkade 1316/ 8 April 1899; BOA. MF. MKT. 387/7. 19 Şevval 1315/ 13 March 1898; BOA. MF. MKT. 449/ 36. 11 Muharrem 1317/ 22 May 1898.

106 *Mümeyyiz* is called anyone who measures the knowledge of a new madrasa graduate with an exam.

107 BOA. A.} DVN 150/ 97. 15 Şaban 1276/ 8 March 1860.

108 Mehmet İpşirli, "Mülazemet," in *TDV İslam Ansiklopedisi* 31 (Istanbul: Türkiye Diyanet Vakfı Yayınları, 2006), 537.

109 Uzunçarşılı, *Osmanlı İlmiye Merkez Teşkilatı'nda Reform*, 45.

110 For instance, MA. USAD. no: 242. Abdülhalim Efendi of Kastamonu. 23 Mayıs 1326/5 June 1910. Abdülhalim Efendi of Kastamonu was appointed as *dersiam* in 1881 after took his *icazet* from Hafiz Ali Rıza Efendi, who was a famous Beyazıt Dersiam, and passed the *rüus* exam the same year; MA. USAD. no: 171. Hasan Tahsin Efendi of Konya. 24 Haziran 1309/ 6 June 1893. Hasan Tahsin Efendi of Konya was appointed as a naib in Trablusgarp in 1884 after passing the exam and at the end of the waiting period that averaged three years; MA. USAD. no: 229. Yusuf Efendi of Trabzon. 7 Receb 1328/ 15 July 1910. Yusuf Efendi of Trabzon was appointed as a naib in Kasımpaşa at the age of thirty-five

in 1903 following a seven-year *mülazemet* period after he passed the *rüus* exam in 1886.

111 For instance, MA. USAD. no: 1315. Mustafa Cemaleddin Efendi of Konya. 29 Teşrinisani 1321/ 12 December 1905. Mustafa Cemaleddin Efendi of Konya worked as a court scribe during his mülazemet period until being appointed as Bursa müderris.

112 MA. USAD. no:2. Ahmed Efendi of Ankara. 14 Kanunuevvel 1311/ 26 December 1895; MA. USAD. no: 201. Halil Fehmi Efendi of Hüdavendigar. 14 Teşrinievvel 1308/ 26 October 1892; MA. USAD. no: 18. Hüseyin Efendi of Trabzon. 19 Muharrem 1311/ 2 August 1893; MA. USAD. no: 1014. İsmail Hakkı Efendi of Hüdavendigar. 28 Kanunusani 1309/ 9 February 1894; MA. USAD. no: 594. Mehmed Rüşdü Efendi of Konya. 29 Mart 1312/ 10 April 1896; MA. USAD. no: 229. Yusuf Efendi of Trabzon. 7 Receb 1328/ 15 July 1910; MA. USAD. no: 171. Hasan Tahsin Efendi of Konya. 24 Haziran 1309/ 06 July 1893; MA. USAD. no: 1315. Mustafa Cemaleddin Efendi of Konya. 29 Teşrinisani 1311/ 12 December 1905.

113 MA. USAD. no: 1315. Mustafa Cemaleddin Efendi of Konya. 29 Teşrinisani 1311/ 12 December 1905. Mustafa Cemaleddin Efendi worked in the Sharia court as a scribe and received no salary while he was in his *mülazemet* period. Further examples may be cited, see MA. USAD. no: 594. Mehmed Rüşdü Efendi of Konya, 29 Mart 1312/ 10 April 1896. Mehmed Rüşdü of Konya did not receive a salary for a total of seven years during the *mülazemet* period; MA. USAD. no: 1305. Ali Mürteza Efendi of Konya, 9 Kanunusani 1310/ 21 January 1895. Ali Mürteza Efendi of Konya did not receive any salary during his *mülazemet* period despite his position as court scribe in the sharia courts of various provincial districts until being appointed as a naib in Erzurum in 1866.

114 MA. USAD. no: 201. Halil Fehmi Efendi of Hüdavendigar. 14 Teşrinievvel 1308/ 26 October 1892. Halil Fehmi Efendi of Balıkesir's *mülazemet* lasted from 1873 to 1883, but in this period the state paid a salary of 250 piasters; MA. USAD. no: 1014. İsmail Hakkı Efendi of Hüdavendigar. 28 Kanunusani 1309/ 9 February 1894. İsmail Hakkı Efendi of Kütahya waited out his *mülazemet* with a 100-piaster salary before being appointed as *defter-i hakani kalemi*. Further examples may be cited, see MA. USAD. no: 199. Ahmed Hulusi Efendi of Ankara. 21 Teşrinievvel 1308/ 2 October 1892. Ahmet Hulusi Efendi, who waited for nine months for civil service, was paid a salary of 1,250 piasters in 1893.

115 MA. USAD. no: 845. Hafiz Mehmed Yeseri Efendi of Aydın. 14 Teşrinisani 1326/ 27 November 1910. Hafiz Mehmed Yeseri Efendi waited in his hometown until he was appointed to civil service in the Ilmiye hierarchy.

116 MA. USAD. no: 1576. Mustafa Lütfi Efendi of Konya. 7 Cemaziyelahir 1328/ 16 June 1910. Mustafa Lütfi Efendi gave private courses until he was appointed to an Ilmiye position in the official government system.

117 BOA. Y. MTV. 104/ 73. 2 Eylül 1310/ 14 September 1894.
118 BOA. ŞD. 2927/ 32. 20 Muharrem 1309/ 26 August 1891.

4 Ulema's Professional Career (1880–1920)

1 For instance, MA. USAD. no: 2453. İsmail Temel Efendi of Trabzon. 7 Kanunuevvel 1326/ 20 December 1910. İsmail Temel Efendi stated that he was tested by a commission in 1899.
2 BOA. BEO. 4649/ 348606. 12 Zilhicce 1338/ 27 August 1920. Being military regiment mufti was equal to major rank. (*Binbaşı*)
3 BOA. BEO. 1687/ 126519. 24 Rabiyülevvel 1319/ 11 July 1911.
4 Zeki Salih Zengin, *Tanzimat Dönemi Osmanlı Örgün Eğitim Kurumlarında Din Eğitimi ve Öğretimi (1839-1876)*, PhD Diss. (Kayseri: Erciyes Üniversitesi Sosyal Bilimler Enstitüsü, 1997), 120.
5 For the examples of long waiting period, see MA. USAD. no: 201. Halil Fehmi Efendi of Hüdavendigar. 14 Teşrinievvel 1308/ 26 October 1892; MA. USAD. no: 229. Yusuf Efendi of Trabzon. 7 Receb 1328/ 15 July 1910
6 BOA. BEO. 1849/ 138641. 5 Mayıs 1318/ 18 May 1902.
7 MA. USAD. no: 2282. Osman Zeki Efendi of Ankara. 6 Ağustos 1308/ 18 August 1892.
8 MA. USAD. no: 568. Mehmed Kazım Efendi of Konya. 21 Muharrem 1310/ 15 August 1892.
9 For instance, MA. USAD. no: 467. Haci Mehmed Şakir Efendi of Kastamonu. 11 Haziran 1326/ 24 June 1910; MA. USAD. no: 1576. Mustafa Lütfi Efendi of Konya. 7 Cemaziyelahir 1328/ 16 June 1910; MA. USAD. no: 2282. Süleyman Şakir Efendi of Hüdavendigar. 17 Temmuz 1326/ 30 July 1910.
10 BOA. BEO. 3746/ 280920. 27 Rabiyülahir 1328/ 8 May 1910.
11 Uzunçarşılı, *Osmanlı İlmiye Merkez Teşkilatı'nda Reform*, 195–205.
12 BOA. ŞD. 199/ 26. 15 Şaban 1331/ 20 July 1913; BOA. EV. BRT. 315/ 10. 18 Zilhicce 1323/ 13 February 1906.
13 *Takvim-i Vekayi*, No: 1938, 16 Cemaziyelahir 1294/28 June 1877.
14 BOA. C. MF. 78/ 3890. 25 Şevval 1282/ 13 March 1866.
15 BOA. A.} MKT. 118/ 37. 29 Rabiyülahir 1294/ 13 May 1877; BOA. Y. EE. 123/ 24. 06 Cemaziyelevvel 1317/ 12 September 1899.
16 See Gibb and Bowen, *Islamic Society and the West*, 85. They claim that the highest legal official was the mufti, not the kadı. However, they do not indicate that a şeyhülislam was appointed only after a long career as a kadı.

17 BOA. HR. SFR. 04. 469/ 4. 17 Temmuz 1319/ 30 July 1903; BOA. BEO. 2761/ 207064. 20 Zilhicce 1323/ 15 February 1906; BOA. HR. SFR. 04. 469/ 17. 04 Ekim 1904/ 4 October 1904.

18 Ahmet Cevdet Paşa, *Tezakir-i Cevdet* 21-39 (Ankara: Türk Tarih Kurumu, 1953), 150.

19 BOA. BEO. 1349/ 101155. 15 Haziran 1315/ 27 June 1899; BOA. BEO. 3703/ 277716. 1 Şubat 1326/ 14 February 1911.

20 For instance, MA. USAD. no: 451. Mehmed Sadık Efendi of Adana. 1 Muharrem 1310/ 26 Temmuz 1892. Mehmed Sadık Efendi of Adana, who was elected by the people, was able to begin his duty as mufti after receiving the approval of the şeyhülislam Hasan Efendi in 1876.

21 For instance, MA. USAD. no: 605. Ebubekir Sıtkı Efendi of Ankara. 16 Ağustos 1308/ 28 August 1892; MA. USAD. no:3328. Mustafa Mahfi Efendi of İzmit. 22 Teşrinievvel 1308/ 3 November 1892; MA, USAD no: 541. Hacı Mehmed Şaban Efendi of Trabzon. 2 Şaban 1332/ 26 June 1914. All of these worked as müderris and mufti at the same time.

22 For instance, MA. USAD. no: 2777. Hasan Hüsnü Efendi of Van. 14 Şubat 1326/ 27 February 1911. Hasan Hüsnü Efendi of Van became a mufti in 1908 in addition to his duty as a *muallim*, which he had started in 1897. After 1908, he performed both duties together; MA. USAD. no: 359 Haci Mahmud Hamdi Efendi of Erzurum. 29 Eylül 1308/11 October 1892. Haci Mahmud Hamdi Efendi of Erzurum held two positions—as *muallim* and mufti—at the same time; MA. USAD. no: 2302. Mehmed Şakir Efendi of Diyarbakır. 18 Temmuz 1327/31 July 1911. Mehmed Şakir Efendi of Diyarbakır became a mufti in 1908 in additional to his duty as a *muallim* that he had been performing since 1899.

23 For instance, MA. USAD. no: 2282. Süleyman Şakir Efendi of Hüdavendigar. 17 Temmuz 1326/ 30 July 1910. Süleyman Şakir Efendi of Kütahya was appointed as mufti to the Gediz district of Kütahya in 1909 while serving as Müderris in a madrasa. Another similar example, MA. USAD. no: 1576. Mustafa Efendi of Konya. 7 Cemaziyelahir 1328/ 16 June 1910. Mehmed Şükrü Efendi was a *dersiam* in the Beyazıt Madrasa and a military regimentmufti *(alay* mufti*)* in the first imperial army, performing the two tasks at the same time in 1899.

24 MA. USAD. no: 3328. Mustafa Mahfi Efendi of İzmit. 22 Teşrinievvel 1308/ 3 November 1892.

25 For instance, MA. USAD. no: 1248. Ahmet Hilmi Efendi of Diyarbakır. 8 Eylül 1308/ 20 September 1892. Ahmet Hilmi Efendi of Diyarbakır had two books about hadiths and *kıraat* that affected his choice as mufti in 1882.

26 BOA. Y. MTV. 102/ 4. 1 Safer 1312/ 4 August 1894.

27 MA. USAD. no: 1207, Mustafa Hulusi Efendi of Aydın. 31 Kanunusani 1307/ 31 January 1921. This is a recommendation letter for the appointment Mustafa Hulusi

Efendi with the signatures of thirty-two prominent persons from the Mutki district of Bitlis and members of the sect of Kadiriye (*Tarikat-ı Kadiriye*).

28 BOA. HR. SFR. 04. 469/ 4. 17 Temmuz 1319/ 30 July 1903.

29 Akiba, "From Kadi to Naib: Reorganization of the Ottoman Sharia Judiciary in the Tanzimat Period," 53.

30 For the *Tarik-i İlmiyeye Dair Ceza Kanunnamesi*, see Çadırcı, "Tanzimat'ın İlanı Sıralarında Osmanlı İmparatorluğu'nda Kadılık Kurumu ve Tarik-i İlmiyeye Dair Ceza Kanunnamesi", 148–158.

31 Jun Akiba, "A New Scholl for Qadis: Education of the Sharia Judges in the Late Ottoman Empire," *Turcica* 35 (2003): 143–144.

32 BOA. BEO. 4413/ 330973. 30 Nisan 1332/ 13 May 1916.

33 MA. USAD. no: 464. Halil Hulusi Efendi of Adana. 5 Kanunuevvel 1326/ 29 December 1910.

34 MA. USAD. no:2. Ahmed Efendi of Ankara. 14 Kanunuevvel 1311/ 26 December 1895.

35 MA. USAD. no: 201. Halil Fehmi Efendi of Hüdavendigar. 14 Teşrinievvel 1308/ 26 October 1892.

36 MA. USAD. no: 750. Ahmed Raşid Efendi of Aydın. 12 Temmuz 1326/ 25 July 1910. Ahmed Raşid Efendi, who started his career as a court scribe while still studying at the madrasa, was appointed as a naib with a 1225—piaster salary as soon as he graduated in 1874.

37 The re-assignment of naibs was generally made every two years. For instance, MA. USAD. no: 167. Ahmed Hamid Efendi of Ankara. 22 Muharrem 1310/ 16 August 1892. Ahmed Halil Efendi has rotated to another region every two years; MA. USAD. no: 464. Halil Hulusi Efendi of Adana. 5 Kanunuevvel 1326/ 29 December 1910. Similarly, Halil Hulusi Efendi was relocated every two years. This rotation of naib offices was not an option but the prerequisite for naibs. The duration of the position of naibs could vary from region to region though the average was two years. For instance, see MA, USAD no: 1492. İbrahim Edhem Efendi of Aydın. 24 Teşrinisani 1313/ 6 December 1897; MA. USAD. no: 1981. İsmail Efendi of Hüdavendigar. 7 Mayıs 1327/ 20 May 1911. The period of duty of İbrahim Ethem Efendi lasted two years between 1894 and 1896 in the Laşid district of Girit. In the Kandiye district of Girit, his duty lasted only eleven months from February to December 1896. On the other hand, İsmail Efendi of Kütahya maintained his naib duty in the Kürki district of Kütahya for six years.

38 MA. USAD. no: 1021. Halil Fahri Efendi of Erzurum. 3 Teşrinisani 1308/ 15 November 1892.

39 MA. USAD. no:432. Halil İbrahim Efendi of Konya. 16 Kanunusani 1308/ 28 January 1893.

40 BOA. BEO. 4413/ 330973. 30 Nisan 1332/ 13 May 1916.

41 Ş. Tufan Buzpınar, "Nakibüleşraf," in *TDV İslam Ansiklopedisi* 32 (Istanbul: Türkiye Diyanet Vakfı Yayınları, 2006), 322.
42 BOA. Y. PRK. AZJ. 44/ 62. 24 Rabiyülahir 1320/ 31 July 1902; BOA. ŞD. 3088/3. 02 Şaban 1335/ 24 May 1917.
43 BOA. EV. d. 39419/ 5. 29 Mayıs 1333/ 29 May 1917.
44 BOA. EV. d. 39419/ 3. 15 Eylül 1330/ 29 September 1914.
45 MA. USAD. no: 1248. Ahmed Hilmi Efendi of Diyarbakır. 8 Eylül 1308/ 20 September 1892.
46 MA. USAD. no: 201. Halil Fehmi Efendi of Hüdavendigar. 14 Teşrinievvel 1308/ 26 October 1892.
47 MA. USAD. no: 1159. Mesud Efendi of Diyarbakır. 24 Kanunuevvel 1309/ 5 January 1894.
48 MA. USAD. no: 853. Mustafa Bahri Efendi of Aydın. 15 Şubat 1325/ 28 February 1910.
49 BOA. BEO. 1943/ 145661. 28 Receb 1320/ 31 October 1902.
50 BOA. ZB. 453/ 37. 25 Mart 1323/ 7 April 1907.
51 MA. USAD. no: 3420. Abdüllatif Lütfi Efendi of Mamuratülaziz. 24 Mayıs 1326/ 9 June 1910.
52 MA. USAD. no: 2302. Şakir Efendi of Diyarbakır. 18 Temmuz 1327/ 31 July 1911.
53 MA. USAD. no: 187. Mustafa Asım Efendi of Trabzon. 24 Mayıs 1326/ 6 June 1910.
54 MA. USAD. no: 918. İsmail Hakkı Efendi of Kastamonu. 27 Mayıs 1326/ 9 June 1910.
55 For instance, MA. USAD. no: 433. Hafiz Mehmed İzzet Efendi of Kastamonu. 9 Kanunusani 1308/ 21 January 1893.
56 For instance, MA. USAD. no: 169. Mehmed Tevfik Efendi of Ankara. 15 Safer 1310/ 8 September 1892. Mehmet Tevfik of Ankara reached the paye of Rumeli kazaskeri at the end of 21 years; MA. USAD. no: 3469. Mehmed Emin Efendi of İzmit. 17 Haziran 1326/ 30 June 1910. Hafiz Emin Efendi of İzmit reached the Süleymaniye paye at the end of twenty-seven years.
57 MA. USAD. no: 169. Mehmed Tevfik Efendi of Ankara. 15 Safer 1310/ 8 September 1892. Since Mehmet Tevfik Efendi was the son of Seyyid Osman Efendi. He took the rank of İstanbul *rüus* in 1835 before he had even graduated from the madrasa. He also reached the ranks of Halep *Mevleviyet* in 1857, Mısır *Mevleviyet* in 1867, Medine-i Münevvere *Mevleviyet* and then 5th class order of *Osmani* in 1871, the paye of Istanbul in 1882, the rank of Anatolian kazasker and 1st class order of *Mecidi* in 1889.
58 For instance, MA. USAD. no: 23. Hüseyin Avni Efendi of Ankara. 24 Receb 1316/ 8 December 1898; MA. USAD. no: 3391. Mustafa Fevzi Efendi of Ankara. 30 Haziran 1326/ 13 July 1910.

59 MA. USAD. no: 23. Hüseyin Avni Efendi of Ankara. 24 Receb 1316/ 8 December 1898.

60 BOA. C. MF. 50/ 7479. 16 Kanunuevvel 1313/ 28 December 1857; for instance MA. USAD. no: 1902. Mehmed Kamil Efendi of Hüdavendigar. 5 Ağustos 1309/ 17 August 1893.

61 MA. USAD. no: 169. Mehmed Tevfik Efendi of Ankara. 15 Safer 1310/ 8 September 1892; MA. USAD. no: 1902, Mehmed Kamil Efendi of Hüdavendigar. 5 Ağustos 1309/ 17 August 1893; MA. USAD. no: 3469. Mehmed Emin Efendi of İzmit. 17 Haziran 1326/ 30 June 1910; MA. USAD. no:384. Osman Nuri Efendi of Sivas. 27 Mayıs 1326/ 9 June 1910.

62 *Arpalık* was given as a salary for civil servants in the Ottoman Empire—and as a retirement pension once they left government service.

63 BOA. Y. MTV. 55/ 87. 29 Rabiyülevvel 1309/ 2 November 1892; BOA. A.} MKT. NZD. 204/ 49. 11 Rabiyülahir 1273/ 9 December 1856.

64 BOA. İ. MVL. 305/ 12589. 11 Şaban 1270/ 9 May 1854; BOA. MF. MKT. 6/ 81. 13 Şaban 1289/ 16 October 1872; BOA. MVL. 416/ 89. 3 Zilkade 1279/ 22 April 1863.

65 BOA. Y.PRK. BŞK. 28/ 49. 07 Cemaziyelevvel 1310/ 27 November 1892; BOA. EV. d. 23980. 23 Receb 1298/ 21 June 1881.

66 Akiba, "From Kadi to Naib: Reorganization of the Ottoman Sharia Judiciary in the Tanzimat Period," 51.

67 MA. USAD. no: 1635. Mehmed Rıfat Efendi of Ankara. 26 Temmuz 1330/ 8 August 1914.

68 MA. USAD. no: 2282. Süleyman Şakir Efendi of Hüdavendigar. 17 Temmuz 1326/ 30 July 1910.

69 MA. USAD. no:2961. Ahmed Hamdi Efendi of Kastamonu. 27 Kanunusani 1328/ 9 July 1913.

70 MA. USAD. no: 945. Yusuf Ziya Efendi of Bitlis. 4 Kanunusani 1325/ 17 January 1910.

71 MA. USAD. no: 1420. Abdülkadir Efendi of Trabzon. 21 Temmuz 1326/ 3 August 1910.

72 MA. USAD. no: 1465. Ömer Faruk Efendi of Uşak. 30 Kanunusani 1331/ 12 February 1916.

73 BOA. MF. MKT. 452/ 32. 07 Safer 1317/ 17 June 1899.

74 For the "*mazuliyet* salary" see Nadir Özbek, "Osmanlı İmparatorluğu'nda Sosyal Yardım Uygulamaları," in *Tanzimat Değişim Sürecinde Osmanlı İmparatorluğu*, 405. Officers dismissed from the Ottoman government bureaucracy were called *mazul*, and the pensions paid to them for the period they were fired was a kind of insurance system known as the *mazuliyet* salary. This salary was given until the assignment to a new task.

75 For instance, the *müderrises'* monthly wages in the Süleymaniye Madrasa ranged from 2500 to 5000 piasters. While the müderris of Sahn-ı Seman Madrasa earned between 1500–2500 piasters, the İbtida-yi Hariç and Dahil *müderrises* earned between 600–1500 piasters. *Düstur*, Tertib-i Sani, IX, 598–601.

76 Ali Akyıldız, *Tanzimat Dönemi Osmanlı Merkez Teşkilatında Reform (1839-1856)* (Istanbul: Eren Yayıncılık, 1993), 147.

77 Ibid., 157.

78 For instance, MA. USAD. no: 1635. Mehmed Rıfat Efendi of Ankara. 26 Temmuz 1330/ 8 August 1914; MA. USAD. no: 2961. Ahmed Hamdi Efendi of Kastamonu. 27 Kanunusani 1328/ 9 July 1913. Both Mehmed Rıfat Efendi of Ankara and Ahmed Hamdi Efendi of Kastamonu received salaries for their position of mufti.

79 BOA. DH. MKT. 2905/ 57. 3 Şaban 1327/ 20 August 1900.

80 For instance, MA. USAD. no: 1015, Rüşdü Efendi of Mamuratülaziz. 10 Kanunuevvel 1308/ 22 December 1892. Haci Hasan Rüşdü Efendi of Mamuratülaziz worked as a mufti without salary from 1871 to 1889.

81 For instance, MA. USAD. no: 2329. Hafiz Mehmed Necib Efendi of Sivas, 28 Temmuz 1308/ 9 August 1892. Hafiz Mehmed Necib Efendi of Sivas started to work as a mufti without a salary starting in 1890.

82 BOA. Y. MTV. 286/ 95. 18 Rabiyülahir 1324/ 11 June 1906.

83 MA. USAD. no: 1492 İbrahim Edhem Efendi of Aydın. 24 Teşrinisani 1313/ 6 December 1897.

84 For instance, MA. USAD. no: 171. Hasan Tahsin Efendi of Konya. 24 Haziran 1309/ 06 July 1893. While Hasan Tahsin Efendi of Konya worked in Trablusgarp as a naib with a salary of 1000 piasters in 1884, he was appointed to Konya with a salary of 500 piasters in 1888. This proves that the salary of naibs changed according to the region in which they worked.

85 MA. USAD. no: 464. Halil Hulusi Efendi of Adana. 5 Kanunuevvel 1326/ 29 December 1910.

86 MA. USAD. no: 467. Mehmed Şakir Efendi of Kastamonu. 11 Haziran 1326/ 24 June 1910.

87 MA. USAD. no: 10. Ali Rıza Efendi of Erzurum. 15 Kanunusani 1308/ 27 January 1893.

88 BOA. DH. MKT. 668/ 63. 2 Teşrinisani 1318/ 15 November 1902.

89 BOA. A.} MKT. UM. 532/ 24. 12 Receb 1278/ 13 January 1862.

90 Afaf Lutfi al-Sayyid Marsot, "The Ulema of Cairo in the Eighteenth and Nineteenth Centuries," in *Scholars Saints and Sufis: Muslim Religious Institutions Since 1500*, 153.

91 BOA. BEO. 4575/343071. 20 Şaban 1337/ 21 May 1919.

92 MA. USAD. no: 890. Mustafa Asım Efendi of Bitlis. 21 Haziran 1327/ 4 July 1911.

93 MA. USAD. no: 2282. Süleyman Şakir Efendi of Hüdavendigar. 17 Temmuz 1326/ 30 July 1910.

94 For instance, MA. USAD. no: 451. Mehmed Sadık Efendi of Adana. 1 Muharrem 1310/ 26 Temmuz 1892; MA. USAD. no: 169. Mehmed Tevfik Efendi of Ankara. 15 Safer 1310/ 8 September 1892. Sultan Mahmut II gave 5000 piasters to Mehmed Tevfik Efendi of Ankara in 1837.

95 BOA. DH. MKT. 1950/ 89. 20 Şevval 1309/ 12 May 1892.

96 BOA. DH. MKT. 2155/ 74. 19 Şaban 1316/ 2 January 1899.

97 BOA. DH. MKT. 1580/ 6. 26 Rabiyülahir 1306/ 30 December 1888.

98 Nadir Özbek, "Osmanlı İmparatorluğu'nda Sosyal Yardım Uygulamaları," in *Tanzimat: Değişim Sürecinde Osmanlı İmparatorluğu*, 585, 597, 598.

99 BOA. BEO. 473/ 35431. 11 Rabiyyülevvel 1312/ 22 September 1894.

100 Şeref Gözübüyük and Suna Kili, *Türk Anayasa Metinleri*, (Ankara: Ankara Üniversitesi Siyasal Bilgiler Fakültesi Yayınları, 1982), 32. Article 39 of the Kanun-i esasi concerns the conditions and duration of civil service in the government hierarchy. This article stipulates that civil servants will remain in civilian service for life unless they are legally dismissed or resing.

101 MA. USAD. no: 3328. Mustafa Mahfi Efendi of İzmit. 22 Teşrinievvel 1308/ 3 November 1892. The fact that provincial administrators embarked on a quest for a new mufti upon the death of the Murad Fuad Efendi of İzmit reveals that muftis functioned for life.

102 *Düstur*, Tertib-i Evvel, IV, 773–789.

103 *Düstur*, Tertib-i Sani, I, 667.

104 *Düstur*, Tertib-i Sani, I, 667.

105 *Düstur*, Tertib-i Sani, I, 667.

106 *Düstur*, Tertib-i Sani, I, 668.

107 BOA. BEO. 764/ 57292. 29 Şevval 1313/ 13 April 1896.

108 *Düstur*, Tertib-i Sani, I, 668; BOA. BEO. 387/ 288610. 23 Muharrem 1329/ 24 January 1911; BOA. BEO. 473/ 35431. 11 Rabiyülevvel 1312/ 22 September 1894.

109 *Düstur*, Tertib-i Sani, I, 670.

110 *Düstur*, Tertib-i Sani, I, 672; BOA. ŞD. 2800/ 36. 10 Cemaziyelahir 1329/ 8 June 1911.

111 BOA. A.} DVN. MKL. 22/ 24. 8 Zilhicce 1299/ 21 October 1882.

112 *Düstur*, Tertib-i Sani, I, 326–333.

113 MA. USAD. no: 1981. İsmail Efendi of Hüdavendigar. 7 Mayıs 1327/ 20 May 1911.

114 MA. USAD. no: 181. Ali Fahreddin of Bolu. 28 Mayıs 1326/ 22 May 1910.

115 MA. USAD. no: 2303. Mehmed Tahir Efendi of Diyarbakır. 7 Haziran 1326/ 22 April 1915.

116 For instance, MA. USAD. no: 10. Ali Rıza Efendi of Erzurum. 15 Kanunusani 1308/ 27 January 1893. Ali Efendi from Erzurum reports in a complaint letter to Meclisi Mebusan that there were examples of individuals continuing to work

despite reaching age sixty-five. He also indicated that he was retired because no one protected him.

117 MA. USAD. no: 10. Ali Rıza Efendi of Erzurum. 15 Kanunusani 1308/ 27 January 1893.

118 MA. USAD. no: 4014. Mehmed Emin Efendi of Aydın. 31 Rabiyülevvel 1333/ 15 February 1915.

119 *Düstur*, Tertib-i Sani, I, 667; BOA. BEO. 4111/308325. 01 Zilhicce 1330/ 11 November 1912.

120 There were many documents in the archive with this topic regarding the exemption from age limit, see; BOA. ŞD. 28/ 36. 20 Mart 1327/2 April 1911; BOA. BEO. 3703/ 277716. 20 Şubat 1325/ 10 March 1910; BOA. BEO. 4056/ 304153. 14 Mayıs 1327/ 27 May 1911.

121 BOA. MV. 216/ 133. 30 Zilkade 1337/ 27 August 1919.

122 MA. USAD. no: 4014. Mehmed Emin Efendi of Aydın. 31 Rabiyülevvel 1333/ 15 February 1915.

123 BOA. BEO. 3703/ 277716. 20 Şubat 1325/ 10 March 1910; BOA. DH. MUİ. 66/ 2. 7 Rabiyülevvel 1328/ 19 March 1910.

124 MA. USAD. no: 3328. Mustafa Mahfi Efendi of İzmit. 22 Teşrinievvel 1308/ 3 November 1892.

125 BOA. BEO. 3703/ 277716. 20 Subat 1325/ 10 March 1910.

126 MA. USAD. no: 1981. İsmail Efendi of Hüdavendigar. 7 Mayıs 1327/ 20 May 1911.

127 BOA. BEO. 764/ 57292. 29 Şevval 1313/13 April 1896.

128 BOA. Y. PRK. MYD. 7/109. 22 Zilhicce 1305/ 30 August 1888.

129 BOA. BEO. 1349/ 101155. 15 Haziran 1315/ 27 June 1899.

130 MA. USAD. no: 23. Hüseyin Avni Efendi of Ankara. 24 Receb 1316/ 08 December 1898.

131 BOA. Y. PRK. MYD. 7/ 110. 22 Zilhicce 1305/ 30 August 1838.

132 MA. USAD. no: 3662. Mustafa Vasfi Efendi of Bolu. 21 Mayıs 1326/ 3 June 1910.

133 BOA. İ. TAL. 80/ 54. 5 Zilhicce 1312/ 30 May 1895.

134 BOA. Y. PRK. DH. 10/ 98. 14 Zilhicce 1316/ 25 April 1899.

135 BOA. BEO. 3542/ 265639. 14 Rabiyülahir 1327/ 5 May 1909

136 BOA. DH. SYS. 52/ 4. 7 Rabiyülahir 1330/ 26 March 1912.

137 MA. USAD. No: 8. Abdullah Şevket Efendi of Konya. 16 Eylül 1325/ 29 September 1909; MA. USAD. no: 2432. Yusuf Efendi of Trabzon. 2 Eylül 1326/ 15 September 1910; MA. USAD. no: 467. Mehmed Şakir Efendi of Kastamonu. 11 Haziran 1326/ 24 June 1910; MA. USAD. no: 1015. Rüşdü Efendi of Mamratülaziz. 10 Kanunuevvel 1308/ 22 December 1892; MA. USAD. no: 3420. Abdüllatif Lütfi Efendi of Mamratülaziz. 24 Mayıs 1326/ 6 June 1910; BOA. DH. EUM. AYŞ. 67/34. 06 Rabiyülevvel 1338/ 29 November 1919; BOA. MKT. 232/49. 29 Şevval 1311/ 5 May 1894;

138 MA. USAD. no: 3420. Abdüllatif Lütfi Efendi of Mamuratülaziz. 24 Mayıs 1326/ 9 June 1910.
139 MA. USAD. no: 467. Mehmed Şakir Efendi of Kastamonu. 11 Haziran 1326/ 24 June 1910.
140 MA. USAD. no: 1015. Rüşdü Efendi of Mamratülaziz. 10 Kanunuevvel 1308/ 22 December 1892.
141 MA. USAD. no: 2432. Yusuf Efendi of Trabzon. 2 Eylül 1326/ 15 September 1910.
142 MA. USAD. No: 8. Abdullah Şevket Efendi of Konya. 16 Eylül 1325/ 29 September 1909.
143 BOA. DH. EUM. AYŞ. 67/34. 06 Rabiyülevvel 1338/ 29 November 1919.
144 BOA. MKT. 232/49. 29 Şevval 1311/ 5 May 1894.
145 BOA. BEO. 213/ 15929. 16 Mayıs 1309/ 28 May 1893.
146 BOA. BEO. 2800/ 209944. 24 Mart 1322/ 6 April 1906.
147 BOA. MF. MKT. 263/ 19. 29 Haziran 1310/ 11 July 1894.
148 The salary known as arpalık in the classical period was called a tarik salary in the Tanzimat period.
149 MA. USAD. no: 3420. Abdüllatif Lütfi Efendi of Mamuratülaziz 24 Mayıs 1326/ 9 June 1910.
150 MA. USAD. no: 359. Salih Nazım Efendi of Erzurum. 15 Mayıs 1326/ 28 May 1910.
151 MA. USAD. no: 853. Mustafa Bahri Efendi of Aydın. 15 Şubat 1325/ 28 February 1910.
152 MA. USAD. no: 967. Ahmed Sami Efendi of Konya. 22 Teşrinisani 1308/ 4 December 1892.
153 MA. USAD. no: 2720. Mustafa Efendi of Konya. 20 Haziran 1326/ 3 July 1910.
154 MA. USAD. no: 918. İsmail Hakkı Efendi of Kastamonu. 27 Mayıs 1326/ 9 June 1910.
155 MA. USAD. no: 451 Mehmed Sadık Efendi of Adana. 1 Muharrem 1310/ 26 Temmuz 1892.
156 MA. USAD. no: 594. Mehmed Rüşdü Efendi of Konya, 29 Mart 1312/ 10 April 1896.
157 MA. USAD. no: 3413. Mehmed Fevzi Efendi of Konya. 27 Mayıs 1326/ 9 June 1910; MA. USAD. no: 2842. Osman Efendi of Mamuratülaziz. 12 Teşrinievvel 1326/ 25 December 1910; MA. USAD. no: 4439. Abdurrahman Halis Efendi of Urfa. 20 Mart 1334/ 20 March 1918.
158 MA. USAD. no: 890. Mustafa Asım Efendi of Bitlis. 21 Haziran 1327/ 4 July 1911.
159 MA. USAD. no: 1575. Nadir Cemil Efendi of Adana. 14 Eylül 1323/ 27 September 1907.
160 MA. USAD. no: 181. Ali Fahreddin Efendi of Bolu, 28 Mayıs 1326/ 22 May 1910.

161 MA. USAD. no: 1354. Ali Kemal Efendi of Hüdavendigar. 21 Temmuz 1326/ 3 August 1910.
162 MA. USAD. no: 304. Abdülhamid Hilmi Efendi of Trabzon. 14 Haziran 1326/ 27 June 1910.
163 BOA. BEO. 623/ 46720. 23 Zilkade 1312/ 18 May 1895.
164 BOA. ZB. 453/ 37. 25 Mart 1323/ 7 April 1907.
165 MA. USAD. no: 464. Halil Hulusi Efendi of Adana. 5 Kanunuevvel 1326/ 29 December 1910.
166 MA. USAD. no: 1248. Ahmed Hilmi Efendi of Diyarbakır. 8 Eylül 1308/ 20 September 1892.
167 MA. USAD. no: 638. İsmail Efendi of Ankara. 15 Rabiyülevvel 1329/ 16 March 1911.
168 BOA. DH. MKT. 1275/ 45. 6 Receb 1326/ 4 August 1908.
169 Abdülhamit Kırmızı, *Rulers of the Provincial Empire: Ottoman Governors and The Administration of Provinces 1895-1908*, PhD Diss. *(Istanbul: Boğaziçi University, 2005)*, 4.
170 MA. USAD. no: 451. Mehmed Sadık Efendi of Adana. 1 Muharrem 1310/ 26 Temmuz 1892.
171 MA. USAD. no: 5281. Mahmud Celaleddin of Adana. 16 Teşrinisani 1336/ 16 November 1920.
172 MA. USAD. no: 1575. Nadir Cemil Efendi of Adana. 14 Eylül 1323/ 27 September 1907.
173 MA. USAD. no: 3880. Rıfat Efendi of Ankara. 7 Nisan 1327/ 20 April 1911.
174 BOA. MF.MKT. 387/ 7. 19 Şevval 1315/ 13 March 1898; BOA. MF. MKT 452/ 32. 07 Safer 1317/ 17 June 1899. For instance, MA, USAD no: 1465 Ömer Faruk Efendi of Uşak. 30 Kanunusani 1331/ 12 February 1916; MA. USAD. no: 918. İsmail Hakkı Efendi of Kastamonu. 27 Mayıs 1326/ 9 June 1910; MA. USAD. no: 939 Abdullah Efendi of Konya 21 Temmuz 1326/ 3 August 1910; MA. USAD. no:1052. Yusuf Talat Efendi of Konya. 4 Temmuz 1320/ 17 July 1904; MA. USAD. no: 1579. Ahmed Naci Efendi of Konya. 30 Haziran 1326/ 13 July 1910.; MA. USAD. no: 3428. Süleyman Sırrı Efendi of Konya. 4 Mart 1325/ 17 March 1909; MA. USAD. no:384. Osman Nuri Efendi of Sivas. 27 Mayıs 1326/ 9 June 1910; MA. USAD. no: 1207, Mustafa Hulusi Efendi of Aydın. 31 Kanunusani 1307/ 31 January 1921; MA. USAD. no: 2416. İsmail Sabri Efendi of Sivas. 5 Şubat 1330/ 18 February 1915; MA. USAD. no:2431. Hasan Tahsin Efendi of Sivas. 11 Rabiyyülahir 1310/ 2 November 1892; MA. USAD. no: 3709. Mehmed Emin Efendi of Sivas. 30 Eylül 1326/ 13 October 1910; MA. USAD. no: 1420. Abdülkadir Efendi of Trabzon. 21 Temmuz 1326/ 3 August 1910; MA. USAD. no: 4439. Abdurrahman Halis Efendi of Urfa. 20 Mart 1334/ 20 March 1918; MA. USAD. no: 2194. Abdülkadir Efendi of Urfa. 15 Şevval 1309/ 13 May 1892; MA. USAD.

no: 2777. Hasan Hüsnü Efendi of Hakkari. 14 Şubat 1326/ 27 February 1911. MA, USAD no: 23, Hüseyin Avni Efendi of Ankara, 24 Receb 1316/ 8 December 1898; MA. USAD. no: 839. Mehmed Halid Efendi of Aydın. 16 Şubat 1326/ 1 March 1911; MA. USAD. no: 2287. İbrahim Efendi of Diyarbakır. 19 Temmuz 1308/ 31 July 1892; MA. USAD. no: 2299. Hüseyin Efendi of Diyarbakır. 1 Mart 1326/ 14 March 1910; MA. USAD no: 2302. 18 Temmuz 1327/ 31 July 1911; MA. USAD. no: 359. Salih Nazım Efendi of Erzurum. 15 Mayıs 1326/ 28 May 1910; MA. USAD. no: 529. Hacı Ahmet Necati of Erzurum. 22 Kanunuevvel 1329/ 4 January 1910; MA. USAD. No: 2513. Halil Efendi of İzmit. 1 Şubat 1326/ 14 February 1911; MA. USAD. no: 3328. Mustafa Mahfi Efendi of İzmit. 22 Teşrinievvel 1308/ 3 November 1892; MA. USAD. no: 3469. Mehmed Emin Efendi of İzmit. 17 Haziran 1326/ 30 June 1910. MA. USAD. no: 176. Ahmed Nazif Efendi of Kastamonu. 26 Ağustos 1308/ 7 September 1892; MA. USAD. no: 433. Mehmed İzzet Efendi of Kastamonu. 9 Kanunusani 1308/ 21 January 1893. All of these worked in the general madrasas and the newly established schools at the same time.

175 MA. USAD. no: 3428. Süleyman Sırrı Efendi of Konya. 4 Mart 1325/ 17 March 1909.

176 MA. USAD. no: 3428. Süleyman Sırrı Efendi of Konya. 4 Mart 1325/ 17 March 1909; MA. USAD. no: 3413. Mehmed Fevzi Efendi of Konya. 27 Mayıs 1326/ 9 June 1910; MA. USAD. no: 650. Halit Efendi of Kastamonu. 29 Haziran 1330/ 12 July 1914; MA. USAD. no: 918. İsmail Hakkı Efendi of Kastamonu. 27 Mayıs 1326/ 9 June 1910; MA. USAD. no: 1207. Mustafa Hulusi Efendi of Aydın. 31 Kanunusani 1307/ 31 January 1921.

177 MA. USAD. no: 1354. Ali Kemal Efendi of Hüdavendigar. 21 Temmuz 1326/ 3 August 1910.

178 MA. USAD. no: 2303. Mehmed Tahir Efendi of Diyarbakır. 7 Haziran 1326/ 22 April 1915.

179 MA. USAD. no: 650. Halit Efendi of Kastamonu. 29 Haziran 1330/ 12 July 1914.

180 MA. USAD. no: 384. Osman Nuri Efendi of Sivas. 27 Mayıs 1326/ 9 June 1910.

181 MA. USAD. no: 1605. Mustafa Efendi of Adana. 1 Kanunuevvel 1327/ 14 December 1911.

182 MA. USAD. no: 918. İsmail Hakkı Efendi of Kastamonu. 27 Mayıs 1326/ 9 June 1910.

183 MA. USAD. no: 1354. Ali Kemal Efendi of Hüdavendigar. 21 Temmuz 1326/ 3 August 1910.

184 MA. USAD. no: 2777. Hasan Hüsnü Efendi of Hakkari. 14 Şubat 1326/ 27 February 1911.

185 BOA. BEO. 1453/ 108935. 7 Zilkade 1317/ 9 March 1900.

186 For instance, MA. USAD. no: 605. Ebubekir Sıtkı Efendi of Ankara. 16 Ağustos 1308/ 28 August 1892.

187 BOA. BEO. 4056/ 304153. 14 Mayıs 1327/ 27 May 1911. In the process of appointing Hasan Hilmi Efendi as mufti in 1911, Hasan Efendi's commitment and love for the constitutional monarchy were highlighted by the governor.

5 Social Profile of the Ulema: A Prosopographical Study

1 For "prosopography," see Lawrence Stone, "Prosopography," *Daedalus* 100, 1 (Winter 1971): 46–47. Prosopography is the investigation of common background characteristics of a group of actors in history by studying their collective lives.
2 Findley, *The Bureaucratic Reform in The Ottoman Empire: The Sublime Porte, 1789-1922,* 65, 167. The bureaucratic centralization in the Ottoman Empire was accompanied by a great increase in the total number of personnel who served as civil officials in service at the beginning of the nineteenth century. The total number of men serving in the bureaucracy reached approximately 50,000 to 100,000 under the rule of Sultan Abdülhamid II from 1,000–1,500 men at the end of the eighteenth century. The total size of the officials in the Şeyhülislam Office was about six thousand within the total number of Ottoman officials.
3 For instance, we learn from these biographies that the majority of the members of the ulema were hazel-eyed, wheat-skinned, and medium-sized. There were also tall, dark-skinned ulema. Again, according to these documents, most ulema had one wife and others had no wives.
4 For instance, MA. USAD. no: 2961. Ahmed Hamdi Efendi of Kastamonu. 27 Kanunusani 1328/ 9 July 1913.
5 See MA. USAD. no: 1207. Mustafa Hulusi Efendi of Aydın. 31 Kanunusani 1307/ 31 January 1921
6 Zerdeci, *Osmanlı Ulema Biyografilerinin Arşiv Kaynakları*, 45.
7 Ibid., 45.
8 Ibid., 46.
9 Carter Vaughn Findley, *Kalemiyeden Mülkiyeye Osmanlı Memurlarının Toplumsal Tarihi* (Istanbul: Tarih Vakfı Yurt Yayınları, 1996).
10 Ahmet Şamil Gürer, *Gelenekle Modernite Arasında Bir Meşrutiyet Şeyhülislamı: Musa Kazım Efendi (1861-1920).* PhD Dissertation, (Ankara: Hacettepe University, 2003).
11 Further examples may be cited. See, for instance, BOA, Y. PRK. BŞK. 62/81. 10 Rabiyülevvel 1318/ 8 July 1900. Abdulkadir Reşid Efendi, who participated in the classes of *huzur-u hümayun* was assigned as *Bab-ı Meşihat Müsteşarı*, which was a high-level position in the office of Şeyhülislam.

12 MA. USAD. no: 1902. Mehmed Kamil Efendi of Hüdavendigar. 5 Ağustos 1309/ 17 August 1893.

13 MA. USAD. no: 169. Mehmed Tevfik Efendi of Ankara. 15 Safer 1310/ 8 September 1892. "*Sultan mahmud hazretleri tarafından davet buyrulmağla beraber deraliyeye gelip pederime hürmet-i mahsusa olmak üzere müşarünileyh Sultan Mahmud han hazretlerinin huzuru hümayunlarına müşerref.*"

14 MA. USAD. no: 169. Mehmed Tevfik Efendi of Ankara. 15 Safer 1310/ 8 September 1892.

15 MA. USAD. no: 653. Mehmed Emin Efendi of Kastamonu. 28 Haziran 1330/ 11 July 1914.

16 MA. USAD. no: 890, Mustafa Asım Efendi of Bitlis. 21 Haziran 1327/ 4 July 1911.

17 MA. USAD. no: 653. Mehmed Emin Efendi of Kastamonu. 28 Haziran 1330/ 11 July 1914.

18 MA. USAD. no: 2431. Hasan Tahsin Efendi of Sivas. 11 Rabiyülahir 1310/ 2 November 1892.

19 MA. USAD. no: 428. Ali Vehbi Efendi of Trabzon. 28 Teşrinievvel 1308/ 10 January 1913.

20 See MA. USAD. no: 384. Osman Nuri Efendi of Sivas. 27 Mayıs 1326/ 9 June 1910.

21 See MA. USAD. no: 653. Mehmed Emin Efendi of Kastamonu. 28 Haziran 1330/ 11 July 1914; MA. USAD. no: 229. Yusuf Efendi of Trabzon. 7 Receb 1328/ 15 July 1910.

22 MA. USAD. no: 199. Ahmed Hulusi Efendi of Ankara. 21 Teşrinievvel 1308/ 2 October 1892.

23 MA. USAD. no: 1575. Nadir Cemil Efendi of Adana. 14 Eylül 1323/ 27 September 1907.

24 MA. USAD. no: 433. Mehmed İzzet Efendi of Kastamonu. 9 Kanunusani 1308/ 21 January 1893.

25 MA. USAD. no: 199. Ahmed Hulusi Efendi of Ankara. 21 Teşrinievvel 1308/ 2 October 1892.

26 MA. Meclis-i Mesalih Talebe Defterleri no: 2195, 2196, 2197, 2198, 2199, 2200, 2201, 2203.

27 MA. USAD. no: 3420. Lütfi Efendi of Mamuratülaziz. 24 Mayıs 1326/ 9 June 1910; MA. USAD. no: 901. Ahmed Cevdet Efendi of Aydın. 18 Cemaziyelahir 1326/ 18 June 1908.

28 MA. USAD. no: 3585. Hüseyin Hilmi Efendi of Konya. 10 Mart 1336/ 10 March 1910. "Although Hüseyin of Konya graduated from a Konya madrasa in the Akseki district, he attained the highest teaching position, the Fatih Dersiamship.

29 Kemal Karpat, "Ottoman Population Records and Census of 1881/82-1893," *International Journal of Middle East Studies* 9, 2 (1978): 237–274.

30 Zerdeci, *Osmanlı Ulema Biyografilerinin Arşiv Kaynakları*, 45.

31 Ibid., 45.

32 MA. USAD. no: 2282. Süleyman Şakir Efendi of Hüdavendigar. 17 Temmuz 1326/ 30 July 1910.

33 For instance, MA. USAD. no: 30. Mehmed Raşid Efendi of Trabzon. 25 Zilkade 1310/ 10 June 1893.

34 For a detailed account of this new school for judges see Akiba, "A New School for Qadis: Education of the Sharia Judges in the Late Ottoman Empire," 2003.

35 For instance, MA. USAD. no: 23, Hüseyin Avni Efendi of Ankara, 24 Receb 1316/ 8 December 1898. While Beşiktaş Naib Hüseyin Avni Efendi was educated in the Fatih Camii Madrasa, he also entered Darulmuallim, and he graduated from both successfully.

36 For research on the late Ottoman education system and schools, see Benjamin C. Fortna, *Imperial Classroom: Islam, The State, and Education in the Late Ottoman Empire* (Oxford: Oxford University Press, 2002); Benjamin C. Fortna, "Islamic Morality in late Ottoman 'Secular' Schools," *International Journal of Middle Eastern Studies* 32, 3 (2000).

37 MA. USAD. no: 2431. Hasan Tahsin Efendi of Sivas. 11 Rabiyyülahir 1310/ 2 November 1892.

38 MA. USAD. no: 242. Abdülhalim Efendi of Kastamonu. 23 Mayıs 1326/ 5 June 1910.

39 MA. USAD. no: 2431. Hasan Tahsin Efendi of Sivas. 11 Rabiyülahir 1310/ 2 November 1892.

40 MA. USAD. no: 871. Ahmed Cemil Efendi of Diyarbakır. 9 Mayıs 1326/ 22 May 1910.

41 For instance, MA. USAD. no: 2553. Abdullah Efendi of Konya. 8 Temmuz 1330/ 21 July 1914. Abdullah of Konya founded a madrasa in Ermenek, was appointed to the duty of müderris in this madrasa, and started to work for a salary of 150 piasters.

42 *Arpalık* means payments in addition to the salaries of members of the Ilmiye.

43 Ibid., 392–393.

44 BOA. İ. DH 1267/ 99649. 13 Şubat 1307/ 25 February 1892.

45 MA. USAD. no: 432. Halil İbrahim Efendi of Konya. 16 Kanunusani 1308/ 28 January 1893.

46 MA. USAD. no: 1929. Mehmed Hamdi Efendi of Hüdavendigar. 14 Temmuz 1326/ 27 July 1910.

47 MA. USAD. no: 2961. Ahmed Hamdi Efendi of Kastamonu. 27 Kanunusani 1328/ 9 July 1913.

48 MA. USAD. no: 2329. Mehmed Necib Efendi of Sivas. 28 Temmuz 1308/ 9 August 1892.

49 MA. USAD. no: 2303. Ahmed Hilmi Efendi of Diyarbakır. 7 Cemaziyelahir 1333/ 20 June 1910.

50 MA. USAD. no: 2303. Mehmed Tahir Efendi of Diyarbakır. 7 Haziran 1326/ 22 April 1915.

51 MA. USAD. no: 204. İlyas Avni Efendi of Kastamonu. 23 Cemaziyelevvel 1328/ 2 June 1910.

6 Ulema in the Context of Everyday Social Life

1 An earlier version of this chapter has been published in *Middle Eastern Studies*; Erhan Bektaş, "The Role of Ottoman Ulema in Peaceful Conflict Resolution," *Middle Eastern Studies*, 56:6, (2020), 772–783.

2 Albert Hourani, Philip Khoury, Mary C. Wilson. eds. *The Modern Middle East* (New York: I. B. Tauris, 2004), 89.

3 Ibid., 89-90.

4 Gibb and Bowen, *Islamic Society and the West,* 81.

5 Denis Dragovic, *Religion and Post-Conflict Statebuilding: Roman Catholic and Sunni Islamic Perspectives* (London: Palgrave Macmillan, 2015).

6 For those recent studies, see, Abdülhamid Kırmızı, "Rulers of the Provincial Empire: Ottoman Governors and the Administration of Provinces, 1895–1908" (PhD diss., Boğaziçi University, 2005); Marc Aymes A Provincial History of the Ottoman Empire: Cyprus and the Eastern Mediterranean in the Nineteenth Century (London: SOAS/ Routledge Studies on the Middle East, 2013); John Bragg, Ottoman Notables and Participatory Politics: Tanzimat Reform in Tokat, 1839–1876 (New York: Routledge, 2014); Ipek Yosmaoğlu, Blood Ties: Religion, Violence, and the Politics of Nationhood in Ottoman Macedonia, 1878–1908 (Ithaca, NY: Cornell University Press, 2016); and Yücel Terzibaşoğlu, "Land Disputes and Ethno-Politics: North-western Anatolia, 1877–1912" in S. Engerman and J. Metzer (eds), Ethno-Nationality, Property Rights in Land and Territorial Sovereignty in Historical Perspective (London: Routledge, 2004).

7 Kırmızı, "Rulers of the Provincial Empire: Ottoman Governors and the Administration of Provinces, 1895–1908", pp. 156–60.

8 Bragg, Ottoman Notables and Participatory Politics: Tanzimat Reform in Tokat, 1839–1876.

9 Yonca Köksal, *Local Intermediaries and Ottoman State Centralization: A Comparison of the Tanzimat Reforms in the Provinces of Ankara and Edirne (1839-1878),* PhD Diss., (Colombia: Colombia University, 2002), 103.

10 Albert Hourani, "Ottoman Reform and the Politics of Notables," in *The Modern Middle East*, 41–68.

11 Green, *The Tunisian Ulama 1873-1915: Social Structure and Response to Ideological Currents*, 63.

12 Ira M. Lapidus, *Muslim Cities in the Later Middle Ages* (Massachusetts: Harvard University Press, 1967), 107–115.

13 BOA. DH. TMIK. M. 221/ 43. 8 Rabiyülevvel 1324/ 2 May 1906.

14 BOA. Y. PRK. BŞK. 63/ 76. 3 Nisan 1318/ 16 April 1902.

15 BOA. Y. EE. 131/ 28. 22 Zilkade 1313/ 5 May 1896.

16 BOA. BEO. 382/ 286. 5 Haziran 1311/ 15 June 1895.

17 BOA. DH. MKT. 2858/ 69. 29 Cemaziyelahir 1327/ 18 July 1909.
18 BOA. BEO. 2589/ 194166. 29 Rabiyülahir 1323/ 3 July 1905.
19 BOA. HR. TO. 513/ 62. 15 Cemaziyelevvel 1293/ 8 June 1876.
20 BOA. Y. PRK. UM. 4/ 78. 27 Şubat 1298/ 11 March 1883.
21 BOA. HR. TO. 513/ 62. 15 Cemaziyelevvel 1293/ 8 June 1876.
22 BOA. DH. MUİ. 63/ 36. 28 Mart 1328/ 10 April 1912.
23 BOA. HSDTFR1. 1/ 7. 6 Mart 1309/ 18 March 1893.
24 BOA. A.} MKT. MHM. 660/ 25. 8 Haziran 1284/ 20 June 1868.
25 BOA. BEO. 3039/ 227873. 10 Nisan 1323/ 23 April 1907.
26 BOA. DH. MKT. 808/ 17. 25 Kanunuevvel 1319/ 5 January 1904.
27 Nadir Özbek, "Policing the Countryside: Gendarmes of the Late 19th-Century Ottoman Empire (1876-1908)," *International Journal of Middle East Studies* 40 (2008): 52. Özbek says that the Ottoman Empire created gendarmerie regiments and battalions in each province and district during the 1870s in order to ensure social order in society. These military officers were seen as a solution to disturbances, political uprisings, and separatist movements. However, the number of the battalions was inadequate particularly in the Balkans and the eastern provinces of the empire to suppress rebels and control the regions due to the budget difficulties. In such regions and conditions, the government needs other mediatory forces.
28 BOA. DH. MKT. 2751/ 24. 21 Subat 1324/ 6 March 1909.
29 BOA. BEO. 862/ 64641. 25 Teşrinievvel 1312/ 6 November 1896.
30 BOA. Y. PRK. MYD 7/ 138. 29 Zilhicce 1305/ 6 September 1888.
31 BOA. Y. PRK. BŞK. 14/ 15. 18 Eylül 1304/ 30 September 1888; BOA. Y. PRK. MYD. 7/ 37. 27 Eylül 1304/ 9 October 1888.
32 BOA. Y. PRK. MYD. 7/ 121. 21 Ağustos 1304/ 2 September 1888.
33 BOA. Y. PRK. MYD. 7/ 138. 29 Zilhicce 1305/ 6 September 1888; BOA. DH. MKT. 1567/ 2. 8 Teşrinisani 1304/ 20 November 1888.
34 BOA. Y. MTV. 35/ 2. 29 Ağustos 1304/ 10 September 1888; BOA. Y. PRK. MYD. 7/ 125. 8 Ağustos 1304/ 20 August 1888.
35 BOA. Y. PRK. ASK. 51/ 33. 17 Teşrinievvel 1304/ 29 December 1888.
36 BOA. Y. PRK. MYD. 7/ 54. 2 Ağustos 1304/ 14 August 1888.
37 BOA. Y. PRK. MYD. 7/ 46. 31 Temmuz 1304/ 12 August 1888.
38 BOA. Y. MTV. 34/ 91. 21 Ağustos 1304/ 2 September 1888.
39 BOA. ŞD. 314/ 29. 21 Ağustos 1304/ 2 September 1888.
40 BOA. Y. PRK. MYD. 7/ 109. 18 Ağustos 1304/ 30 August 1888; BOA. Y. PRK. MYD. 7/ 110. 18 Ağustos 1304/ 30 August 1888.

Bibliography

ARCHIVES

Meşihat Archive *(Meşihat Arşivi)*, MA
Personnel Records of the Ulema *(Sicill-i Ahval Dosyaları)*, USAD
Prime Ministry Ottoman Archives *(Başbakanlık Osmanlı Arşivi)*, BOA:

BOA. A.} MKT. MVL.
BOA. A.} MKT. NZD.
BOA. A.} MKT. MHM.
BOA. A.} AMD.
BOA. A.} DVN.
BOA. BEO.
BOA. C. ADL.
BOA. C. MF.
BOA. DH. MKT.
BOA. DH. MUİ.
BOA. DH. SYS.
BOA. DH. EUM. AYŞ.
BOA. DH. TMIK. M.
BOA. EV.d.
BOA. EV. BRT.
BOA. FTG.f.
BOA. HSDTFR1.
BOA. HR. TO.
BOA. HR. SFR.4.
BOA. HSDTFR1.
BOA. İ. DH.
BOA. İ. DUİT.
BOA. İ. MVL.
BOA. İ. MMS.
BOA. İ. TAL.
BOA. MV.
BOA. MF. MKT.
BOA. ŞD.
BOA. TS. MA.e.

BOA. Y. PRK. UM.
BOA. Y. PRK. DH.
BOA. Y. EE.
BOA. Y. MTV.
BOA. Y. PRK. BŞK.
BOA. Y. PRK. ASK.
BOA. Y. PRK. AZJ.
BOA. ZB.

PERIODICALS

Düstur, Tertib-i Evvel, IV
Düstur, Tertib-i Sani, I, II, VI, VII, IX
İlmiye Salnamesi, Matbaa-i Amire, Darü'l-hilafet'il-aliyye, 1334

NEWSPAPERS

Takvim-i Vekayi, 14 April 1873, 28 June 1877

BOOKS AND ARTICLES

Abou-El-Haj, Rifa'at Ali. *Formation of the Modern State: The Ottoman Empire, Sixteenth to Eighteenth Centuries*. Albany: State University of New York Press, 1991.

Ahmad, Feroz. *The Making of Modern Turkey*. London: Routledge, 1993.

Ágoston, Gábor. "A Flexible Empire, Authority, and Its Limits on the Ottoman Frontiers." *International Journal of Turkish Studies* 9, nos. 1–2 (2003): 15–31.

Akiba, Jun. "A New School for Qadis: Education of the Sharia Judges in the Late Ottoman Empire." *Turcica* 35 (2003): 125–163.

——. "From Kadi to Naib: Reorganization of the Ottoman Sharia Judiciary in the Tanzimat Period." In *Frontiers of Ottoman Studies: State, Province and the West*, edited by C. Imber and K. Kiyotaki, 43–60. London: I.B. Tauris, 2005.

——. "The Practice of Writing Curricula Vitae among the Lower Government Employees in the Late Ottoman Empire: Workers at the Şeyhülislam's Office." *European Journal of Turkish Studies* Thematic Issue, no. 6 (2007).

Akgündüz, Murat. *XIX Asır Başlarına Kadar Osmanlı Devleti'nde* Şeyhülislam*lık*. İstanbul: Beyan Yayınları, 2012.

Albayrak, Sadık. *Son Devir Osmanlı Uleması, İlmiye Ricalinin Teracim-i Ahvali*, 4 vols. Istanbul: Medrese Yayınevi, 1980.

Algar, Hamid. *Religion and State in Iran 1785-1906*. London: University of California Press, 1980.

Altuntaş, Zeynep. "Sultan Abdülmecid Dönemi Osmanlı Uleması." PhD Diss., Marmara University, 2013.

Argun, Selim. "Elite Configurations and Clusters of Power: The Ulema, Waqf, and Ottoman State (1789-1839)." Ph.D. Diss., McGill University, 2013.

Ashiwa, Yoshiko and Wank David L., eds. *Making Religion, Making the State*. Stanford: Stanford University Press, 2009.

Atçıl, Abdurrahman. *Scholars and Sultans in the Early Modern Ottoman Empire*. Cambridge: Cambridge University Press, 2017.

Aydın, Bilgin. "Osmanlı Yenileşme Döneminde Bab-ı Meşihat'in Bürokratik Yapısı ve Evrak İdaresi." Master's thesis, Marmara University, 1996.

——. "Osmanlı Devleti'nde Tekkeler Reformu ve Meclis-i Meşayihin Şeyhülislamlık'a Bağlı Olarak Kuruluşu, Faaliyetleri ve Arşivi." *İstanbul Araştırmaları* 7, (Fall 1998): 93–109.

——, İlhami Yurdakul, and İsmail Kurt, eds. Şeyhülislam*lık (Bab-ı Meşihat) Arşivi Defter Kataloğu*. Istanbul: İslam Araştırmaları Merkezi, 2006.

Aydoğdu, Rukiye. "19. Yüzyıl Osmanlı Toplumunda Tasavvuf-Hadis İlişkisi- Ahmed Ziyaeddin Gümüşhanevi Özelinde." Master's thesis, Ankara University, 2008.

Azra, Azyumardi. *The Origins of Islamic Reformism in Southeast Asia*. Australia: University of Hawai'i Press, 2004.

Baer, Gabriel, ed. *The "Ulama" in Modern History, Studies in Memory of Professor Uriel Heyd*. Jerusalem: Israel Oriental Society, 1971.

Baltacı, Cahit. "Arpalık." In *TDV İslam Ansiklopedisi* 3, 392–93. Istanbul: Türkiye Diyanet Vakfı Yayınları, 1991.

——. "Osmanlı Devleti'nde Eğitim ve Öğretim." *Türkler* XI (2002): 446–462.

Barkey, Karen. *Empire of Difference: The Ottomans in Comparative Perspective*. Cambridge: Cambridge University Press, 2008.

Barter, Shane Joshua. "Ulama, the State and War: Community Islamic Leaders in the Aceh Conflict." *Cont Islam* 5 (2011): 19–36.

Bayezit, Yasemin. "Tanzimat Devri Şeyhülislamlarından Meşrepzade Arif Efendi ve Kadılık Kurumundaki İstihdam Sorunu." *Bilig Türk Dünyası Sosyal Bilimler Dergisi* 54 (Summer 2010): 47–74.

Bayraktar, Faruk. *Türkiye'de Vaizlik Tarihçesi ve Problemleri*. Istanbul: Marmara Üniversitesi İlahiyat Fakültesi Yayınları, 1997.

Bein, Amit. *Ottoman Ulema, Turkish Republic: Agents of Change and Guardians of Tradition*. Stanford: Stanford University Press, 2011.

Bereketzade, İsmail Hakkı. *Yad-ı Mazi*. İstanbul: Nehir Yayınları, 1997.

Berkes, Niyazi. *The Development of Secularism in Turkey*. Montreal: McGill University Press, 1964.

Bilici, Faruk. "İmparatorluktan Cumhuriyete Geçiş Döneminde Türk Uleması." In *V. Milletlerarası Türkiye Sosyal ve İktisat Tarihi Kongresi (21–25 Ağustos 1989)*. Ankara: Türk Tarih Kurumu, 1990: 709–719.

Black, Antony. *The History of Islamic Political Thought: From the Prophet to the Present*. Edinburgh: Edinburgh University Press, 2011.

Buzpınar, Tufan Ş. "Nakibüleşraf." In *TDV İslam Ansiklopedisi* 32, 322–24. Istanbul: Türkiye Diyanet Vakfı Yayınları, 2006.

Ceylan, Ebubekir. "Ottoman Centralization and Modernization in the Province of Baghdad, 1831-1872." PhD Diss., Boğaziçi University, 2006.

Chambers, Richard L. "The Ottoman Ulema and the Tanzimat." In *Scholars, Saints, and Sufis: Muslim Religious Institutions in the Middle East since 1500*, edited by Nikki R. Keddie, 33–46. Berkeley: University of California Press, 1978.

Cihan, Ahmet. *Reform Çağında Osmanlı İlmiyye Sınıfı*. Istanbul: Birey, 2004.

Crecelius, Daniel. "Nonideological Responses of the Egyptian Ulama to Modernization." In *Scholars, Saints, and Sufis: Muslim Religious Institutions in the Middle East since 1500*, edited by Nikki R. Keddie, 167–210. Berkeley: University of California Press, 1978.

Çadırcı, Musa. "Tanzimat'ın İlanı Sıralarında Osmanlı İmparatorluğu'nda Kadılık Kurumu ve 1838 Tarihli Tarik-i İlmiyeye Dair Ceza Kanunnamesi, 12 Eylül 1838, 25 Ramazan 1254." *Ankara Üniversitesi Dil Tarih Coğrafya Fakültesi Tarih Araştırmaları Dergisi* 25 (1981): 148–158.

Çetin, Atilla. "Sicill-i Ahval Defterleri ve Dosyaları Hakkında Bir Araştırma." *Vakıflar Dergisi* 29 (2005): 87–104.

Davison, Roderic H. *Reform in the Ottoman Empire, 1856-1876*. Princeton: Princeton University Press, 1963.

Dede, İsmail. "Sebilürreşad Dergisi'nde Madrasa Öğrencilerinin Madrasayi Değerlendirmeleri." Master's thesis, Çanakkale Onsekiz Mart Üniversitesi, 2006.

Demirpolart, Anzavur and Gürsoy Akça. "Osmanlı Toplumunda Modernleşme ve Ulema." *Ekev Akademi Dergisi* 36 (Summer 2008): 119–132.

Devellioğlu, Ferit. *Osmanlıca-Türkçe Ansiklopedik Lügat: Eski ve Yeni Harflerle*. Ankara: Aydın Kitabevi Yayınları, 2011.

Dragovic, Denis. *Religion and Post-Conflict Statebuildung: Roman Catholic and Sunni Islamic Perspectives*. London: Palgrave Macmillan, 2015.

Erbay, Halil İbrahim. "Teaching and Learning in the Madrasas of Istanbul During The Late Ottoman Period." Ph.D. Diss., London: SOAS, University of London. 2009.

Ergün, Mustafa. "II. Meşrutiyet Devrinde Medreselerin Durumu ve Islah Çalışmaları." *Ankara Üniversitesi Dil ve Tarih-Coğrafya Fakültesi Dergisi* 1–2 (1982): 59–89.

Es-Sakkar, Sami. "Muid." In *TDV İslam Ansiklopesi* 31, 86–87. İstanbul: Türkiye Diyanet Vakfı Yayınları, 2006.

Findley, Carter Vaughn. *Bureaucratic Reform in the Ottoman Empire: The Sublime Porte 1789-1922*. Princeton: Princeton University Press, 1980.

——. *Ottoman Civil Officialdom: A Social History*. Princeton: Princeton University Press, 1989.

Fortna, Benjamin C. "Education and Autobiography at the End of the Ottoman Empire." *Die Welt des Islams* 41, no.1 (2001): 1–31.

Gelvin, James L. *The Modern Middle East*. New York: Oxford University Press, 2011.

Georgeon, François. *Sultan Abdülhamid*. Ali Berktay (trans.). İstanbul: İletişim Yayınları, 2012.

Gerber, Haim. *State, Society, and Law in Islam: Ottoman Law in Comparative Perspective*. Albany: State University of New York Press, 1994.

Gibb, H. A. R., and Harold Bowen. *Islamic Society and the West*. Vol. 1. London: Oxford University Press, 1957.

Gilbert, Joan E. "Institutionalization of Muslim Scholarship and Professionalization of the Ulama in Medieval Damascus,' *Studia Islamica* 52 (1980): 5–34.

Green, Arnold H. *The Tunisian Ulama 1873-1915*. Leiden: E. J. Brill, 1978.

Gunasti, Susan. *The Qur'an Between the Ottoman Empire and the Turkish Republic : An Exegetical Tradition*. Routledge: Routledge Studies, 2019.

Güldöşören, Arzu. "II. Mahmud Dönemi Osmanlı Uleması." PhD Diss., Marmara University, 2013.

Gündüz, İrfan. *Osmanlılarda Devlet-Tekke Münasebetleri*. Ankara: Seha Neşriyat, 1989.

Gürer, Ahmet Şamil. "Gelenekle Modernite Arasında Bir Meşrutiyet Şeyhülislamı: Musa Kazım Efendi (1861-1920)." PhD Diss., Hacettepe University, 2003.

Hatina, Meir, ed. *Guardians of Faith in Modern Time: "Ulama" in the Middle East*. Leiden: Brill, 2009.

——. "Historical Legacy and the Challenge of Modernity in the Middle East: The Case of al-Azhar in Egypt." *The Muslim World* 93, 1 (2003): 51–68.

Heyd, Uriel. "The Ottoman 'Ulema and Westernization in the Time of Selim III and Mahmud II." In *The Modern Middle East*, edited by Albert Habib Hourani, Philip S. Khoury and Mary C. Wilson, 29–59. Berkeley: University of California Press, 1993.

——, and Encümend Kuran. "Ilmiyye." In *Encyclopedia of Islam* vol. III, *Second Edition*, edited by P. Bearman, Th. Bianquis, C.E. Bosworth, E. van Donzel and W.P. Heinrichs. 1152–1155. New York: MacMillan, 2004.

——. "Some Aspects of the Ottoman Fetva." *School of Oriental and African Studies, University of London Bulletin* 32, 1 (1969): 35–56.

Hourani, Albert and Philip Khoury and Mary C. Wilson, eds. *The Modern Middle East*. New York: I. B. Tauris, 2004.

İhsanoğlu, Ekmeleddin. "Ottoman Educational and Scholarly-Scientific Institutions." In *History of the Ottoman State, Society and Civilization*, edited by Ekmeleddin İhsanoğlu, 357–515. Istanbul: IRCICA, 2001.

İnalcık, Halil. *The Ottoman Empire: The Classical Age, 1300-1600*. London: Phoenix, 1997.

İpşirli, Mehmet. "Osmanlı İlmiye Mesleği Hakkında Gözlemler: XVI-XVII. Asırlar." *Osmanlı Araştırmaları* 7 (1988): 273–285.

——. "İlmiye." In *TDV İslam Ansiklopedisi* 22, 141–145. Istanbul: Türkiye Diyanet Vakfı Yayınları, 2000.

——. "Osmanlı'da İlmiyeye Dair Çalışmalar Üzerine Gözlemler." In *Dünden Bugüne Osmanlı Araştırmaları: Tesbitler, Problemler, Teklifler*, edited by Ali Akyıldız, Ş. Tufan Buzpınar, and Mustafa Sinanoğlu, 267–277. Istanbul: İsam Yayınları, 2007.

——. "II. Mahmud Döneminde Vakıfların İdaresi." In *Sultan II. Mahmut ve Reformları Semineri*. Istanbul: İstanbul Üniversitesi Edebiyat Fakültesi, 1990: 49–57.

——. "Kazasker." In *TDV İslam Ansiklopedisi* 25, 140–143. Istanbul: Türkiye Diyanet Vakfı Yayınları, 2002.

——. "Çömez." In *TDV İslam Ansiklopedisi* 8, 380. Istanbul: Türkiye Diyanet Vakfı Yayınları, 1993.

——. "Mülazemet." In *TDV İslam Ansiklopedisi* 31, 537–539. Istanbul: Türkiye Diyanet Vakfı Yayınları, 2006.

——. "Cer." In *TDV İslam Ansiklopedisi* 7, 388–389. Istanbul: Türkiye Diyanet Vakfı Yayınları, 1993.

Kafadar, Cemal. *The Question of Ottoman Decline. Harward Middle Eastern and Islamic Review* 4 (1997–98): 30–75.

Kara, İsmail. *Din ile Modernleşme Arasında, Çağdaş Türk Düşüncesinin Meseleleri*. Istanbul: Dergah Yayınları, 2003.

——. "Turban and Fez: Ulema as Opposition." In *Late Ottoman Society: The Intellectual Legacy*, edited by Elisabeth Özdalga, 162–200. London: Routledge Curzon, 2005.

——. "Ulema-Siyaset İlişkisine Dair Önemli Bir Metin: Muhalefet Yapmak, Muhalefete Katılmak." *Divan* 3, 4 (1998): 1–25.

——. "Ulema Siyaset İlişkisine Dair Metinler II: Ey Ulema Bizim Gibi Konuş!." *Divan* 7 (1999): 65–134.

Kara, Mustafa. *Din, Hayat ve Sanat Açısından Tekkeler ve Zaviyeler*. Istanbul: Dergah Yayınları, 1980.

Karateke, Hakan T., and Maurus Reinkowski. *Legitimizing the Order the Ottoman Rhetoric of State Power*. Leiden: Brill, 2005.

Karon D. Salch. "Şeyhülislam and The Tanzimat." Ph.D. Diss., McGill University, 1980.

Karpat, Kemal H. *The Politicization of Islam: Reconstructing Identity, State, Faith, and Community in the Late Ottoman State*. London: Oxford University Press, 2001.

——. "Ottoman Population Records and Census of 1881/82-1893." *International Journal of Middle East Studies* 9, no. 2 (1978): 237–274.

Kaya, Kamil. "Sosyolojik Açıdan Türkiye'de Din-Devlet İlişkileri ve Diyanet İşleri Başkanlığı." PhD Diss., Istanbul: İstanbul University, 1994.

Keddie, Nikki R. "The Roots of the Ulama's Power in Modern Iran." In *Scholars, Saints, and Sufis: Muslim Religious Institutions in the Middle East since 1500*, edited by Nikki R. Keddie, 211-30. Berkeley: University of California Press, 1978.

Kellner-Heinkele, Barbara. "Family Politics of Ottoman Ulema. The Case of Sheykhulislam Seyyid Feyzullah Efendi and His Descendants." In *Kinship in the Altaic World: Proceedings of the 48th Permanent International Altaistic Conference, Moscow 10-15 July 2005*, edited by E. V. Bojkova and Rostislav B. Rybakov, 191–198. Wiesbaden: Harrassowitz, 2006.

Kenar, Ceren. "Bargaining Between Islam and Kemalism: An Investigation of Official Islam through Friday Sermons." Master's thesis, Boğaziçi University, 2011.

Kırlı, Cengiz. "Kahvehaneler ve Hafiyeler: 19. Yüzyıl Ortalarında Osmanlı'da Sosyal Kontrol." In *Tanzimat: Değişim Sürecinde Osmanlı İmparatorluğu,* edited by Halil İnalcık-Mehmet Seyitdanlıoğlu, 425–446. Istanbul: Phoenix Yayınları, 2011.

——. "Yolsuzluğun İcadı: 1840 Ceza Kanunu, İktidar ve Bürokrasi." *Tarih ve Toplum* 4 (2006): 45–119.

Kırmızı, Abdülhamid. "Rulers of the Provincial Empire: Ottoman Governers and the Administration of Provinces, 1895-1908." PhD Diss., Boğaziçi University, 2005.

Kirilina, Svetlana, "Islamic Institutions in the Ottoman Egypt in the 18th-Beginning of the 19th Century: Ulama and Sufis," *Essays Ottoman Civilization: Proceedings of the 12th Congress of the Comite International d'Etudes Pre-Ottomanes, Praha 1996,* Praha: N.P. 1998.

Koca, Ferhat. "Fetvahane." In *TDV İslam Ansiklopedisi* 12, 496–500. Istanbul: Türkiye Diyanet Vakfı Yayınları, 1995.

Köksal, Yonca. "Local Intermediaries and Ottoman State Centralization: A Comparison of the Tanzimat Reforms in the Provinces of Ankara and Edirne (1839-1878)." PhD Diss., Colombia University, 2002.

Kuran, Ercüment and Mümtazer Türköne. *Türkiye'nin Batılılaşması ve Milli Meseleler.* Ankara: Türkiye Diyanet Vakfı Yayınları, 2007.

Kushner, David. "The Place of the Ulema in the Ottoman Empire during the Age of Reform (1838-1918)." *Turcica* 19 (1987): 51–74.

——. "Career Patterns Among the Ulama in the Late Nineteenth Century and Early Twentieh Centuries." In *Tanzimat'ın 150. Yıldönümü Uluslararası Sempozyum; (Ankara, 31 Ekim- 3 Kasım 1989).* Ankara: Türk Tarih Kurumu, 1994: 165–172.

Kütükoğlu, Mübahat. "Darü'l-Hilafeti'l-Aliyye Medresesi ve Kuruluşu Arefesinde İstanbul Medreseleri." *İslam Tetkikleri Enstitüsü Dergisi* 7, 1–2 (1978): 1–212.

Lapidus, Ira M. *Muslim Cities in the Later Middle Ages.* Massachusetts: Harvard University Press, 1967.

Levy, Avigdor. "Military Reforms and the Ulema in the Reign of Mahmud II." In *II. Mahmud: Istanbul in the Process of Being Rebuilt,* edited by Coşkun Yılmaz, 150-161. Istanbul: İstanbul Avrupa Kültür Başkenti, 2010.

——. "The Ottoman Ulema and the Military Reforms of Sultan Mahmud II." *Asian & African Studies* 7 (1971): 13–39.

Lewis, Bernard. *The Emergence of Modern Turkey.* London: Oxford University Press, 1968.

Makdisi, George. *The Rise of Colleges: Institutions of Learning in Islam and the West.* Edinburgh: Edinburgh University Press, 1981.

Mansurnoor, Iık Arifin. "Religious Scholars and State: Patterns of Recruitment among the Ottoman Ulama." *Islamic Studies* 31 (Spring 1992): 35–51.

Maoz, Moshe. "The Ulama and the Process of Modernization in Syria during the mid-Nineteenth Century." In *The "Ulama"in Modern History, Studies in Memory of*

Professor Uriel Heyd, edited by Gabriel Baer, 277–301. Jerusalem: Israel Oriental Society, 1971.

Marsot, Afaf Lutfi al-Sayyid. "The Ulama of Cairo in the Eighteenth and Nineteenth Centuries." In *Scholars, Saints, and Sufis: Muslim Religious Institutions in the Middle East since 1500*, edited by Nikki R. Keddie, 149-165. Berkeley: University of California Press, 1978.

Meeker, Michael E. *A Nation of Empire, the Ottoman Legacy of Turkish Modernity*. Berkeley: University of California Press, 2001.

Mert, Nuray. "Early Republican Secularism in Turkey: A Theoretical Approach." PhD Diss., Boğaziçi University, 1992.

Müller, Rainer A. "Student Education, Student Life." In *A History of the University in Europe* vol. II, edited by Hilde de Ridder-Symoens, 326–354. Cambridge: Cambridge University Press, 1996.

Namlı, Tuncer. "Tanzimat ve Sonrası Dönem Kanunlaştırmaları Karşısında İslam Alimlerinin Aldığı Tavır ve Bunun Neticeleri." Master's thesis, Erciyes University, 1988.

Ortaylı, İlber. *İmparatorluğun En Uzun Yüzyılı*. Istanbul: Timaş Yayınları, 2009.

——. "Kadı." In *TDV İslam Ansiklopedisi* 24, 69–73. Istanbul: Türkiye Diyanet Vakfı Yayınları, 2001.

Öcal, Mustafa. "Amin Alayı." In *TDV İslam Ansiklopedisi* 3, 63. Istanbul: Türkiye Diyanet Vakfı Yayınları, 1991.

Ölmez, Adem. "II. Meşrutiyet Devrinde Osmanlı Medreselerinde Reform Çabaları ve Merkezileşme." *Vakıflar Dergisi* 41 (June 2014): 127–140.

Özbek, Nadir. "The Politics of Welfare: Philanthropy, Voluntarism and Legitimacy in the Ottoman Empire, 1876-1914." PhD Diss., Binghamton University, 2001.

——. "Policing the Countryside: Gendarmes of the Late 19th-Century Ottoman Empire (1876-1908)." *International Journal of Middle East Studies* 40 (2008): 47–67.

——. "Osmanlı İmparatorluğu'nda Sosyal Yardım Uygulamaları." In *Tanzimat: Değişim Sürecinde Osmanlı İmparatorluğu*, edited by Halil İnalcık-Mehmet Seyitdanlıoğlu, 401–424. Istanbul: Phoenix Yayınları, 2011.

Özcan, Tahsin. "Osmanlılar-Dini Hayat." In *TDV İslam Ansiklopedisi* 33, 538–541. Istanbul: Türkiye Diyanet Vakfı Yayınları, 2007.

Özkul, Osman. *Gelenek ve Modernite Arasında Osmanlı Uleması*. Istanbul: Birharf Yayınları, 2005.

Özzorluoğlu, Süleyman Tevfik. *Abdülhamid'in Cinci Hocası Şeyh Ebü'l-Hüda*, Istanbul: Yeditepe Yayınları, 2011.

Pakalın, Mehmet Zeki. *Osmanlı Tarih Deyimleri ve Terimleri Sözlüğü*. Istanbul: Milli Eğitim Bakanlığı Yayınları, 1983.

Polat, Ayşe. "Osmanlı'da Matbu İslam'ın Onay ve Denetimi: Tedkik-i Mesahif ve Müellefat-i Şer'iyye Meclisi," *FSM İlmi Araştırmalar İnsan ve Toplum Bilimleri Dergisi*, 11 (2018): 87–120.

Repp, Richard Cooper. *The Mufti of Istanbul: A Study in the Development of the Ottoman Learned Hierarchy*. London: Ithaca Press, 1986.

Saby, Yusny. "Islam and Social Change: The Role of Ulama in Acehnese Society." Ph.D. Diss., Temple University. 1995.

Saçmalı, Muhammet Habib. "Compliance and Negotiation: The Role of Turkish Diyanet in the Production of Friday Khutbas." Master's thesis, Boğaziçi University, 2013.

Sakallıoğlu, Ümit. "Parameters and Strategies of Islam- State Interaction in Republican Turkey." *International Journal of Middle East Studies* 28, 2 (May 1996): 232.

Sarıkaya, Yaşar. *Medreseler ve Modernleşme*. Istanbul: İz Yayıncılık, 1997.

——. *Merkez ile Taşra Arasında Bir Osmanlı Alimi: Ebu Said El-Hadimi*. Istanbul: Kitap Yayınevi, 2008.

Shaw, Stanford J., and Ezel Kural Shaw. *History of the Ottoman Empire and Modern Turkey*. Vols. 1. 2. Cambridge: Cambridge University Press, 1976.

Smith, Donald Eugene. *Religion and Political Modernization*. New York: Yale University Press, 1974.

Stone, Lawrance. "Prosopography." *Daedalus* 100, 1 (Winter 1971): 46–79.

Şeker, Fatih M. *Modernleşme Devrinde İlmiye*. Istanbul: Dergah Yayınları, 2011.

Şeref Gözübüyük, Suna Kili. *Türk Anayasa Metinleri*. Ankara: Ankara Üniversitesi Siyasal Bilgiler Fakültesi Yayınları, 1982.

Şimşek, Veysel. "Ottoman Military Recruitment and the Recruit: 1826-1853." Master's thesis, Bilkent University, 2005.

Taş, Kemaleddin. *Türk Halkının Gözüyle Diyanet*. Istanbul: İz Yayıncılık, 2002.

Uluğ, Nimet Elif. "Elemterefiş: Superstitious Beliefs and Occult in Ottoman Empire (1839-1923)." PhD Diss., Boğaziçi University, 2013.

Uğur, Ali. *The Ottoman Ulema in the Mid-17th Century: An Analysis of the Vakaiül-Fuzala of Mehmed Şeyh Efendi*. Berlin: Klaus Schwars Verlag, 1986.

Unan, Fahri. "Osmanlı Resmi Düşüncesinin İlmiye Tariki İçindeki Etkileri: Patronaj İlişkileri." *Türk Yurdu* 45, XI (1991): 33–41.

——. "Paye." In *TDV İslam Ansiklopedisi* 34, 193–194. Istanbul: Türkiye Diyanet Vakfı Yayınları, 2007.

Uzunçarşılı, İsmail Hakkı. *Osmanlı Devleti'nin İlmiye Teşkilatı*. Ankara: TTK Basımevi, 1988.

——, and Enver Ziya Karal, *Osmanlı Tarihi*, 8 vols. Ankara: Türk Tarih Kurumu Yayınları, 1972.

Ünüvar, Kerem. "Economic and Moral Organization of the Ottoman Society in the Tanzimat Period: Sadık Rıfat Paşa's Ahlak Risalesi." Master's thesis, Boğaziçi University, 2004.

Ünver, Süheyl. *Istanbul Üniversitesi Tarihine Başlangıç: Fatih Külliyesi ve Zamanı İlim Hayatı* (The Commencement of the History of Istanbul University: Fatih Complex and Period Scholarly Life). Istanbul: İstanbul Üniversitesi Tıp Fakültesi, 1946.

Varol, Muharrem. "Osmanlı Devleti'nin Tarikatları Denetleme Siyaseti ve Meclis'i Meşayihin Bilinen; Ancak Bulunamayan İki Nizamnamesi." *Türk Kültürü İncelemeleri Dergisi* 23 *(2010)*: 39–68.

Weber, Max. *Economy and Society: An Outline of Interpretive Sociology*, ed. Guenther Roth and Claus Wittich. 2 vols., New York: Bedminster Press, 1968.

Yakut, Esra. Şeyhülislam*lık: Yenileşme Döneminde Devlet ve Din*. İstanbul: Kitap Yayınevi, 2005.

Yalçınkaya, M. Alper. *Learned Patriots : Debating Science, State, and Society in the Nineteenth- Century Ottoman Empire*. Chicago: The University of Chicago Press, 2015.

Yurdakul, İlhami. *Osmanlı İlmiye Merkez Teşkilatında Reform*. İstanbul: İletişim, 2008.

Zengin, Zeki Salih. "Osmanlılar'da II. Meşrutiyet Döneminde Yeni Açılan Medreseler ve Din Görevlisi Yetiştirme Çalışmaları." *İslam Araştırmaları Dergisi 36* (2016): 33–61.

——. "Tanzimat Dönemi Osmanlı Örgün Eğitim Kurumlarında Din Eğitimi ve Öğretimi (1839-1876)." PhD Diss., Erciyes Üniversitesi Sosyal Bilimler Enstitüsü, 1997.

——. *Tanzimat Dönemi Osmanlı Örgün Eğitim Kurumlarında Din Eğitimi ve Öğretimi (1839-1876)*. Ankara: Milli Eğitim Bakanlığı, 2004.

Zerdeci, Hümeyra. *Osmanlı Ulema Biyografilerinin Arşiv Kaynakları*. Ankara: Türkiye Diyanet Vakfı Yayınları, 2008.

Zilfi, Madeline C. "The Ottoman Ulema." In *The Cambridge History of Turkey Volume 3: The Later Ottoman Empire, 1603–1839*, edited by Suraiya N. Faroqhi, 209–225. Cambridge: Cambridge University Press, 2006.

Zilfi, Madeline C. *The Politics of Piety: The Ottoman Ulema in the Postclassical Age (1600-1800)*. Minneapolis, MN: Bibliotheca Islamica, 1988.

Zürcher, Eric J. *Turkey: A Modern History*. London: I. B. Tauris, 199.

Index

www.ingramcontent.com/pod-product-compliance
Lightning Source LLC
Chambersburg PA
CBHW062220300426
44115CB00012BA/2151
9780755645510